Instruction Selection

Gabriel Hjort Blindell

Instruction Selection

Principles, Methods, and Applications

 Springer

Gabriel Hjort Blindell
Computer Systems Laboratory (CSL)
Royal Institute of Technology (KTH)
Kista
Sweden

ISBN 978-3-319-81658-6   ISBN 978-3-319-34019-7   (eBook)
DOI 10.1007/978-3-319-34019-7

Printed on acid-free paper

This Springer imprint is published by Springer Nature
The registered company is Springer International Publishing AG Switzerland

*För mina föräldrar
och min bror*

Foreword

Compilers are ideal software projects: You have relatively stable and well-defined, partly even formal specifications for the input and the output, and lots of interesting subproblems in between.

In particular, the scanning part of compilers has been formalized using regular languages and is expressed in regular expressions, which have become not only popular for scanning programming languages, but for many other tasks as well. The parsing part has been formalized with context-free grammars in (extended) BNF and that has led to the development of parser generators that are quite popular in language implementations.

Formal specifications have been used for specifying the input language of compilers beyond context-free grammars, such as Van Wijngaarden grammars in ALGOL 68, or various formal semantics of programming languages. Among theses formalisms, attribute grammars seem to be the most popular, judging by the tool support available, but even that does not seem to be very popular: most language designers prefer the flexibility of natural language; most compiler writers prefer to specify work beyond the parser in a general-purpose programming language.

This book is about the other end of the compiler, the output part, in particular the part that has to do with the instruction set of the target processor. One might think that a similar development to frontends takes place here; but while the instruction sets of many processors are also specified in a relatively formal way, no common standard analogous to regular expressions or (extended) BNF has established itself.

One reason is that there are many different purposes for an instruction set description: assembly programming, code generation, performing assembly, simulation, automatic hardware generation, etc.

Still, for specifying instruction selection, retargetable compilers usually use machine description languages, rather than falling back to a general-purpose language, and these languages correspond to some formalism used in the instruction selector, e.g., a tree grammar in tree-parsing instruction selection. However, the qmachine description languages used differ significantly, because of differences in the instruction selection methods, and in the intermediate representations of the compilers.

One significant difference between compiler frontend and backend is that the frontend must interpret the input in only one way, while the backend can generate a variety of machine code programs for the input program, all of them correct. Therefore, the machine description is usually arranged as mapping the intermediate representation to machine instructions rather than the other way round, leading to compiler-specific machine descriptions.

Among the possible correct code sequences, the compiler will ideally select the one that is best in terms of speed, size or some other metric, so we have an optimization problem at hand, and like many compiler problems, this one is NP-complete in the general case.

Moreover, there are additional goals in instruction selection, such as short compilation time and ease of compiler development, resulting in a large variety of different instruction selection methods; some methods have been superseded, and are mainly of historical interest, but others are used because they offer a useful trade-off for various design goals. For example, Chris Fraser (who contributed to Davidson-Fraser code generation, and several tree-parser generators) once told me that he worked on tree parsing for fast compilation, but would use Davidson-Fraser if better generated code was more important.

Probably because there is no canonical instruction selection specification formalism comparable to BNF, instruction selection has been mostly neglected for a long time in many compiler textbooks. Even those textbooks that cover instruction selection have to limit themselves to just one or two techniques for space reasons.

If you want to know more, read this book! It gives a broad survey over the large body of literature on instruction selection. Also, if, after reading this book, you desire an even deeper knowledge of a particular method, this book points you to the original papers that you can then read, and it also provides background knowledge that is useful for understanding these papers.

This book is not just useful for students who are looking for knowledge beyond the compiler textbook level, but also for experts: I have published in this area, yet a lot of this material, especially the early work, was new to me when I got this book for review.

Vienna, Austria
March 2016

M. Anton Ertl
TU Wien

Preface

Like most doctoral students, I started my studies by reviewing the existing, most prominent approaches in the field. A couple of months later I thought I had acquired a sufficient understanding of instruction selection and felt confident enough to begin developing new methods.

That confidence was short-lived.

When exploring my new ideas, I would soon face a number of problems about instruction selection that I didn't fully understand, prompting me to read more papers until I did. Empowered with new knowledge, I would resume my research, only to shortly after be confronted with yet another set of problems. After doing this for another few months, the pile of related work had grown so large that I started to wonder how many more papers the collection would need before it contained everything ever published on instruction selection. So I set out to find those missing papers. Several months later, my findings had been compiled into a 109-page technical report—which grew to 139 pages in a second revision—and although it was written primarily to be shared with others, I wrote it equally as much for myself to be used later as a manual of reference. At this point my supervisors and I believed the material to be of sufficient quality for publication, but it was simply too long to be accepted by any journal in its current form. Fortunately, Springer agreed to publish my work as a book, which is the one you are currently reading.

The ambition of this book is to (i) introduce instruction selection as an interesting problem—what it is, and why it matters—and (ii) present an exhaustive, coherent, and accessible survey on the existing methods for solving this problem. In most cases, the goal is to convey the main intuition behind a particular technique or approach. But for methods that have had a significant impact on instruction selection, the discussions are more in-depth and detailed. The prerequisites are kept to a minimum to target as wide an audience as possible: it is assumed that the reader has a basic background in computer science, is familiar with complexity theory, and has some basic skills in logic and maths. However, no expectations are made regarding prior knowledge on instruction selection, and very little on compilers in general. Hence the material presented herein should be useful to anyone interested in instruction selection, including:

- novice programmers, who have used a compiler but know nothing about its internals;
- intermediate and advanced students, who may already have taken a course on compilers; and
- expert practitioners, who have decades of experience in compiler development.

Stockholm, Sweden   *Gabriel Hjort Blindell*
January 2016   KTH Royal Institute of Technology

Acknowledgments

I am indebted to several persons, who, one way or another, have had a hand in shaping the material and appearance of this book.

First and foremost, I want to thank my main supervisor Christian Schulte, my colleague Roberto Castañeda Lozano, and my co-supervisor Mats Carlsson—their insightful feedback and helpful suggestions have had a significant impact in clarifying and improving much of the material.

I want to thank Ronan Nugent for taking care of the administrative tasks of publishing this book. I am especially grateful to Ronan for organizing the peer review, and I want to thank all the reviewers who agreed to participate—your comments have been invaluable. I also want to thank Karl Johansson and Jaak Randmets, who pointed out some of the errors that appeared in the earlier, report version.

I am grateful to the *Swedish Research Council* for funding this research,[1] and to the *Swedish Institute of Computer Science* for letting me use their office equipment and drink their delicious coffee.[2]

I want to thank everyone at *TEX StackExchange*[3] for helping me with all the LATEX-related problems I encountered in the course of writing this book. Without their help, the material would undoubtedly have been much less comprehensible.

Last—but certainly not least—I am indebted to Emily Fransson, who has been a dear friend since a long time and given me tremendous solace when I faced hard times during my doctoral studies. Without her support, this book might not have seen the light of day.

---

[1] VR grant 621-2011-6229.

[2] I am not certain which of the two played the most pivotal role in bringing this work together.

[3] http://tex.stackexchange.com/

Contents

List of Figures

Chapter 1
Introduction

A *compiler* is primarily and foremost a tool that enables programs to be executed by a computer. This means that virtually every undertaking of implementing a piece of software—be it a GUI-based Windows application, a high-performance Fortran program for mathematical computations, a smartphone app written in Java, or that tiny C program which controls your refrigerator—necessitates a compiler in one form or another. Since a computer is only as useful as the programs it executes, compilation has consequently been under active research ever since the first computers started to appear in the 1940s, which makes it one of the oldest and most studied areas of computer science.

In order to perform its task, a compiler must tackle a broad range of intermediate problems. The most important problems include *syntactic analysis*, *program optimization*, and *code generation*, which is the task of generating code for a given program and a particular hardware. Code generation in turn consists of three sub-problems: *instruction selection*—the task of deciding which instructions to use; *instruction scheduling*—the task of scheduling the selected instructions; and *register allocation*—the task of assigning *registers* to the variables of the program. This book focuses on the first of these tasks.

Compared to many other aspects of compilation and code generation, instruction selection has received far less attention. Most compiler textbooks discuss instruction selection only briefly and thus provide little insight. For example, in the compiler textbooks [8, 18, 85, 130, 231, 257, 339]—a collection comprising over 4,600 pages—fewer than 160 pages are devoted to instruction selection, and in these there is tremendous overlap and they typically only describe methods based on a single approach. In addition, the existing surveys conducted by Cattell [68], Ganapathi et al. [150], Leupers [227], and Boulytchev and Lomov [53] are either too old or incomplete. This book addresses both these shortcomings by presenting an exhaustive and coherent survey of the existing techniques, spanning over 45 years of research, and includes both conventional designs as well as the state of the art. To facilitate access to this vast amount of work on instruction selection, the survey is structured along two dimensions: the techniques are organized and discussed according to (i) their intrinsic approach, and (ii) the extent of their machine instruction support.

© Springer International Publishing Switzerland 2016
G. Hjort Blindell, *Instruction Selection*,
DOI 10.1007/978-3-319-34019-7_1

The book is organized as follows. The rest of this chapter describes the task of instruction selection (and why it is needed), establishes a common taxonomy, discusses common issues when comparing existing methods, and briefly covers the first publications on code generation. Chapters 2 through 5 then examine a fundamental *principle* to instruction selection: macro expansion, tree covering, DAG covering, and graph covering. Chapter 6 ends the book with conclusions through which I attempt to identify directions for future research.

The book also contains several appendices. Appendix A provides a table which summarizes all techniques covered in the book. Appendix B contains a diagram illustrating the distribution of publications over time for each principle of instruction selection. Appendix C gives a set of formal definitions regarding graphs. Appendix D contains a summary of the taxonomy which is used throughout this book.

1.1 What Is Instruction Selection?

In order to describe the task of instruction selection, we will begin by briefly outlining the common structure of a program, the characteristics of the designated hardware, and the anatomy of a typical compiler.

1.1.1 The Program Under Compilation

We assume that a *program* consists of a set of directives, written according to the syntactic and semantic rules specified by some *programming language*. This body of directives is commonly called the *source code* of the program. Without loss of generality we can also assume that all programs are composed of a set of *program functions*, which we will simply call *functions* unless there is risk of confusion. A function is defined as a series of computations and function calls, interspersed with

```
1:  int factorial(int n) {
2:      int f = 1;
3:      for (; n > 1; n--) {
4:          f = f * n;
5:      }
6:      return f;
7:  }
```

```
1:  int factorial(int n) {
2:  init:
3:      int f = 1;
4:  loop:
5:      if (n <= 1) goto end;
6:      f = f * n;
7:      n--;
8:      goto loop;
9:  end:
10:     return f;
11: }
```

(a) Factorial function, written in C   (b) Same function, but with *goto*s

Fig. 1.1: Source code example

control-flow operations such as *if-then-else* statements and *for* loops (see Fig. 1.1a
for an example using the factorial function). We also assume each program has
exactly one function which represents the program's entry point of execution.

Each function in turn is said to consist of a set of *basic blocks* (or simply *blocks*).
A block is a group of statements where a change in control flow only occurs at the
end of the block. By rewriting the aforementioned factorial function to only use *goto*
statements for control flow (see Fig. 1.1b), we achieve the following set of blocks:

- lines 2 through 3 form a block, since execution can jump to line 4;
- lines 4 through 5 form a block, since there is a jump at line 5;
- lines 6 through 8 form a block, for the same reason as above; and
- lines 9 through 10 form the last block.

The notion of blocks will be needed when we discuss the scope of instruction
selection.

1.1.2 The Target Machine

The hardware for which a given program is compiled is commonly referred to as the
target machine. A target machine comprises a processor that continuously interprets
and executes *machine code*. The machine code consists of a series of 1s and 0s that are
bundled by the processor into *machine instructions* (or simply *instructions*), which
are subsequently executed. The set of available instructions, called the *instruction
set*, and their behavior is specified by the target machine's *instruction set architecture
(ISA)*, which means that machine code using instructions from a specific ISA can
be executed on any target machine supporting the same ISA. The complexity of
the instruction set may range from simple, single-operation instructions (such as
arithmetic addition) to highly elaborate instructions (for example, "copy the content
of one memory location to another, increment the address pointers, and then repeat
until a certain stop value is encountered").

Although it is technically feasible to write programs directly as machine code, it
is obviously extremely cumbersome to do so in practice. Such programs are instead
written in an *assembly language*, which enables the instructions to be referred to using
mnemonic names instead of specific bit patterns. Code written in assembly language
is called *assembly code*, and an example will be shown shortly. The assembly code is
then converted into machine code by an *assembler*.

Compared to the relatively high-level programming languages, the assembly
language is typically much more austere. For example, control flow can usually
only be expressed using compare-and-jump instructions, and much of what is done
implicitly in programming languages, such as memory accesses, must be done
explicitly in the assembly language. Moreover, certain operations appearing in the
source code may not necessarily have a directly corresponding operation in the
assembly language, and must instead be emulated using multiple instructions.

Hence there is a gap between the programming language in which the program is expressed, and the assembly language understood by the target machine that will execute the program. This gap is bridged by the compiler.[1]

1.1.3 Inside the Compiler

Figure 1.2 illustrates the infrastructure of a typical compiler. First a *frontend* parses and validates the source code of the program, ensuring that it is free from syntactic and semantic errors which would violate the rules of the programming language. Next the frontend translates the source code into an equivalent form known as the *intermediate representation (IR)*. The IR code is a format used internally by the compiler, which also isolates the rest of its components from the characteristics of a particular programming language. Hence multiple programming languages can be supported by the same compiler infrastructure simply by replacing the frontend.

The IR code is then passed on to the *optimizer*, which attempts to improve the efficiency of the program. Examples of common program optimizations include *dead-code elimination* (removing code that will never be executed), *constant folding* (evaluating computations with constant values during compilation), and *loop unrolling* (performing several iterations at once within the same loop in order to reduce the loop maintenance overhead). Although the optimizer is not strictly necessary for bridging the gap between program and target machine, a vast majority of the implementation effort goes into this component (for production-quality compilers such as GCC and LLVM, it is in the order of hundreds of man-years).

Lastly the optimized program is passed on to the *backend*, also called the *code generator*, where the IR code will be converted into assembly code, typically one function at a time. The first task that the backend must perform is to decide which

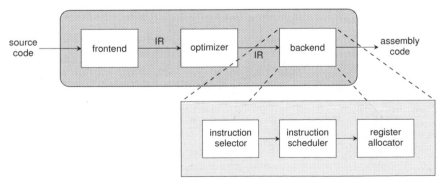

Fig. 1.2: Overview of a typical compiler infrastructure

---

[1] It should be mentioned that the compiler itself is also a program that must be compiled in order to be executable. This gives rise to a curious Catch 22 dilemma: How was the first compiler compiled?

```
1:  factorial:
2:      mov  t0,$a0
3:      addi t1,$r0,1
4:      subi t2,t0,1
5:  head:
6:      blez t2,end
7:  loop:
8:      mul  t1,t1,t2
9:      subi t2,t2,1
10:     j head
11: end:
12:     mov $v0,t1
13:     jr  $ra
```

```
1:  factorial:
2:      mov  t0,$a0
3:      {addi t1,$r0,1;
        subi t2,t0,1}
4:  head:
5:      blez t2,end
6:  loop:
7:      mul  t1,t1,t2
8:      subi t2,t2,1
9:      j head
10: end:
11:     mov $v0,t1
12:     jr  $ra
```

```
1:  factorial:
2:      {addi $v0,$r0,1;
        subi $t0,$a0,1}
3:  head:
4:      blez $t0,end
5:  loop:
6:      mul  $v0,$v0,$t0
7:      subi $t0,$t0,1
8:      j head
9:  end:
10:     jr  $ra
```

(a) After instruction selection   (b) After instruction scheduling   (c) After register allocation

Fig. 1.3: The factorial function, expressed in assembly for a multi-issue MIPS architecture

instructions of the target machine to use for implementing the IR code (see Fig. 1.3a). This is the responsibility of the instruction selector. For the selected instructions, the backend must also decide in what order they appear in the assembly code (see Fig. 1.3b). This is taken care of by the instruction scheduler. Finally, the backend must decide how to use the limited set of registers available on the target machine (see Fig. 1.3c), which is managed by the register allocator.

1.1.4 The Instruction Selector

For a given piece of IR code *P*—depending on the scope, this may constitute an entire program, a function, a block, or only part of a block—the instruction selector must first and foremost select instructions such that they implement the same behavior on the target machine as that specified by *P*. However, depending on the target machine, some sequences of instructions are more efficient than others in performing a specific task. This is especially true for *digital signal processors (DSPs)*, which provide many customized instructions in order to improve the performance of certain algorithms. According to a 1994 study [357], the clock-cycle overhead of compiler-generated assembly code from C programs targeting DSPs could be as much as 1,000% compared to hand-written assembly code when failing to take full advantage of the target machine's capabilities. Consequently, as a secondary objective the instruction selector should pick instructions that result in high-quality assembly code.

As we will see later, the semantics of the instructions can be captured as patterns, which allows us to reformulate the task of instruction selection as the following subproblems:

The *pattern matching* problem. Finding the instructions that can be used to implement a given piece of IR code.

The *pattern selection* problem. Deciding upon a combination of instructions to implement the IR code.

The first subproblem is concerned with finding instruction candidates—most instruction sets are seldom orthogonal, meaning there is typically more than one way of implementing the same behavior—whereas the second subproblem is concerned with selecting a subset from these candidates. Some techniques combine both subproblems into a single step, but most keep them separate and predominantly differ in how they solve the pattern selection problem. In general, the latter problem is formulated as an optimization problem: each instruction is assigned a cost, and the goal is to minimize the total cost of the selected instructions. The cost is an abstraction of a property that one would like to minimize in the generated assembly code, for example its execution time, code size, or energy consumption. It is most common to minimize the execution time in order to maximize performance.

1.2 Comparing Different Instruction Selection Methods

As discussed in the previous section, the instruction set can consist of many different kinds of instructions. However, it is common to all contemporary designs that none is capable of handling every instruction available in the instruction set. As a result, when discussing a new instruction selection technique, most papers differ on the instruction set under consideration. For example, in the early literature a "complex instruction" refers to a memory load or store instruction that computes the memory address using schemes of varying complexity. These schemes are called *addressing modes*, and using these appropriately can reduce code size as well as increase performance. As an example, let us assume that we need to load the value at a particular position in an array A of 1-byte values that reside in memory. The memory address of our wanted value is thus @A + offset, where @A represents the memory address of the first element in A (usually called the *base address*), and offset represents the memory distance from the base address to the wanted value. A reasonable approach to fetching this value is to first execute an add instruction to compute @A + offset into some register r_x, and then execute a load instruction that reads from the memory address specified by r_x. Such load instructions are said to have *absolute* or *direct* addressing modes. But if the instruction set provides a load with *indexed* addressing mode, where base address and offset are provided directly as arguments to the instruction, then we only need to use a single instruction. As efficient handling of such addressing modes nowadays is trivial for the most part, a complex instruction in modern literature typically refers an instruction which produces more than one value, or an instruction which can only be used (or not used) in particular situations.

1.2.1 Introducing the Notion of Machine Instruction Characteristics

To mitigate these problems—and to enable us to more conveniently compare the different methods of instruction selection—I will introduce and define *machine instruction characteristics*, each of which refers to a certain class of instructions. The first three characteristics form sets of instructions which are disjoint from one another, but the last two characteristics can be combined as appropriate with any of the other characteristics.

Single-output Instructions

The simplest kind of instruction forms the set of *single-output instructions*. These produce only a single observable output, in the sense that "observable" means a value that can be read and accessed by the assembly code. This includes all machine instructions that implement a single operation (such as addition, multiplication, and bit operations), but it also includes more complicated instructions that implement several operations like the aforementioned memory operations with complicated addressing modes. As long as the observable output constitutes a single value, a single-output instruction can be arbitrarily complex.

This class comprises the majority of instructions in most instruction sets, and in simple *reduced instruction set computer (RISC)* architectures, such as MIPS, nearly all instructions are single-output instructions. Needless to say, all instruction selectors are expected to support this kind of instruction.

Multi-output Instructions

As expected, *multi-output instructions* produce more than one observable output from the same input. Examples include `divmod` instructions, which compute both the quotient and the remainder of two input values, as well as arithmetic instructions that, in addition to computing the result, also set one or more *status flags*. A status flag (sometimes also known as a *condition flag* or a *condition code*) is a single bit that signifies additional information about the result of a computation, for example if there was a carry overflow or the result was equal to 0. For this reason such instructions are often said to have *side effects*, but in reality these bits are nothing else but additional output values produced by the instruction, and will thus be referred to as multi-output instructions. `Load` and `store` instructions, which access a value in memory and then increment the address pointer, are also considered multi-output instructions.

Many architectures such as X86, ARM, and Hexagon provide instructions of this class, although they are typically not as common as single-output instructions.

Disjoint-output Instructions

Instructions which produce many observable output values from many different input values are referred to as *disjoint-output instructions*. These are similar to multi-output instructions with the exception that all output values in the latter originate from the same input values. Another way to put it is that if one formed the patterns that correspond to each output, all these patterns would be disjoint from one another (how such patterns are formed will be explained in Chapter 2). This typically includes *single-instruction, multiple-data (SIMD) instructions*, which execute the same operations simultaneously on many distinct input values.

Disjoint-output instructions are very common in high-throughput graphics architectures and DSPs, but also appear in X86 as extensions with names like SSE and AVX [186]. Recently, certain ARM processors are also equipped with such extensions [23].

Inter-block Instructions

Instructions whose behavior essentially spans across multiple blocks are referred to as *inter-block instructions*. Examples of such instructions are saturated arithmetic[2] and hardware loop instructions, which repeat a fixed sequence of machine instructions a certain number of times.

Instructions with this characteristic typically appear in customized architectures and DSPs such as ARM's Cortex-M7 processor [24] and TI's TMS320C55x processor [322]. But because of their complexity, these instructions require sophisticated techniques for capturing their behavior which are not provided by most compilers. Instead, individual instructions are supported either via customized program optimization routines or through so-called compiler intrinsics, which are special types of nodes in the IR code. If no such routine or compiler intrinsic is available, making use of these machine instructions requires the program to be written directly in assembly language.

Interdependent Instructions

The last class is the set of *interdependent instructions*. This includes instructions which exhibit additional constraints that appear when they are combined with other instructions in certain ways. An example includes an add instruction, again from the

---

[2] In saturated arithmetic, the computed value is "clamped" within a specific range. For example, if the permitted range is $-128 \leq x \leq 127$, then the saturated sum of $100 + 80$ is 127. This is common in signal processing applications, and it is typically implemented by first performing a regular arithmetic operation and then checking whether the result exceeds the bounds. In fact, a request was recently made to extend the LLVM compiler with saturated arithmetic *compiler intrinsics* to facilitate selection of such instructions [51].

TMS320C55x instruction set, which cannot be combined with an `rpt` instruction if a particular addressing mode is used for the `add` instruction.

Interdependent instructions are rare and may be found in complex, heterogeneous architectures such as DSPs. As we will see, this is another class of instructions that most instruction selectors struggle with, mainly because such instructions typically violate the set of assumptions made by the underlying techniques.

1.2.2 What Does It Mean for Instruction Selection to Be "Optimal"?

When using the term *optimal instruction selection*, most literature assumes—often implicitly—the following definition:

Definition 1.1. For a particular set I of instructions, where each instruction $i \subset I$ has a cost c_i, an instruction selector is *optimal* if and only if for any given input P it finds a multiset[3] S from I such that S implements P and there exists no other multiset S' that also implements P and $\sum_{s' \in S'} c_{s'} < \sum_{s \in S} c_s$.

In other words, if no assembly code with lower cost can be achieved using the same set of instructions, then the instruction selector is said to be optimal.

This definition has two shortcomings. First, the "set I of instructions" does not necessarily need to contain every instruction available on the target machine. It is therefore most common to only include the instructions that can be supported by the instruction selector and simply ignore all other instructions available on the target machine, even though they may in certain cases lead to more efficient assembly code. While the clause enables comparison between instruction selectors with similar instruction support, it also allows two instruction selectors with very different instruction support to both be considered optimal even though one clearly produces more efficient assembly code than the other. One solution is to require the set I to include all available instructions, but this also renders essentially all existing instruction selection techniques as suboptimal as there always seems to exist—excluding the simplest of instruction sets—some non-supported instruction that would improve the code quality for a particular program. Note also that an instruction selector which is optimal for programs represented in one form is not necessarily optimal when they are represented in another. Hence even two optimal instruction selectors that both handle the same instruction set, but accept programs in different forms, are not necessarily comparable [17].

Second, two comparable instruction selectors may select different sets of instructions that ultimately yield assembly code of disproportionate quality after instruction scheduling and register allocation has been performed. For example, let us assume that we need to select instructions for implementing a set of operations that can be executed independently from one another. The instruction set provides two options:

---

[3] A multiset is a set where duplicates are allowed.

either use two machine instructions, each taking two cycles (thus yielding a total cost of 4); or use a single instruction which takes three cycles (total cost 3). According to the aforementioned definition, the second solution is preferred as its total cost is lower. However, if the target machine can execute multiple instructions in parallel, then the first solution is preferred since it would only take two cycles to execute both machine instructions. Hence the costs are not always additive, but depend on the optimization criteria and the properties of the target machine.

However, the second solution is only better if the instruction scheduler is capable of scheduling the two instructions in parallel. Hence, decisions made by the instruction selector have an impact on the decisions to be made by the instruction scheduler. A similar dependence exists between the instruction selector and register allocator for heterogeneous architectures with multiple *register classes*; if not all instructions can access all registers, then selecting particular instructions may force the register allocator to keep data in certain registers, which could potentially have a negative impact on code quality. This highlights a well-known property of code generation: instruction selection, instruction scheduling, and register allocation are all interconnected, forming a complex system that affects the quality of the final assembly code in complicated and often counterintuitive ways. Therefore, to produce truly optimal assembly code, all three tasks must be performed in unison. Several attempts to do this have been made, some of which are covered in this book.

But if the idea of optimal instruction selection as an isolated concept is of limited significance, why then has it become so firmly established in the compiler community and literature? The first part of the answer is that it makes sense when code generation is performed in stages, which is the case for most compilers. The second part is that it makes it easier to write the so-called machine description [17], which we will introduce in Chapter 2. Adding a new machine instruction or rule to an instruction will never degrade the quality of code generated by an optimal instruction selector, whereas this new extension may cause a greedy instruction selector to make poor decisions in certain situations.

Due to these aforementioned problems, I will make as little use as possible of the term *optimal instruction selection* and instead use *optimal pattern selection*, which will be introduced Chapter 3 and has a less problematic definition (although it, too, is not perfect).

1.3 The Prehistory of Instruction Selection

The first papers on code generation [15, 133, 262, 291] appeared in the early 1960s and were predominantly concerned with how to compute arithmetic expressions on target machines based on *accumulator registers*. An accumulator register is a register which acts both as an input value and destination for an instruction (for example $a \leftarrow a + b$). These were prevalent in the early target machines as the processor could be built using only a few registers. Although this simplified the hardware manufacturing process, it was not straightforward to generate assembly code which evaluates an expression and at the same time minimizes the number of transfers between the accumulator registers and main memory.

Sethi and Ullman [305] later expanded these first methods to target machines with n general-purpose registers. In a paper from 1970, Sethi and Ullman introduce an algorithm that evaluates arithmetic statements with common subexpressions and generates assembly code with as few instructions as possible. This work was later extended in 1976 by Aho and Johnson [3], who applied dynamic programming to develop a code generation algorithm that could handle target machines with more complex addressing modes such as indirection. We will revisit this method later in the book as it has influenced many subsequent instruction selection techniques.

Common among these early techniques is that the instruction selection problem was effectively ignored or circumvented. For instance, both Sethi and Ullman's and Aho and Johnson's designs assume that the target machines exhibit precise mathematical properties and are devoid of any exotic instructions and multiple register classes. Since no, or very few, machines have such characteristics, these algorithms were not directly applicable in practice.

Lacking formal methods, the first instruction selectors were typically written by hand and based on ad hoc algorithms. This meant a trade-off between efficiency and retargetability: if the instruction selector was too general, the generated assembly code might not be efficient; if it was tailored too tightly to a particular target machine, it could constrain the compiler's support for other target machines. Retargeting such instruction selectors therefore involved manual modifications and rewrites of the underlying algorithms. For irregular architectures, with multiple register classes and different instructions to access each class, the original instruction selector might not even be usable at all.

But even if the instruction selector was built to facilitate compiler retargeting, it was still not immediately clear how to achieve this goal. Thus we will begin by examining the first methods that attacked this problem.

Chapter 2
Macro Expansion

The selection of techniques in this chapter includes all those discussed in earlier surveys by Cattell [68] and Ganapathi et al. [150]. In the latter, the principle discussed in this chapter is called *interpretative code generation*. Several of these techniques are also discussed in depth by Lunell [244].

2.1 The Principle

The first papers to introduce methods that specifically dealt with instruction selection as a separate problem appeared in the late 1960s and applied a principle known as *macro expansion*. In these designs the instruction selector

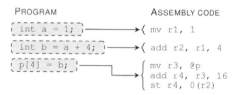

operates by matching *templates* over the program. Upon a match a corresponding *macro* is executed by a *macro expander*, using the matched program string as argument. Each programming language construct has its own macro definition which is responsible for emitting the assembly code that implements the corresponding semantics on the target machine. To make better use of the instruction set, multiple language constructs can also be combined into a single template. For a given program the instruction selector will operate in a procedural manner of traversing the program, matching the code against the templates, and executing the macros that match. If some portion of the code cannot be matched against any template, then the instruction selector will fail and report an error, indicating that it is unable to produce valid assembly code for that particular program against the specific target machine (which preferably should never happen).

Using the terms introduced in Chapter 1, the process of matching templates corresponds to the pattern matching problem, and the process of choosing between multiple matching macros corresponds to the pattern selection problem. To the best

© Springer International Publishing Switzerland 2016
G. Hjort Blindell, *Instruction Selection*,
DOI 10.1007/978-3-319-34019-7_2

of my knowledge, all macro-expanding instruction selectors immediately select the macro that matches first, thereby sidestepping the latter problem entirely.

Keeping the implementation of these macros separate from the implementation of the core of the instruction selector—that is, the part that takes care of matching the template and executing the macros—means that the effort of retargeting the compiler against a different target machine is lessened as only the macros need to be redefined. Compare this with the earlier, monolithic designs, which often necessitated complete rewrites of the entire code generator.

2.2 Naïve Macro Expansion

2.2.1 Early Applications

We will refer to instruction selectors that directly apply the principle just described as *naïve macro expanders*, for reasons that will soon become apparent. In the first such implementations the macros were either written by hand (like in the Pascal compiler developed by Ammann et al. [12, 13]) or generated automatically from a specification of the target machine, called the *machine description*, which was typically written in some dedicated language. Consequently, many such languages and related tools have appeared—and then disappeared—over the years (see for example [59] for an early survey).

One such example is SIMCMP, a macro expander developed in 1969 by Orgass and Waite [273]. Designed to facilitate *bootstrapping*,[1] SIMCMP read its input line by line, compared the line against the templates of the available macros, and then executed the first macro that matched. An example of such a macro is given in Fig. 2.1.

Another example is the *Generate Coding Language (GCL)*, developed by Elson and Rake [108], which was used in a PL/1 compiler for generating assembly code from *abstract syntax trees (ASTs)*. An AST is a graph-based representation of the program's source code and is always shaped like a tree (Appendix C provides an exact definition of graphs, trees, nodes, edges, and other related terms which we will

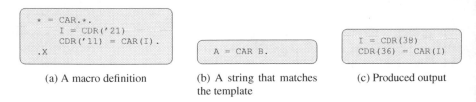

(a) A macro definition   (b) A string that matches   (c) Produced output
                                     the template

Fig. 2.1: Language transfer example using SIMCMP [273]

---

[1] Bootstrapping is the process of writing a compiler in the programming language it is intended to compile.

encounter throughout this book). The most important feature of these trees is that
only a syntactically valid program can be transformed into an AST, which simplifies
the task of the instruction selector. However, the basic principle of macro expansion
remains the same.

Using an Intermediate Representation Instead of Abstract Syntax Trees

Performing instruction selection directly on the program's source code, either in
its textual form or on the AST, carries the disadvantage of tightly coupling the
code generator to a particular programming language. Most compiler infrastructures
therefore rely on some lower-level, machine-independent IR which isolates the
subsequent program optimization routines and the backend from the details of the
programming language.[2] The IR code is often represented as a *program tree*, which
is a data-flow graph where each node represents an operation in the program and each
edge represents a data dependency between two operations. An example is shown
in Fig. 2.2. In this book we will consistently draw trees with their root on top, but
note that the convention differs from one paper to another. It is also common to omit
any intermediate variables from the program tree and only keep those signifying
the input and output values of the expression, as shown in the example. This also
means that a program tree can only represent a set of computations performed within
the same block, which thus may contain more than one program tree. Since these
representations only capture data flow, the program's control flow is represented
separately as a *control-flow graph*.

   One of the first IR-based schemes was developed by Wilcox [338]. Implemented
in a PL/C compiler, the AST is first transformed into machine-independent code
consisting of *source language machine (SLM) instructions*. The instruction selector
then maps each SLM instruction into one or more target-specific instructions using
macros defined in a language called *Interpretive Coding Language (ICL)* (see Fig. 2.3
for an example).

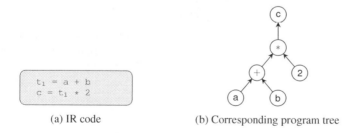

(a) IR code   (b) Corresponding program tree

Fig. 2.2: Example of a piece of IR code represented as a program tree

---

[2] This need was in fact recognized in the late 1950s [83, 315].

```
ADDB    BR      A,ADDB1         If A is in a register, jump to ADDB1
        BR      B,ADDB2         If B is in a register, jump to ADDB2
        LGPR A                  Generate code to load A into register

ADDB1   BR      B,ADDB3         If B is in a register, jump to ADDB3
        GRX A,A,B               Generate A+B
        B       ADDB4           Merge

ADDB3   GRR     AR,A,B          Generate A+B
ADDB4   FREE B                  Release resources assigned to B
ADDB5   POP     1               Remove B descriptor from stack
        EXIT

ADDB2   GRI     A,B,A           Generate A+B
        FREE A                  Release resources assigned to A
        SET     A,B             A now designates result location
        B       ADDB5           Merge
```

Fig. 2.3: A binary addition macro in ICL [338]

In practice, these macros turned out to be tedious and difficult to write. Many details, such as addressing modes and data locations, had to be dealt with manually from within the macros. In the case of ICL, the macro writer also had to keep track of which variables were part of the final assembly code, and which variables were auxiliary and only used to aid the code generation process. In an attempt to simplify this task, Young [350] proposed (but never implemented) a higher-level language called *Template Language (TEL)* that would abstract away some of the implementation-oriented details. The idea was to first express the macros as TEL code and then to automatically generate the lower-level ICL macros from the machine description.

2.2.2 *Generating the Macros from a Machine Description*

As with Wilcox's design, many of the early macro-expanding instruction selectors depended on macros that were intricate and difficult to write. In addition, many compiler developers often incorporated register allocation into these macros, which further exacerbated the problem. For example, if the target machine exhibits multiple register classes and has special instructions to move data from one register class to another, a record must be kept of which program values reside in which registers. Then, depending on the register assignment, the instruction selector needs to emit the appropriate data-transfer instructions in addition to the rest of the assembly code. Due to the exponential number of possible situations, the complexity that the macro designer has to manage can be immense.

Automatically Inferring the Necessary Data Transfers

The first attempt to address this problem was made by Miller [255]. In his master's thesis from 1971, Miller introduces a code generation system called DMACS that automatically infers the necessary data transfers between memory and different register classes. By encapsulating this information in a separate machine description, DMACS was also the first system to allow the details of the target machine to be declared separately instead of being implicitly embedded into the macros.

DMACS relies on two proprietary languages: *Machine-Independent Macro Language (MIML)*, which declares a set of procedural two-argument commands that serves as the IR format (see Fig. 2.4 for an example); and a declarative language called *Object Machine Macro Language (OMML)* for implementing the macros that will transform each MIML command into assembly code. So far this scheme is similar to the one applied by Wilcox.

When adding support for a new target machine, a macro designer first specifies the set of available register classes (including memory) as well as the permissible transfer paths between these classes. The macro designer then defines the OMML macros by providing, for each macro, a list of instructions that implements the corresponding MIML command on the target machine. If necessary, a sequence of instructions can be given to emulate the effect of a single MIML command. Lastly, constraints are added that force the input and output data to reside in the locations expected of the instruction. Fig. 2.5 shows excerpts of an OMML specification for an IBM machine.

DMACS uses this information to generate a collection of *finite state automata* (or *state machines*, as they are also called) to determine how a given set of input values can be transferred into locations that are permissible for a given OMML macro. Each state machine consists of a directed graph where a node represents a specific configuration of register classes and memory, some of which are marked as permissible. The edges indicate how to transition from one state to another, and are labeled with the machine instruction that will enable the transition when executed on a particular input value. During compilation the instruction selector consults the appropriate state machine as it traverses from one MIML command to the next, using the input values of the former to initialize the state machine. As the state machine transitions from one state to another, the machine instructions appearing on the edges are emitted until the state machine reaches a permissible state.

1:	SS	C,J
2:	IMUL	1,D
3:	IADD	2,B
4:	SS	A,I
5:	ASSG	4,3

Fig. 2.4: An example on how an arithmetic expression A[I] = B + C[J] * D can be represented as MIML commands. The SS command is used for data referencing and the ASSG command assigns a value to a variable. The arguments to the MIML commands are referred to either by a variable symbol or by line number [255]

```
rclass REG:r2,r3,r4,r5,r6
rclass FREG:fr0,fr2,fr4,fr6
...
rpath WORD->REG: L REG,WORD
rpath REG->WORD: ST REG,WORD
rpath FREG-WORD: LE FREG,WORD
rpath WORD->FREG: STE FREG,WORD
...
ISUB s1,s2
from REG(s1),REG(s2) emit SR s1,s2  result REG(s1)
from REG(s1),WORD(s2) emit S s1,s2  result REG(s2)

FMUL m1,m2 (commutative)
from FREG(m1),FREG(m2) emit MER m1,m2  result FREG(m1)
from FREG(m1),WORD(m2) emit ME m1,m2   result FREG(m1)
```

Fig. 2.5: Partial machine description for IBM-360 in OMML. The `rclass` command declares a register class, and the `rpath` command declares a permissible transfer between a register class and memory (or vice versa) along with the instruction that implements the transfer [255]

The work by Miller was pioneering but limited: DMACS only handled arithmetic expressions consisting of integer and floating-point values, its addressing mode support was limited, and it could not model other target machine classes such as stack-based architectures. In his 1973 doctoral dissertation, Donegan [101] extended Miller's ideas by proposing a new language called *Code Generator Preprocessor Language (CGPL)*. Donegan's proposal was put to the test in the 1978 master's thesis by Maltz [247], and was later extended by Donegan et al. [100]. Similar techniques have also been developed by Tirrell [319] and Simoneaux [309], and in their survey Ganapathi et al. [150] describe another state machine-based compiler called UGEN, which was derived from a virtual machine called U-CODE [280].

Further Improvements

In 1975, Snyder [310] implemented one of the first fully operational and portable C compilers, where the target machine-dependent parts could be automatically generated from a machine description. The design is similar to Miller's in that the frontend first transforms the program into an equivalent representation for an abstract machine. In Snyder's design this representation consists of *abstract machine operations (AMOPs)*, which are then expanded into target-specific instructions via macros. The abstract machine and macros are specified in a machine description language which is also similar to Miller's, but handles more complex data types, addressing modes, alignment, as well as branching and function calls. If needed, more complicated macros can be defined as customized C functions. We mention Snyder's work primarily because it was later adapted by Johnson [191] in his implementation of PCC, which we will discuss in Chapter 3.

Fraser [140, 141] also recognized the need for human knowledge to guide the code generation process, and implemented a system with the aim of facilitating the addition of handwritten rules when these are required. First the program is transformed into a representation based on a programming language called *Extensible Language (XL)*, which is akin to high-level assembly language. For example, XL provides primitives for array accesses and *for* loops. As in the cases of Miller and Snyder, the instructions are provided via a separate description that maps directly to a distinct XL primitive. If some portion of the program cannot be implemented by any of the available instructions, the instruction selector will invoke a set of rules to rewrite the XL code until a solution is found. For example, array accesses are broken down into simpler primitives, and the same rule base can also be used to improve the code quality of the generated assembly code. Since these rules are provided as a separate machine description, they can be customized and augmented as needed to fit a particular target machine.

As we will see, this idea of "massaging" the program until a solution can be found has been applied, in one form or another, by many instruction selectors that both predate and succeed Fraser's design. Although they represent a popular approach, a significant drawback of such schemes is that the instruction selector may get stuck in an infinite loop if the set of rules is incomplete for a particular target machine, and determining if this is the case is often far from trivial. Moreover, such rules tend to be hard to reuse for other target machines.

2.2.3 Reducing Compilation Time with Tables

Despite their already simplistic nature, macro-expanding instruction selectors can be made even more so by representing the 1-to-1 or 1-to-n mappings as sets of tables. This further emphasizes the separation between the machine-independent core of the instruction selector from the machine-dependent mappings, as well as allows for denser implementations that require less memory and potentially reduce the *compilation time*, which is the time it takes to compile a given program.

Representing Instructions as Coding Skeletons

In 1969 Lowry and Medlock [243] introduced one of the first table-driven methods for code generation. In their implementation of *Fortran H Compiler (FHC)*, Lowry and Medlock used a bit string, called a *coding skeleton*, for each instruction. The bits represent the restrictions of the instructions, such as the modes permitted for the operands and the

```
L  B2,D(0,BD)  XXXXXXXX00000000
LH B2,D(0,B2)  0000111100000000
LR R1,R2       0000110100001101
```

result (for example, "load from memory," "load from register," "do not store," "use this or that base register"). These coding skeletons are then matched against the bit strings corresponding to the program under compilation. An 'X' appearing in the coding skeleton means that it will always match any bit.

The main disadvantage of Lowry and Medlock's design was that the tables could only be used for the most basic of instructions, and had to be written by hand in the case of FHC. More extensive designs were later developed by Tirrell [319] and Donegan [101], but these also suffered from similar disadvantages of making too many assumptions about the target machine, which hindered compiler retargetability.

Expanding Macros Top-Down

Later Krumme and Ackley [218] introduced a table-driven design which, unlike the earlier techniques, exhaustively enumerates all valid combinations of selectable instructions, schedules, and register allocations for a given program tree. Implemented in a C compiler targeting DEC-10 machines, the technique also allows code size to be factored in as an optimization goal, which was an uncommon feature at the time. Krumme and Ackley's backend applies a recursive algorithm that begins by selecting instructions for the root in the program tree, and then working its way down. In comparison, the bottom-up techniques we have examined so far all start at the leaves and then traverse upwards. We settle with this distinction for now as we will resume and deepen the discussion of bottom-up vs. top-down instruction selection in Chapter 3.

Enumerating all valid combinations in code generation leads to a combinatorial explosion, thus making it impossible to actually produce and check each and every one of them. To curb this immense complexity, Krumme and Ackley applied a strategy known as *branch-and-bound search*. The idea behind branch-and-bound search is straightforward: during search, always remember the best solution found so far and then prune away all parts of the search space which can be proven to yield a worse solution.[3] The problem is how to prove that a given branch in the search space will definitely lead to solutions that are worse than what we already have (and can thus be skipped). Krumme and Ackley only partially tackled this problem by pruning away branches that for sure will eventually lead to failure and thus yield no solution whatsoever. Without going into too much detail, this is done by using not just a single instruction table but several—one for each so-called *mode*—which are constructed in a hierarchical manner. In this context, a mode is oriented around the result of an expression, for example whether it is to be stored in a register or in memory. Using these tables, the instruction selector can look ahead and detect whether the current set of already-selected instructions will lead to a dead end. With this as the only method of branch pruning, however, the instruction selector will make many needless revisits in the search space, and consequently does not scale to larger program trees.

---

[3] In their paper, Krumme and Ackley actually call this α-β *pruning*, which is an entirely different search strategy, but their description of it fits more the branch-and-bound approach. Both are well explained in [297].

2.2.4 Falling Out of Fashion

Despite the improvements we have just discussed, they still do not resolve the main disadvantage of macro-expanding instruction selectors, namely that they can only handle macros that expand a single AST or IR node at a time. The limitation can be somewhat circumvented by allowing information about the visited nodes to be forwarded from one macro to the next, thereby postponing assembly code emission in the hopes that more efficient instructions can be used. However, if done manually—which was often the case—this quickly becomes an unmanageable task for the macro writer, in particular if backtracking becomes necessary due to faulty decisions made in prior macro invocations.

Thus naïve macro expanders are effectively limited to supporting only single-output instructions.[4] As this has a detrimental effect on code quality for target machines exhibiting more complicated features, such as multi-output instructions, instruction selectors based solely on naïve macro expansion were quickly replaced by newer, more powerful techniques when these started to appear in the late 1970s. One of these we will discuss later in this chapter.

Rekindled Application in the First Dynamic Code Generation Systems

Having fallen out of fashion, naïvely macro-expanding instruction selectors later made a brief reappearance in the first dynamic code generation systems that were developed in the 1980s and 1990s. In such systems the program is first compiled into *byte code*, which is a kind of target-independent machine code that can be interpreted by an underlying runtime environment. By providing an identical environment on every target machine, the same byte code can be executed on multiple systems without having to be recompiled.

The cost of this portability is that running a program in interpretive mode is typically much slower than executing native machine code. This performance loss can be mitigated by incorporating a compiler into the runtime environment. First, the byte code is profiled as it is executed. Frequently executed segments, such as inner loops, are then compiled into native machine code. Since the code segments are compiled at runtime, this scheme is called *JIT compilation*, which allows performance to be increased while retaining the benefits of the byte code. If the performance gap between running byte code instead of native machine code is large, then the compiler can afford to produce assembly code of low quality in order to decrease the overhead in the runtime environment. This was of great importance for the earliest dynamic runtime systems where hardware resources were typically scarce, which made macro-expanding instruction selection a reasonable option. A few examples include interpreters for SMALLTALK-80 [96] and OMNIWARE [1] (a predecessor to Java), and code generation systems, such as VCODE [113], GBURG [139] (which

---

[4] This is a truth with modification: a macro expander can emit multi-output instructions, but only one of its output values will be retained in the assembly code.

was used within a small virtual machine), and GNU LIGHTNING [16] (which was directly inspired by VCODE).

As technology progressed, however, dynamic code generation systems also began to transition to more powerful techniques for instruction selection such as tree covering, which will be described in Chapter 3.

2.3 Improving Code Quality with Peephole Optimization

An early but still applied method of improving the quality of generated assembly code is to perform a subsequent program optimization step that attempts to combine and replace several instructions with shorter, more efficient alternatives. These routines are known as *peephole optimizers* for reasons which will soon become apparent.

2.3.1 What Is Peephole Optimization?

In 1965, McKeeman [254] advocated the use of a simple but often neglected program optimization procedure which, as a post-step to code generation, inspects a small sequence of instructions in the assembly code and attempts to combine two or more adjacent instructions with a single instruction. Similar ideas were also suggested by Lowry and Medlock [243] around the same time. Doing this reduces code size and also improves performance as using complex instructions is often more efficient than using several simpler instructions to implement the same functionality.[5] Because of its narrow window of observation, this technique became known as *peephole optimization*.

Modeling Instructions with Register Transfer Lists

Since this kind of optimization is tailored for a particular target machine, the earliest implementations were (and still often are) done ad hoc and by hand. For example, in 2002, Krishnaswamy and Gupta [216] wrote a peephole optimizer by hand which reduces code size by replacing known patterns of ARM code with smaller equivalents. Recognizing the need for automation, Fraser [136] introduced in 1979 the first technique that allowed peephole optimizers to be generated from a formal description. The technique is also described in a longer article by Davidson and Fraser [93].

Like Miller, Fraser described the semantics of the instructions separately in a symbolic machine description. The machine description describes the observable effects that each instruction has on the target machine's registers. Fraser called these effects *register transfers (RTs)*, and each instruction thus has a corresponding *register*

---

[5] On a related note, this idea was applied by Cho et al. [75] for reselecting instructions in order to improve iterative modulo schedules for DSPs.

transfer list (RTL). For example, assume that we have a three-address add instruction which adds an immediate value imm to the value in register r_s, stores the result in register r_d, and sets a zero flag Z. For this instruction, the corresponding RTL would be expressed as

$$RTL(\text{add}) = \left\{ \begin{array}{l} r_d \leftarrow r_s + \text{imm} \\ Z \leftarrow (r_s + \text{imm}) \leftrightarrow 0 \end{array} \right\}.$$

The RTLs are then fed to a program called *Peephole Optimizer (PO)*, which produces a program optimization routine that makes two passes over the generated assembly code. The first pass runs backwards across the assembly code to determine the observable effects (that is, the RTL) of each instruction in the assembly code. This allows effects that have no impact on the program's observable behavior to be removed. For example, if the value of a status flag is not read by any subsequent instruction, it is considered to be *unobservable* and can thus be ignored. The second pass then checks whether the combined RTLs of two adjacent instructions are equal to that of some other instruction (in PO this check is done via a series of string comparisons). If such an instruction is found, the pair is replaced and the routine backs up one instruction in order to check the combination of the new instruction with the following instruction in the assembly code. This way replacements can be cascaded and many instructions reduced into a single equivalent, provided there exists an appropriate instruction for each intermediate step.

Pioneering as it was, PO also had several limitations. The main drawbacks were that it only supported combinations of two instructions at a time, and that these had to be lexicographically adjacent in the assembly code. The instructions were also not allowed to cross block boundaries, meaning that they had to belong to the same block. Davidson and Fraser [91] later removed the limitation of lexicographical adjacency by making use of data-flow graphs instead of operating directly on the assembly code, and they also extended the size of the instruction window from pairs to triples.

Further Developments

Much research has been dedicated to improving automated approaches to peephole optimization. In 1983, Giegerich [156] proposed a formal design that eliminates the need for a fixed-size instruction window. Shortly after, Kessler [202] introduced a method where RTL combinations and comparisons can be precomputed as the compiler is built, thus decreasing compilation time. Kessler [201] later expanded his work to incorporate an *n*-size instruction window, similar to that of Giegerich, although at an exponential cost.

Another scheme was developed by Massalin [253] who implemented a system called the SUPEROPTIMIZER, and similar systems have subsequently been referred to as *superoptimizers*. The SUPEROPTIMIZER accepts small programs written in assembly language, and then exhaustively combines sequences of instructions to find

shorter implementations that exhibit the same behavior as the original program.[6]
Granlund and Kenner [165] later adapted Massalin's ideas into a method that minimizes the number of branches. Both implementations, however, were implemented
by hand and customized for a particular target machine. Moreover, neither makes
any guarantees on correctness. A technique for automatically generating peephole
optimization-based superoptimizers was developed by Bansal and Aiken [38], where
the superoptimizer learns to optimize short sequences of instructions from a set of
training programs. A couple of designs that guarantee correctness have been developed by Joshi et al. [193, 194] and Crick et al. [90], who applied automatic theorem
proving and a method called *answer set programming*, respectively. Recently, a
similar technique based on *quantifier-free bit-vector logic* formulas was introduced
by Srinivasan and Reps [312].

2.3.2 Combining Naïve Macro Expansion with Peephole Optimization

Up to this point peephole optimizers had mainly been used to improve already-
generated assembly code—in other words, *after* instruction selection had been
performed. In 1984, however, Davidson and Fraser [91] developed an instruction
selection technique that incorporates the power of peephole optimization with the
simplicity of macro expansion. Similar yet unsuccessful strategies had already been
proposed earlier by Auslander and Hopkins [33] and Harrison [170], but Davidson
and Fraser struck the right balance between compiler retargetability and code quality, which made their design a viable option for production-quality compilers. This
scheme has hence become known as the *Davidson-Fraser approach*, and variants
of it have been used in several compilers, such as the *Y Compiler (YC)* [92], the
ZEPHYR/VPO system [19], the *Amsterdam Compiler Kit (ACK)* [318], and, most
famously the *GNU Compiler Collection (GCC)* [205, 313].

The Davidson-Fraser Approach

In the Davidson-Fraser approach the instruction selector consists of two parts: an
expander and a *combiner* (see Fig. 2.6). The task of the expander is to transform the
program into a series of RTLs. The transformation is done by executing simple macros
that expand every node in the program tree (assuming the program is represented as
such) into a corresponding RTL that describes the effects of that node. Unlike the
previous macro expanders we have discussed, these macros do not incorporate register

---

[6] The same idea has also been applied by El-Khalil and Keromytis [204] and Anckaert et al. [14],
where the assembly code of compiled programs is modified in order to support *steganography*
(the covert insertion of secret messages). For example, Anckaert et al. used this technique on
nine programs from the SPECint 2000 benchmark suite in order to embed and extract William
Shakespeare's play *King Lear*.

Fig. 2.6: Overview of the Davidson-Fraser approach [91]

allocation. Instead the expander assigns each result to a virtual storage location called a *temporary*, of which it is assumed there exists an infinite amount. A subsequent register allocator then assigns each temporary to a register, potentially inserting additional code that saves some values to memory for later retrieval when the number of available registers is not enough (this is called *register spilling*). After expansion, but before register allocation, the combiner is run. Using the same technique as that behind PO, the combiner tries to improve code quality by combining several RTLs in the program into a single, larger RTL that corresponds to some instruction on the target machine. For this to work, both the expander and the combiner must at every step adhere to a rule, called the *machine invariant*, which dictates that every RTL in the program must be implementable by a single instruction.

By using a subsequent peephole optimizer to combine the effects of multiple RTLs, the instruction selector can effectively extend over multiple nodes in the AST or program tree, potentially across block boundaries. The instruction support in Davidson and Fraser's design is therefore in theory only restricted by the number of instructions that the peephole optimizer can compare at a time. For example, opportunities to replace three instructions by a single instruction will be missed if the peephole optimizer only checks pair combinations. But increasing the window size typically incurs an exponential cost in terms of added complexity, thus making it difficult to handle complicated instructions that require large instruction windows.

Further Improvements

Fraser and Wendt [135] later expanded the work by Davidson and Fraser. In a paper from 1988, Fraser and Wendt describe a method where the expander and combiner are effectively fused together into a single component. The idea is to generate the instruction selector in two steps. The first step produces a naïve macro expander that is capable of expanding a single IR node at a time. Unlike Davidson and Fraser, who implemented the expander by hand, Fraser and Wendt applied an elaborate scheme consisting of a series of *switch* and *goto* statements—effectively implementing a state machine—which allowed their expander to be generated automatically from a machine description. Once produced, the macro expander is executed on a carefully designed training set. Using function calls embedded into the instruction selector, a retargetable peephole optimizer is executed in tandem which discovers and gathers statistics on target-specific optimizations that can be done on the generated assembly code. Based on these results, the beneficial optimization decisions are then selected and incorporated directly into the macro expander. This effectively enables the macro expander to expand multiple IR nodes at a time, thus removing the need for a separate peephole optimizer in the final compiler. Fraser and Wendt argued that as the instruction selector only implements the optimization decisions that are deemed to be "useful," the code quality is improved with minimal overhead. Wendt [335] later improved the technique by providing a more powerful machine description format, also based on RTLs, which subsequently evolved into a compact standalone language used for implementing code generators (see Fraser [134]).

Enforcing the Machine Invariant with a Recognizer

The Davidson-Fraser approach was also recently extended by Dias and Ramsey [98]. Instead of requiring each separate RTL-oriented optimization routine to abide by the machine invariant, Dias and Ramsey's design employs a *recognizer* to determine whether an optimization decision violates the aforementioned restriction (see Fig. 2.7). The idea is that, by doing so, the optimization routines can be simplified and generated automatically as they no longer need to internalize the machine invariant.

In a paper from 2006, Dias and Ramsey demonstrate how the recognizer can be produced from a declarative machine description written in λ-*RTL*. Originally developed by Ramsey and Davidson [288], λ-RTL is a high-level functional language based on ML (which stands for *Metalanguage*) and raises the level of abstraction for writing RTLs (see Fig. 2.8 for an example). In their paper, Dias and Ramsey claim that λ-RTL-based machine descriptions are more concise and simpler to write compared to those of many other designs, including GCC. In particular, λ-RTL is precise and unambiguous, which makes it suitable for automated tool generation and verification. The latter has been explored by Fernández and Ramsey [128] and Bailey and Davidson [34].

The recognizer checks whether an RTL in the program fulfills the machine invariant by performing a syntactic comparison between that RTL and the RTLs of the instructions. However, if a given RTL in the program has n operations, and a given

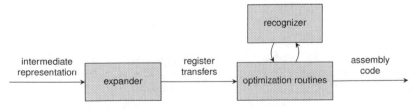

Fig. 2.7: Overview of Dias and Ramsey's design [98]

```
default attribute
    add(rd, rs1, rs2) is $r[rd] := $rs[rs1] + $r[rs2]
```

Fig. 2.8: A PowerPC add instruction specified using λ-RTL [97]

λ-RTL description contains m instructions whose RTL contains l operations, then a naïve implementation would take $O(nml)$ time to check a single RTL. Instead, using techniques to be discussed in Chapter 3, Dias and Ramsey automatically generate the recognizer as a finite state automaton that can compare a given RTL against all RTLs in the λ-RTL description with a single check.

"One Program to Expand Them All"

In 2010, Dias and Ramsey introduced a scheme, described in [97] and [289], where the macro expander only needs to be implemented once per every distinct *architecture family* instead of once per every distinct *instruction set*. For example, register-based and stack-based machines are two separate architecture families, whereas X86, PowerPC, and SPARC are three different instruction sets. In other words, if two target machines belong to the same architecture family, then the same expander can be used despite the differing details in their instruction sets. This is useful because the correctness of the expander only needs to be proven once, which is a difficult and time-consuming process if it is written by hand.

The idea is to have a predefined set of *tiles* that are specific for a particular architecture family. A tile represents a simple operation which is required for any target machine belonging to that architecture family. For example, stack-based machines require tiles for *push* and *pop* operations, which are not necessary on register-based machines. Then, instead of expanding each IR node in the program into a sequence of RTLs, the expander expands it into a sequence of tiles. Since the set of tiles is identical for all target machines within the same architecture family, the expander only needs to be implemented once. After macro expansion the tiles are replaced by the instructions used to implement each tile, and the resulting assembly code can then be improved by the combiner.

A remaining problem is how to find instructions to implement a given tile for a particular target machine. In the same papers, Dias and Ramsey describe a scheme for doing this automatically. By expressing both the tiles and the instructions as λ-RTL, Dias and Ramsey developed a technique where the RTLs of the instructions are combined such that the effects equal that of a tile. In broad outline, the algorithm maintains a pool of RTLs which initially contains those of the instructions found in the machine description. Using algebraic laws and combining existing RTLs to produce new RTLs, the pool is grown iteratively until either all tiles have been implemented, or some termination criterion is reached. The latter is necessary, as Dias and Ramsey proved that the general problem of finding implementations for arbitrary tiles is undecidable.

Although the primary aim of Dias and Ramsey's design is to facilitate compiler retargetability, some experiments suggest that it potentially also yields better code quality than the original Davidson-Fraser approach. When a prototype was compared against the default instruction selector in GCC, the results favored the former. However, this was seen only when all target-independent optimizations were disabled; when they were reactivated, GCC still produced better results.

2.3.3 *Running Peephole Optimization Before Instruction Selection*

In the techniques just discussed, the peephole optimizer runs after code generation. But in a scheme developed in 1989 by Genin et al. [155], a similar routine is executed *before* code generation. Targeting digital signal processors, their compiler first transforms the program into an *internal signal-flow graph (ISFG)*, and then executes a routine—Genin et al. called it a *pattern matcher*—which attempts to find several low-level operations in the ISFG that can be merged into single nodes.[7] Code generation is then done following the conventional macro expansion approach. For each node the instruction selector invokes a rule along with the information about the current context. The invoked rule produces the assembly code appropriate for the given context, and can also insert new nodes to offload decisions that are deemed better handled by the rules corresponding to the inserted nodes.

According to Genin et al., experiments show that their compiler generated assembly code that was five to 50 times faster than that produced by other, contemporary DSP compilers, and comparable with manually optimized assembly code. A disadvantage of this design is that it is limited to programs where prior knowledge about the application area, in this case digital signal processing, can be encoded into specific optimization routines, which most likely has to be done manually.

2.3.4 *Interactive Code Generation*

The aforementioned techniques yield peephole optimizers which are static once they have been generated, meaning they will only recognize and optimize assembly code for a fixed set of patterns. A method to overcome this issue has been designed by Kulkarni et al. [219], which is also the first and only one to my knowledge.

In a paper from 2006, Kulkarni et al. describe a compiler system called VISTA, which is an interactive compilation environment where the user is given greater control over the compiler. Among other things, the user can alter RTLs derived from the program's source code and add new customized peephole optimization patterns. Hence optimization privileges which normally are limited to low-level assembly programmers are also granted to higher-level programming language users. In addition, Kulkarni et al. employed genetic algorithms—these will be explained in Chapter 3— in an attempt to automatically derive a combination of user-provided optimization guidelines to improve the code quality of a particular program. Experiments show that this scheme reduced code size on average by 4% and up to 12% for a selected set of programs.

---

[7] The paper is not clear on how this is done exactly, but presumably Genin et al. implemented the routine as a handwritten peephole optimizer since the intermediate format is fixed and does not change from one target machine to another.

2.4 Summary

In this chapter we have discussed techniques and designs based on a principle known as macro expansion, which was the first approach to perform instruction selection. The idea behind the principle is to expand the nodes in the AST or IR code into one or more target-specific instructions. The expansion is done via template matching and macro invocation, which yields instruction selectors that are resource-effective and straightforward to implement.

But because macro-expanding instruction selectors only visit and execute macros one IR node at a time, they require a 1-to-1 or 1-to-n mapping between the IR nodes and the instructions provided by the target machine in order to generate efficient assembly code. The limitation can be mitigated by incorporating additional logic and bookkeeping into the macros, but this quickly becomes an unmanageable task for the macro writer if done manually. Consequently, the code quality yielded by these techniques will typically be low. Moreover, as instructions are often emitted one at a time, it also becomes difficult to make use of instructions that can have unintended effects on other instructions.

A more robust remedy for improving code quality is to append a peephole optimizer into the component chain of the backend. A peephole optimizer combines the effects of multiple instructions in the assembly code with more efficient alternatives, thereby amending some of the poor decisions made by the instruction selector. Peephole optimization can also be incorporated directly into the instruction selector—a scheme which has become known as the Davidson-Fraser approach—and thereby extend its machine instruction support. Because of this versatility, the Davidson-Fraser approach remains one of the most powerful instruction selection techniques to date (a variant is still applied in GCC as of version 4.8.2).

In Chapter 3 we will explore another principle of instruction selection, which solves the problem of implementing several AST or IR nodes using a single instruction in a more direct fashion.

Chapter 3
Tree Covering

As we saw in Chapter 2, the main limitation of most instruction selectors based on macro expansion is that the scope of expansion is restricted to a single AST or IR node. Hence exploitation of many instructions is excluded, resulting in low code quality. Another problem is that macro-expanding instruction selectors typically combine pattern matching and pattern selection into a single step, thus making it very difficult to consider combinations of instructions and then pick the one that yields the "best" assembly code.

These problems can be solved by employing another principle of instruction selection called *tree covering*, which is also the most common principle of techniques found in the current literature.

3.1 The Principle

Let us assume that the program is represented as a set of program trees, which we are already familiar with from Chapter 2 (see p. 15). Let us further assume that each instruction can be modeled similarly to a *pattern tree*. When there is no risk of confusion, we will refer to these as simply *patterns*. We also say that the set of all patterns available during tree covering constitute the *pattern set*. The task of instruction selection can then be reduced to finding a subset of the pattern set such that every node in the program tree is *covered* by at least one pattern. Here we see clearly how pattern matching and pattern selection constitute two separate problems in

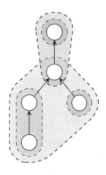

instruction selection. In the former we need to find which patterns are applicable for a given program tree and where they are applicable. We call each such instance a *pattern match* (or simply *match*), and there may exist multiple matches for the same pattern and program tree. In the latter problem we then select from these matches a subset which results in a valid and efficient cover of the program tree. For most

© Springer International Publishing Switzerland 2016
G. Hjort Blindell, *Instruction Selection*,
DOI 10.1007/978-3-319-34019-7_3

target machines there will be a tremendous amount of overlap among the patterns, meaning that one pattern may match (either partially or fully) the nodes matched by another pattern in the program tree. Typically we want to use as few patterns as possible to cover the program tree. This is for two reasons:

- Striving for the smallest number of patterns means favoring larger patterns over smaller ones. This in turn leads to the use of more complex instructions which typically yield higher code quality.
- The amount of overlap between the selected patterns is limited, which means that the same values will be computed multiple times only when necessary. Keeping redundant work to a minimum is another crucial factor for performance as well as for reducing code size.

In general, an optimal solution to the pattern selection problem is not defined as the one that minimizes the *number* of selected patterns, but as the one that minimizes the *total cost* of the selected patterns. This allows the pattern costs to be chosen such that they fit the desired optimization criteria, although there is usually a strong correlation between the number of patterns and the total cost. Note, however, that an optimal solution to the pattern selection problem need not necessarily be an optimal solution for the final assembly code. But unlike optimal *instruction* selection, whose problematic definition was criticized in Chapter 1, optimal *pattern* selection is less controversial since it is clear that we will only consider the patterns currently available in the pattern set instead of all patterns that could potentially be derived from the ISA.

Finding the optimal solution to a tree covering problem is not a trivial task, and it becomes even less so if only certain combinations of patterns are allowed. To be sure, most of us would be hard-pressed just to come up with an efficient method that finds all valid matches of the entire pattern set. We therefore begin by exploring the first methods that address the pattern matching problem, but do not necessarily address the pattern selection problem, and then gradually transition to those that do.

3.2 First Techniques to Use Tree-Based Pattern Matching

In 1972 and 1973, the first code generation techniques known to use tree-based pattern matching were introduced by Wasilew [331] and Weingart [332], respectively. Unfortunately only Weingart's work appears to be recognized by other literature, even though Wasilew's ideas have more in common with later tree-based instruction selection techniques. We will briefly cover both in this book, as described by Lunell [244], who gives a more detailed account in his doctoral dissertation.

To begin with, Wasilew devised an intermediate representation where the programs are represented using a postfix notation (see Fig. 3.1). This is also called *reverse Polish notation*, which we will discuss further in Section 3.3.1. Wasilew also developed his own programming language, which is transformed into IR code as part of compilation. The instructions of the target machine are described in a

```
AWAY m YHPASS assign
K AMA m PMFI 7 - assign
Z K AMA m ANS assign assign
X 8 + m HEAD X 6 + m I1 + m X 6 + m I2 + m assign
X Y FR AA transfer assign
X INC if-AZ BB transfer
OR m MAJ 4FCOID 4FCOIN if-equal2 1 J + transfer
```

Fig. 3.1: An example program expressed using Wasilew's intermediate language [244]

table, where each instruction comprises execution time and code size information, a string constituting the assembly code, and the pattern to be matched against the program. For each line in the program, pattern matching is done starting at a leaf in the tree corresponding to the current line. For this subtree, all matches are found by comparing it against all patterns in the pattern set. The subtree is then grown to include its parent, and the new subtree is again compared against the patterns. This continues until no new matches are found. Once the largest match has been found, the subtree is replaced with the result of the pattern, and the process is repeated for the remaining parts in the tree. If multiple largest matches are found for any subtree, the process is repeated for each such match. This results in an exhaustive search that finds all combinations of patterns for a given tree. Once all combinations have been found, the cheapest combination—whose cost is based on the instructions' execution time and code size—is selected.

Compared to the early macro-expanding instruction selectors (at least those prior to Davidson-Fraser), Wasilew's design had a more extensive instruction support as it could include patterns that extend over multiple IR nodes. However, its exhaustive nature makes it considerably more expensive in terms of compilation time. In addition, the notations used by Wasilew are difficult to read and write.

In comparison to Wasilew, Weingart's design is centered around a single tree of patterns—Weingart called this a *discrimination net*—which is automatically derived from a declarative machine description. Using a single tree of patterns, Weingart argued, allows for a compact and efficient means of representing the pattern set. The process of building the AST is then extended to simultaneously push each new AST node onto a stack. In tandem, the discrimination net is progressively traversed by comparing the nodes on the stack against the children of the current node in the net. A match is found when the process reaches a leaf in the discrimination net, whereupon the instruction associated with the match is emitted.

Like Wasilew's design, Weingart's had a more extensive instruction support compared to the contemporary techniques as it could include patterns extending over multiple AST nodes. However, when applied in practice, the design suffered from several problems. First, structuring the discrimination net to support efficient pattern matching proved difficult for certain target machines; it is known that Weingart struggled in particular with the PDP-11. Second, the design assumes that there exists at least one instruction on the target machine that corresponds to a particular node type of the AST, which turned out to not always be the case. Weingart partly addressed this problem by introducing *conversion patterns*, which could transform mismatched parts of the AST into another form that hopefully would be matched by some pattern at a later stage, but these had to be added manually and could potentially cause the compiler to get stuck in an infinite loop. Third, like its macro-expanding predecessors, the process immediately selects a pattern as soon as a match is found.

Another early pattern matching technique was developed by Johnson [191], which was implemented in the *Portable C Compiler (PCC)*—a renowned system that was the first standard C compiler to be shipped with UNIX. Johnson based his design on the earlier work by Snyder [310] (which we discussed in Section 2.2.2), but replaced the use of macro expansion with a method that performs *tree rewriting*. For each instruction, a program tree is formed together with a *rewrite rule*, subgoals, resource requirements, and an assembly string which is emitted verbatim. This information is given in a machine description format that allows multiple, similar patterns to be condensed into a single declaration. An example is shown in Fig. 3.2.

The pattern matching process is then relatively straightforward: for a given node in the program tree, the node is compared against the root of each pattern. If these match, a similar check is done for each corresponding subtree in the pattern. Once all leaves in the pattern are reached, a match has been found. As this algorithm—whose pseudo-code is given in Fig. 3.3—exhibits quadratic time complexity, it is desirable to minimize the number of redundant checks. This is done by maintaining

```
 1: ASG PLUS,      INAREG,
 2:                SAREG,    TINT,
 3:                SNAME,    TINT,
 4:                          0,        RLEFT,
 5:                          "         add        AL,AR\n",
 6: ...
 7: ASG OPSIM,     INAREG|FORCC,
 8:                SAREG,         TINT|TUNSIGNED|TPOINT,
 9:                SAREG|SNAME|SOREG|SCON,    TINT|TUNSIGNED|TPOINT,
10:                          0,                RLEFT|RESCC
11:                          "                 OI          AL,AR\n",
```

Fig. 3.2: A machine description sample for PCC, consisting of two patterns. The first line specifies the node type of the root (+=, for the first pattern) together with its cookie ("result must appear in an A-type register"). The second and third lines specify the left and right descendants, respectively, of the root. The left subtree of the first pattern must be an `int` allocated in an A-type register, and the right subtree must be a `NAME` node, also of type `int`. The fourth line indicates that no registers or temporaries are required and that the matched part in the program tree is to be replaced by the left descendant of the pattern's root. The fifth and last line declares the assembly string, where lowercase letters are output verbatim and uppercase words indicate a macro invocation—AL stands for "Address form of Left operand", and likewise for AR—whose result is then put into the assembly string. In the second pattern we see that multiple restrictions can be *OR*'ed together, thus allowing multiple patterns to be expressed in a more concise manner [192]

```
FINDMATCHSET(program tree rooted at node n, set P of pattern trees):
 1:  initialize matchset as empty
 2:  for each pattern p ∈ P do
 3:    if MATCHES(n, p) then
 4:      add p to matchset
 5:    end if
 6:  end for
 7:  return matchset

MATCHES(program tree rooted at node n, pattern tree rooted at node p):
 1:  if n matches p and number of children of n and p are equal then
 2:    for each child n' of n and child p' of p do
 3:      if not MATCHES(n', p') then
 4:        return false
 5:      end if
 6:    end for
 7:  end if
 8:  return true
```

Fig. 3.3: A straightforward, tree-based pattern matching algorithm with $O(nm)$ time complexity, where n is the number of nodes in the program tree and m is the total number of nodes in the patterns

a set of code generation goals which are encoded into the instruction selector as an integer. For historical reasons this integer is called a *cookie*, and each pattern has a corresponding cookie indicating the situations in which the pattern may be useful. If both the cookies and the pattern match, an attempt is made to allocate whatever resources are demanded by the pattern (for example, a pattern may require a certain number of registers). If successful, the corresponding assembly string is emitted, and the matched subtree in the program tree is replaced by a single node as specified by the rewrite rule. This process of matching and rewriting repeats until the program tree consists of only a single node, meaning that the entire program tree has been successfully converted into assembly code. If no pattern matches, the instruction selector enters a heuristic mode where the program tree is partially rewritten until a match is found. For example, to match an a = reg + b pattern, an a += b expression could first be rewritten into a = a + b and then another rule could try to force operand a into a register.

Although successful for its time, PCC had several disadvantages. Like Weingart, Johnson used heuristic rewrite rules to handle mismatching situations. Without formal methods of verification there was always the risk that the current set of rules would be inadequate and potentially cause the compiler to never terminate for certain programs. Reiser [293] also noted that the investigated version of PCC only supported unary and binary patterns with a maximum height of 1, thus excluding many instructions, such as those with complex addressing modes. Lastly, PCC—and all other techniques discussed so far—still adhered to the *first-matched-first-served* approach when selecting patterns.

3.3 Using LR Parsing to Cover Trees Bottom-Up

As already noted, a common flaw among the first designs is that they (i) apply the greediest form of pattern selection, and (ii) typically lack a formal methodology. In contrast, syntactic analysis—which is the task of parsing the source code—is arguably the best understood area of compilation, and its methods also produce completely table-driven parsers that are very fast and resource-efficient.

3.3.1 The Graham-Glanville Approach

In 1978, Glanville and Graham [158] presented a seminal paper that describes how techniques of syntactic analysis can be adapted to instruction selection.[1] Subsequent experiments and evaluations showed that this design—which we will refer to as the *Graham-Glanville approach*—proved simpler and more general than contemporary designs [9, 150, 163, 164, 220]. Moreover, due to its table-driven nature, assembly code could be generated very rapidly (although the performance of the first implementations matched that of other instruction selectors used at the time). Consequently the Graham-Glanville approach has been acknowledged as one of the most significant breakthroughs in this field, and these ideas have influenced many later techniques in one way or another. In particular, Henry [177] received his doctoral degree for his research on Graham-Glanville code generators, and his 1984 doctoral dissertation provides an extremely deep and thorough account of the theory and practice of this approach.

Expressing Instructions as a Grammar

To begin with, a well-known method of removing the need for parentheses in arithmetic expressions without making them ambiguous is to use Polish notation. For example, 1 + (2 + 3) can be written as + 1 + 2 3 and still denote the same expression. Glanville and Graham recognized that by using this form the instructions can be expressed as a *context-free grammar* based on *Backus-Naur form (BNF)*. This concept is already well described in most compiler textbooks (see for example [8]), so we will proceed with only a brief introduction.

A context-free grammar consists of a set of *terminals* and *nonterminals*, and we will refer to both as *symbols*. We will distinguish between the two by always writing terminals with an initial capital letter (for example Term), and nonterminals entirely in lowercase (for example nt). For each nonterminal there exists one or more *productions* of the following form:

$+ c * a b$

---

[1] This had also been vaguely hinted at ten years earlier in an article by Feldman and Gries [126].

$$\text{lhs} \rightarrow \text{Right hand Side} \dots$$

A production basically specifies how its left-hand side nonterminal symbol can be replaced by its right-hand side as a string of terminal and nonterminal symbols. Since nonterminals can appear on both sides in a production, most grammars allow for infinite chains of replacements, which is one of the powerful features of context-free grammars. In terms of recursion, one can also think of nonterminals as inducing the recursive case whereas the terminals provide the base case that stops the recursion. Productions are often also called *production rules* or just *rules*, and although they can typically be interchanged without causing confusion, we will be consistent in this book and only use the first term (productions), as rules will hold a slightly different meaning.

To model a set of instructions as a context-free grammar, one would add one or more *rules* for each instruction. Each rule contains a production, a cost, and an *action*. The right-hand side of the production represents the pattern tree to be matched over a program tree, and the left-hand side contains the nonterminal indicating the characteristics of the result of executing the instruction (like a specific register class). The cost should be self-explanatory at this point, and the action would typically be to emit a string of assembly code. We illustrate the anatomy of a rule more succinctly with an annotated example:

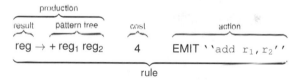

The collection of rules for a particular target machine is called the *instruction set grammar* of that machine.

In most literature, rules and patterns usually have the same connotations. In this book, however, in the context of grammars a rule refers to a tuple of production, cost, and action, and a pattern refers to the right-hand side of the production appearing in a rule.

Tree Parsing

The instruction set grammar provides us with a formal methodology for modeling instructions, but it does not address the problems of pattern matching and pattern selection. For that, Glanville and Graham applied an already-known technique called *left-to-right, right-most derivation (LR) parsing* [208]. Because this technique is mostly associated with syntactic analysis, the same application on trees is commonly referred to as *tree parsing*.

As an example, let us assume that we have the instruction set grammar

	PRODUCTION	COST	ACTION
1	reg $\rightarrow$ + reg$_1$ reg$_2$	1	EMIT ``add r$_1$,r$_2$''
2	reg $\rightarrow$ * reg$_1$ reg$_2$	1	EMIT ``mul r$_1$,r$_2$''
3	reg $\rightarrow$ Int	1	EMIT ``mv r,I''

and that we want to generate assembly code for the program tree

$$+ \; c \; * \; a \; b$$

such that the result of the expression ends up in a register. If a, b, and c all are integers, then we can assume that each node in the program tree is of type Int, *, or +. These will be our terminals.

After transforming the program trees into sequences of terminals, we traverse each from left to right. In doing so we either *shift* the just-traversed symbol onto a stack, or replace symbols currently on the stack via a *rule reduction*. A *reduce* operation consists of two steps. First, the symbols are popped according to those that appear on the pattern of the rule. The number and order of symbols popped must match exactly for a valid rule reduction. Once popped, the nonterminal appearing on the left-hand side is pushed onto the stack, and the assembly code associated with the rule, if any, is also emitted. For a given input the performed rule reductions can also be represented as a *parse tree*, illustrating the terminals and nonterminals which were used to parse the tree. Now, turning back to our example, if we denote a shift by s and a reduce by r_x, where x is the number of the reduced rule, then a valid tree parsing of the program tree

$$+ \; \text{Int}(c) \; * \; \text{Int}(a) \; \text{Int}(b)$$

could be

$$s \; s \; s \; r_3 \; s \; r_3 \; r_2 \; s \; r_3 \; r_1.$$

For this particular tree parsing, the corresponding parse tree and generated assembly code is shown below (the rule numbers are shown next to the nonterminals in the parse tree):

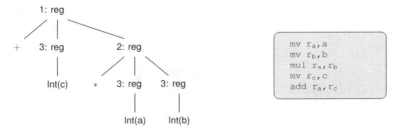

The problem that remains is how to know when to shift and when to reduce. This can be addressed by consulting a state table which has been generated for a specific grammar. How this table is produced is out of scope for this book, but an example, generated from the instruction set grammar appearing in Fig. 3.4, is given in Fig. 3.5, and a walk-through of executing an instruction selector with this state table using an *LR parser* is provided in Fig. 3.6.

The subscripts that appear in some of the productions in Fig. 3.4 are *semantic qualifiers*, which are used to express restrictions that may appear for some of the instructions. For example, all two-address arithmetic instructions store the result in one of the registers provided as input, and using semantic quantifiers this could be expressed as $r_1 \rightarrow + r_1 r_2$, indicating that the destination register must be the same as that of the first operand. To make this information available during parsing, the parser pushes it onto the stacking along with its corresponding terminal or nonterminal symbol. Glanville and Graham also incorporated a register allocator into their parser, thus constituting an entire code generator.

Resolving Conflicts and Avoiding Blocking

As ISAs are rarely nonorthogonal, most instruction set grammars are *ambiguous*, meaning multiple valid parse trees may exist for the same program tree. This causes the instruction selector to have the option of performing either a shift or a reduce, which is known as *shift-reduce conflict*. To solve this kind of conflict, Glanville and Graham's state table generator always decides to shift. The intuition is that this will favor larger patterns over smaller ones as a shift postpones a decision to pattern select while allowing more information about the program tree to accumulate on the stack.[2] Unfortunately, this scheme can cause the instruction selector to fail even though a valid parse tree exists. This is called *syntactic blocking* and requires the grammar designer to augment the instruction set grammar with auxiliary rules that patch the top of the stack, thus allowing the parser to recover from situations when it greedily decides to shift instead of applying a necessary rule reduction.

Likewise, there is also the possibility of *reduce-reduce conflicts*, where the parser has the option of choosing between two or more rules in a reduction. Glanville and Graham resolved these by selecting the rule with the longest pattern. If the grammar contains rules that differ only in their semantic quantifiers, then there may still exist more than one rule to reduce (in Fig. 3.4, rules 5 and 6 are two such rules). These are resolved at parse time by checking the semantic restrictions in the order in which they appear in the grammar (see for example state 20 in Fig. 3.5). If all rules in this set are semantically constrained, then situations can arise where the parser is unable to apply any rule due to semantic mismatch. This is called *semantic blocking* and can be resolved by always providing a default rule that can be invoked when all other semantically constrained rules fail. This fallback rule typically uses multiple, shorter instructions to simulate the effect of the more complex rule, and Glanville and Graham devised a clever trick to infer them automatically. For every semantically constrained rule r, tree parsing is performed over the tree representing the pattern of r, and then the instructions selected to implement this tree constitute the implementation of the fallback rule for r.

---

[2] The approach of always selecting the largest possible pattern is a scheme commonly known as *maximum munch*, which was coined by Cattell in his doctoral dissertation [69].

PRODUCTION	ACTION
1	$r_2 \rightarrow + Ld + C\, r_1\, r_2$	add r_2, C, r_1
2	$r_1 \rightarrow + r_1\, Ld + C\, r_2$	add r_1, C, r_2
3	$r \rightarrow + Ld\, C\, r$	add r, C
4	$r \rightarrow + r\, Ld\, C$	add r, C
5	$r_1 \rightarrow + r_1\, r_2$	add r_1, r_2
6	$r_2 \rightarrow + r_1\, r_2$	add r_2, r_1
7	$\rightarrow = Ld + C\, r_1\, r_2$	store $r_2, *C, r_1$
8	$\rightarrow = + C\, r_1\, r_2$	store r_2, C, r_1
9	$\rightarrow = Ld\, C\, r$	store $r, *C$
10	$\rightarrow = C\, r$	store r, C
11	$\rightarrow = r_1\, r_2$	store r_2, r_1
12	$r_2 \rightarrow Ld + C\, r_1$	load r_2, C, r_1
13	$r_2 \rightarrow + C\, r_1$	load $r_2, =c, r_1$
14	$r_2 \rightarrow + r_1\, C$	load $r_2, =C, r_1$
15	$r_2 \rightarrow Ld\, r_1$	load $r_2, *r_1$
16	$r \rightarrow Ld\, C$	load $r, =C$
17	$r \rightarrow C$	mv r, C

Fig. 3.4: An example of an instruction set grammar. All rules have the same unit cost. C, Ld, $+$, and $=$ are all terminals (C stands for "const" and Ld for "load"), r is a nonterminal indicating that the result will be stored in a register, and subscripts denote the semantic qualifiers [158]

	$	r	c	+	Ld	=
0	*accept*					s1
1		s2	s3	s4	s5	
2		s6	s7	s8	s9	
3		s10	s7	s8	s9	
4		s11	s12	s8	s13	
5		s14	s15	s16	s9	
6	r11	r11	r11	r11	r11	r11
7	r17	r17	r17	r17	r17	r17
8		s11	s17	s8	s13	
9		s14	s18	s19	s9	
10	r10	r10	r10	r10	r10	r10
11		s20	s21	s8	s22	
12		s23	s7	s8	s9	
13		s14	s24	s25	s9	
14	r15	r15	r15	r15	r15	r15
15		s26	s7	s8	s9	
16		s11	s27	s8	s13	
17		s28	s7	s8	s9	
18	r16	r16	r16	r16	r16	r16
19		s11	s29	s8	s13	
20	r5/6	r5/6	r5/6	r5/6	r5/6	r5/6
21	r14	r14	r14	r14	r14	r14
22		s14	s30	s31	s9	
23		s32	s7	s8	s9	
24		s33	s7	s8	s9	
25		s11	s34	s8	s13	
26	r9	r9	r9	r9	r9	r9
27		s35	s7	s8	s9	
28	r13	r13	r13	r13	r13	r13
29		s36	s7	s8	s9	
30	r4	r4	r4	r4	r4	r4
31		s11	s37	s8	s13	
32	r8	r8	r8	r8	r8	r8
33	r3	r3	r3	r3	r3	r3
34		s38	s7	s8	s9	
35		s39	s7	s8	s9	
36	r12	r12	r12	r12	r12	r12
37		s40	s7	s8	s9	
38		s41	s7	s8	s9	
39	r7	r7	r7	r7	r7	r7
40	r2	r2	r2	r2	r2	r2
41	r1	r1	r1	r1	r1	r1

Fig. 3.5: State table generated from the instruction set grammar given in Fig. 3.4. sx indicates a shift to the next state x, ri indicates the reduction of rule i, and a blank entry indicates an error [158]

	STATE STACK	SYMBOL STACK	INPUT	ACTION
1	0		$= + C_a\ r_7 + Ld + C_b\ Ld\ r_7\ Ld\ C_c\ \$$	shift to 1
2	0 1	$=$	$+ C_a\ r_7 + Ld + C_b\ Ld\ r_7\ Ld\ C_c\ \$$	shift to 4
3	0 1 4	$= +$	$C_a\ r_7 + Ld + C_b\ Ld\ r_7\ Ld\ C_c\ \$$	shift to 12
4	0 1 4 12	$= + C_a$	$r_7 + Ld + C_b\ Ld\ r_7\ Ld\ C_c\ \$$	shift to 23
5	0 1 4 12 23	$= + C_a\ r_7$	$+ Ld + C_b\ Ld\ r_7\ Ld\ C_c\ \$$	shift to 8
6	0 1 4 12 23 8	$= + C_a\ r_7 +$	$Ld + C_b\ Ld\ r_7\ Ld\ C_c\ \$$	shift to 13
7	0 1 4 12 23 8 13	$= + C_a\ r_7 + Ld$	$+ C_b\ Ld\ r_7\ Ld\ C_c\ \$$	shift to 25
8	0 1 4 12 23 8 13 25	$= + C_a\ r_7 + Ld +$	$C_b\ Ld\ r_7\ Ld\ C_c\ \$$	shift to 34
9	0 1 4 12 23 8 13 25 34	$= + C_a\ r_7 + Ld + C_b$	$Ld\ r_7\ Ld\ C_c\ \$$	shift to 9
10	0 1 4 12 23 8 13 25 34 9	$= + C_a\ r_7 + Ld + C_b\ Ld$	$r_7\ Ld\ C_c\ \$$	shift to 14
11	0 1 4 12 23 8 13 25 34 9 14	$= + C_a\ r_7 + Ld + C_b\ Ld\ r_7$	$Ld\ C_c\ \$$	reduce rule 15 ($r_c \rightarrow Ld\ r_1$) / assign result to r8 / emit ``load r8,*r7'' / shift to 38
12	0 1 4 12 23 8 13 25 34 38	$= + C_a\ r_7 + Ld + C_b\ r_8$	$Ld\ C_c\ \$$	shift to 9
13	0 1 4 12 23 8 13 25 34 38 9	$= + C_a\ r_7 + Ld + C_b\ r_8\ Ld$	$C_c\ \$$	shift to 18
14	0 1 4 12 23 8 13 25 34 38 9 18	$= + C_a\ r_7 + Ld + C_b\ r_8\ Ld\ C_c$	$\$$	reduce rule 16 ($r \rightarrow Ld\ C$) / assign result to r9 / emit ``load r9,C'' / shift to 41
15	0 1 4 12 23 8 13 25 34 38 41	$= + C_a\ r_7 + Ld + C_b\ r_8\ r_9$	$\$$	reduce rule 1 ($r_2 \rightarrow + Ld + C\ r_1\ r_2$) / emit ``add r9,B,r8'' / shift to 32
16	0 1 4 12 23 32	$= + C_a\ r_7\ r_2$	$\$$	reduce rule 8 ($\rightarrow = + C\ r_1\ r_2$) / emit ``store r9,A,r7''
17	0		$\$$	accept

Fig. 3.6: A walk-through of executing Glanville and Graham's instruction selector on an expression $a = b + c$, where a, b and c are constants residing in memory, which yielded the IR code $= + C_a\ r_7 + Ld + C_b\ Ld\ r_7\ Ld\ C_c$, where r_7 is the base address register. The execution is based on the precomputed table from Fig. 3.5. The proceedings of the reduction steps may need some explanation. A rule reduction may involve two operations: the mandatory reduce operation, followed by an optional operation which may be a shift or another rule reduction. Let us examine step 11. First, a reduce is executed using rule 15, which pops $Ld\ r_7$ from the symbol stack. This is followed by pushing the result of the rule, r_8, on top. At the same time, states 9 and 14 are popped from the stack, which leaves state 34 on top. The top elements of both stacks are now used to consult the state table for inferring the next, additional action (if any). In this case, input symbol r_8 at state 34 leads to a shift to state 38 [158]

Advantages

By relying on a state table, Graham-Glanville-style instruction selectors are completely table-driven and implemented by a core that basically consists of a series of table lookups.[3] Consequently, the time it takes for the instruction selector to generate the assembly code is linearly proportional to the size of the program tree. Although the idea of table-driven code generation was not novel in itself—we have seen several examples of it in Chapter 2—earlier attempts had all failed to provide an automated procedure for producing the tables. In addition, many decisions regarding pattern selection are precomputed by resolving shift-reduce and reduce-reduce conflicts at the time that the state table is generated, thus reducing compilation time.

Another advantage of the Graham-Glanville approach is its formal foundation, which enables means of automatic verification. For instance, Emmelmann [111] presented one of the first methods of proving the completeness of an instruction set grammar.[4] The intuition behind Emmelmann's automatic prover is to find all program trees that can appear in the program but cannot be handled by the instruction selector. Let us denote an instruction set grammar by $\mathscr{G}$ and a grammar describing the program trees by $\mathscr{T}$. If we further use $L(X)$ to represent the set of all trees accepted by a grammar X, we can then determine whether the instruction set grammar is incomplete by checking if $L(\mathscr{T})\backslash L(\mathscr{G})$ yields a nonempty set. Emmelmann recognized that this intersection can be computed by creating a *product automaton* which essentially implements the language that accepts only the trees in this set of counterexamples. From this automaton it is also possible to derive the rules that are missing from the instruction set grammar. Brandner [54] recently extended this method to handle productions that contain predicates—we will discuss these shortly when exploring attribute grammars—by splitting terminals to expose these otherwise-hidden characteristics.

Disadvantages

Although it addressed several of the problems with contemporary instruction selection techniques, the Graham-Glanville approach also had disadvantages of its own. First, since an LR parser can only reason on syntax, any restrictions regarding specific values or ranges must be captured by its own nonterminal. In conjunction with the limitation that each production can match only a single pattern, this typically meant that rules for versatile instructions with several addressing or operand modes had to be duplicated for each such mode. For most target machines this turned out to be

---

[3] Pennello [279] developed a technique to express the state table directly as assembly code, thus eliminating even the need to perform table lookups. This was reported to improve the efficiency of LR parsing by six to ten times.

[4] Note, however, that even though an instruction set grammar has been proven to be complete, a greedy instruction selector may still fail to use a necessary rule. Consequently, Emmelmann's checker assumes that an optimal instruction selector will be used for the proven instruction set grammar.

impracticable. For example, in the case of the VAX machine—a *complex instruction set computer (CISC)* architecture from the 1980s, where each instruction accepted a multitude of operand modes [71]—the instruction set grammar would contain over eight million rules [164]. By introducing auxiliary nonterminals to combine features shared among the rules—a task called *refactoring*—the number was brought down to about a thousand rules, but this had to be done carefully to not have a negative impact on code quality. Second, since the parser traverses from left to right without backtracking, assembly code regarding one operand has to be emitted before any other operand can be observed. This can potentially lead to poor decisions which later have to be undone by emitting additional code, as in the case of recovering from syntactic blocking. Hence, to design an instruction set grammar that was both compact and yielded good code quality, the developer had to possess extensive knowledge about the implementation of the instruction selector.

3.3.2 Extending Grammars with Semantic Handling

In purely context-free grammars there is just no way to handle semantic information. For example, the exact register represented by a reg nonterminal is not available. Glanville and Graham worked around this limitation by pushing the information onto the stack, but even then their modified LR parser could reason upon it using only simple equality comparisons. Ganapathi and Fischer [146, 147, 148, 149] addressed this problem by replacing the use of traditional, context-free grammars with the use of a more powerful set of grammars known as *attribute grammars*. There are also *affix grammars*, which can be thought of as a subset of attribute grammars. In this book, however, we will only consider attribute grammars, and, as with the Graham-Glanville approach, we will discuss how they work only at a high level.

Attribute Grammars

Attribute grammars were introduced in 1968 by Knuth [209], who extended context-free grammars with *attributes*. Attributes are used to store, manipulate, and propagate additional information about individual terminals and nonterminals during parsing, and an attribute is either *synthesized* or *inherited*. Using parse trees as the point of reference, a node with a synthesized attribute forms its value from the attributes of its children, and a node with an inherited attribute copies the value from the parent. Consequently, information derived from synthesized attributes flows *upwards* along the tree while information derived from inherited attributes flows *downwards*. We therefore distinguish between synthesized and inherited attributes by a ↑ or ↓, respectively, which will be prefixed to the attribute of the concerned symbol (for example, the synthesized attribute x of a reg nonterminal is written as reg↑x).

The attributes are then used within *predicates* and actions. Predicates are used for checking the applicability of a rule, and, in addition to emitting assembly code,

	PRODUCTION	PREDICATES	ACTIONS
1	byte↑r → + byte↑a byte↑r	IsOne(↓a), NotBusy(↓r)	EMIT ''incb ↓r''
2	byte↑r → + byte↑r byte↑a	IsOne(↓a), NotBusy(↓r)	EMIT ''incb ↓r''
3	byte↑r → + byte↑a byte↑r	TwoOp(↓a, ↓r)	EMIT ''addb2 ↓a,↓r''
4	byte↑r → + byte↑r byte↑a	TwoOp(↓a, ↓r)	EMIT ''addb2 ↓a,↓r''
5	byte↑r → + byte↑a byte↑b		GETREG(↑r)
			EMIT ''addb3 ↓r,↓a,↓b''

Fig. 3.7: An instruction set expressed as an attribute grammar [148]

actions are used to produce new synthesized attributes. Hence, when modeling
instructions we can use predicates to express the constraints, and actions to indicate
effects, such as code emission, and which register the result will be stored in. Let us
look at an example.

In Fig. 3.7 we see a set of rules for modeling three byte-adding instructions: an
increment version incb (increments a register by 1, modeled by rules 1 and 2); a
two-address version add2b (adds two registers and stores the result in one of the
operands, modeled by rules 3 and 4); and a three-address version add3b (the result
can be stored elsewhere, modeled by rule 5). Naturally, the incb instruction can
only be used when one of the operands is a constant of value 1, which is checked by
the *IsOne* predicate. In addition, since this instruction destroys the previous value
of the register, it can only be used when no subsequent operation uses the old value
(meaning the register is not "busy"), which is checked by the *NotBusy* predicate.
The EMIT action then emits the corresponding assembly code. Since addition is
commutative, we require two rules to make the instruction applicable in both cases.
Similarly, we have two rules for the add2b instruction, but the predicates have
been replaced by a *TwoOp*, which checks if one of the operands is the target of
assignment or if the value is not needed afterwards. Since the last rule does not have
any predicates, it also acts as the default rule, thus preventing situations of semantic
blocking which we discussed when covering the Graham-Glanville approach.

Advantages and Disadvantages

The use of predicates removes the need of introducing new nonterminals for expressing specific values and ranges, resulting in a more concise instruction set grammar
compared to a context-free grammar. For example, for the VAX machine, the use
of attributes leads to a grammar half the size (around 600 rules) compared to that
required for the Graham-Glanville approach, even without applying any extensive
refactoring [147]. Attribute grammars also facilitate incremental development of
the machine descriptions: one can start by implementing the most general rules to
achieve an instruction set grammar that produces correct but inefficient code. Rules
for handling more complex instructions can then can be added incrementally, making
it possible to balance implementation effort against code quality. Another useful
feature is that other program optimization routines, such as constant folding, can be

expressed as part of the grammar instead of as a separate component. Farrow [122] even made an attempt at deriving an entire Pascal compiler from an attribute grammar.

But to permit attributes to be used together with LR parsing, the properties of the instruction set grammar must be restricted. First, only synthesized attributes may appear in nonterminals. This is because an LR parser constructs the parse tree bottom-up and left-to-right, starting from the leaves and working its way up towards the root. Hence an inherited value only becomes available after the subtree of its nonterminal has been constructed. Second, since predicates may render a rule as semantically invalid for rule reduction, all actions must appear last in the rules. Otherwise they may cause effects that must be undone after a predicate fails its check. Third, as with the Graham-Glanville approach, the parser has to take decisions regarding one subtree without any consideration of sibling subtrees that may appear to the right. This can result in assembly code that could have been improved if all subtrees had been available beforehand, and this is again a limitation due to the use of LR parsing. Ganapathi [145] later made an attempt to resolve this problem by implementing an instruction selector in Prolog—a logic-based programming language—but this incurred exponential worst-case time complexity of the instruction selector.

3.3.3 Maintaining Multiple Parse Trees for Better Code Quality

Since LR parsers make a single pass over the program trees—and thus only produce one out of many possible parse trees—the quality of the produced assembly code is heavily dependent on the instruction set grammar to guide the parser in finding a "good" parse tree.

Christopher et al. [76] attempted to address this concern by using the concepts of the Graham-Glanville approach but extending the parser to produce *all* parse trees, and then select the one that yields the best assembly code. This was achieved by replacing the original LR parser with an implementation of Earley's algorithm [104], and although this scheme certainly improves code quality—at least in theory—it does so at the cost of enumerating all parse trees, which is often too expensive in practice.

In 2000, Madhavan et al. [245] extended the Graham-Glanville approach to achieve optimal selection of patterns while allegedly retaining the linear time complexity of LR parsing. By incorporating a new version of LR parsing [307], reductions that were previously executed directly as matching rules were found are now allowed to be postponed by an arbitrary number of steps. Hence the instruction selector essentially keeps track of multiple parse trees, allowing it to gather enough information about the program before committing to a decision that could turn out to be suboptimal. In other words, as in the case of Christopher et al. the design by Madhavan et al. also covers all parse trees, but immediately discards those which are determined to result in less efficient assembly code (this resembles the branch-and-bound search strategy discussed in Chapter 2 on p. 20). To do this efficiently, the design also incorporates offline cost analysis, which we will explore later in

Section 3.6.3. More recently, Yang [347] proposed a similar technique involving the use of *parser cactuses*, where deviating parse trees are branched off a common trunk to reduce space requirements. In both designs, however, the underlying principle still prohibits the modeling of many typical target machine features such as multi-output instructions since their grammars only allow rules that produce a single result.

3.4 Using Recursion to Cover Trees Top-Down

The tree covering techniques we have examined so far—in particular those based on LR parsing—all operate *bottom-up*: the instruction selector begins to cover the leaves in the program tree, and based on the decisions taken for the subtrees it then progressively works it way upwards along the tree until it reaches the root, continually matching and selecting applicable patterns along the way. This is by no means the only method of covering, as it can also be done *top-down*. In such designs, the instruction selector covers the program tree starting from the root, and then recursively works its way downwards. Consequently, the flow of semantic information, such as the particular register in which a result will be stored, is also different: a bottom-up instruction selector lets this information trickle upwards along the program tree—either via auxiliary data structures or through tree rewriting—whereas a top-down implementation decides upon this beforehand and pushes this information downwards. The latter is therefore said to be *goal-driven*, as pattern selection is guided by a set of additional requirements which must be fulfilled by the selected pattern. Since this in turn will incur new requirements for the subtrees, most top-down techniques are implemented recursively. This also enables backtracking, which is a necessary feature, as selection of certain patterns can cause the lower parts of the program tree to become uncoverable.

3.4.1 First Applications

Using Means-End Analysis to Guide Instruction Selection

To the best of my knowledge, Newcomer [263] was the first to develop a scheme that uses top-down tree covering to address instruction selection. In his 1975 doctoral dissertation, Newcomer proposes a design that exhaustively finds all combinations of patterns that cover a given program tree, and then selects the one with lowest cost. Cattell [68] also describes this in his survey paper, which is the main source for the discussion of Newcomer's design.

The instructions are modeled as *T-operators*, which are basically pattern trees with costs and attributes attached. The attributes describe various restrictions, such as which registers can be used for the operands. There is also a set of T-operators that the instruction selector uses to perform necessary transformations of the program—its need will become clear as the discussion continues. The scheme takes an AST as expected input and then covers it following the aforementioned top-down approach: the instruction selector first attempts to find all matching patterns for the root of the AST, and then proceeds to recursively cover the remaining subtrees for each match. Pattern matching is done using a straightforward technique that we know from before (see Fig. 3.3 on p. 35), and for efficiency all patterns are indexed according to the type of their root. The result of this procedure is thus a set of pattern sequences each of which covers the entire AST. Afterwards, each sequence is checked for whether the attributes of its patterns are equal to those of a *preferred attribute set (PAS)*, which corresponds to a goal. If not, the instruction selector will attempt to rewrite the subtree using the transformation T-operators until the attributes match. To guide this process, Newcomer applied a heuristic search strategy known as *means-end analysis*, which was introduced by Newell and Simon [264] in 1959. The intuition behind means-end analysis is to recursively minimize the quantitative difference—how this is calculated is not mentioned in [68]—between the current state (that is, what the subtree looks like *now*) and a goal state (what it *should* look like). To avoid infinite looping, the transformation process stops once it reaches a certain depth in the search space. If successful, the applied transformations are inserted into the pattern sequence; if not, the sequence is dropped. From the found pattern sequences the one with the lowest total cost is selected, followed by assembly code emission.

Newcomer's design was pioneering as its application of means-end analysis made it possible to guide the process of modifying the program until it could be implemented on the target machine, without have to resort to target-specific mechanisms. But the design also had several significant flaws. First, it had little practical application, as Newcomer's implementation only handled arithmetic expressions. Second, the T-operators used for modeling the instructions as well as transformations had to be constructed by hand—a task that was far from trivial—which hindered compiler retargetability. Third, the process of transforming the program could end prematurely due to the search space cut-off, causing the instruction selector to fail to generate any assembly code whatsoever. Lastly, the search strategy proved much too expensive to be usable in practice except for very small program trees.

Making Means-End Analysis Work in Practice

Cattell et al. [67, 70, 234] later improved and extended Newcomer's work into a more practical framework which was implemented in the *Production Quality Compiler-Compiler (PQCC)*, a derivation of the BLISS-11 compiler originally written by Wulf et al. [344]. Instead of performing the means-end analysis as the program is compiled, their design does it as a preprocessing step when generating the compiler itself—much as with the Graham-Glanville approach.

The patterns are expressed as a set of templates which are formed using recursive composition, and are thus similar to the productions found in instruction set grammars. But unlike Glanville and Graham's and Ganapathi and Fischer's designs—where the grammars were written by hand—the templates in PQCC are derived automatically from a target-specific machine description. Each instruction is modeled as a set of *machine operations* that describe the effects of the instruction, and are thus akin to the RTLs introduced by Fraser [136] in Chapter 2. These effects are then used by a separate tool, called the *Code-Generator Generator (CGG)*, to create the templates which will be used by the instruction selector.

In addition to producing the trivial templates corresponding directly to an instruction, CGG also produces a set of single-node patterns as well as a set of larger patterns that combine several instructions. The former ensures that the instruction selector is capable of generating assembly code for all programs (since any program tree can thereby be trivially covered), while the latter reduces compilation time as it is quicker to match a large pattern than many smaller ones. To do this, CGG uses a combination of means-end analysis and heuristic rules which apply a set of axioms (such as $\neg\neg E \Leftrightarrow E$, $E + 0 \Leftrightarrow E$, and $\neg(E_1 \geq E_2) \Leftrightarrow E_1 < E_2$) to manipulate and combine existing patterns into new ones. However, there are no guarantees that these "interesting" patterns will ever be applicable in practice. Once generated, instruction selection is performed in a greedy, top-down fashion that always selects the lowest-cost template matching the current node in the program tree (pattern matching is done using a scheme identical to Newcomer's). If there is a tie, the instruction selector picks the template with the least number of memory loads and stores.

Compared to the LR parsing-based methods discussed previously, the design by Cattell et al. has both advantages and disadvantages. The main advantage is that the instruction selectors is less at risk of failing to generate assembly code for some program. There is the possibility that the set of predefined templates is insufficient to produce all necessary single-node patterns, but then CGG can at least issue a warning (in Ganapathi and Fischer's design this correctness has to be ensured by the grammar designer). The disadvantage is that it is relatively slow: whereas the tree parsing-based instruction selectors exhibit linear time complexity, both for pattern matching and selection, the instruction selector by Cattell et al. has to match each template individually, which could take quadratic time in the worst case.

Recent Designs

To the best of my knowledge, the only recent technique (less than 20 years old) to use this kind of recursive top-down methodology for tree covering is that of Nymeyer et al. [270, 271]. In two papers from 1996 and 1997, Nymeyer et al. introduce a method where A^* *search*—another strategy for exploring the search space (see [297])—is combined with BURS theory. We will discuss BURS theory in more detail later in this chapter—the anxious reader can skip directly to Section 3.6.3—so for now let it be sufficient to say that grammars based on BURS allow transformation rules, such as rewriting $X + Y$ into $Y + X$, to be included as part of the instruction set grammar. This potentially simplifies and reduces the number of rules required for expressing the instructions, but unfortunately the authors did not publish any experimental results, thus making it difficult to judge whether the A^*-BURS theory combination would be an applicable technique in practice.

3.5 A Note on Tree Rewriting vs. Tree Covering

At this point some readers may feel that tree rewriting—where patterns are iteratively selected for rewriting the program tree until it consists of a single node of some goal type—is something entirely different compared to tree covering—where compatible patterns are selected for covering all nodes in the program tree. The same argument applies to DAG and graph covering, although rewriting-based techniques are less common for those principles. Indeed, there appears to be a subtle difference, but a valid solution to a problem expressed using tree rewriting is also a valid solution to the equivalent problem expressed using tree covering, and vice versa. It could therefore be argued that the two are interchangeable, but I regard tree rewriting as a *means* to solving the tree covering problem, which I regard as the fundamental *principle*.

3.5.1 Handling Chain Rules in Purely Coverage-Driven Designs

Another objection that may arise is how tree covering, as a principle, can support *chain rules*. A chain rule is a rule whose pattern consists of a single nonterminal, and the name comes from the fact that reductions using these rules can be chained together one after another. Consequently, chain rules are often used to represent data transfers and other value-preserving transformations (an example of this is given in Chapter 5).

Let us first assume that we have as input the program tree shown in Fig. 3.8a, which will be covered using the following instruction set grammar:

	PRODUCTION
1	$reg_A \rightarrow Int$
2	$reg_B \rightarrow reg_A$
3	$reg_B \rightarrow reg_B + reg_B$

Let us further assume that we have an instruction selector where pattern matching is performed strictly through node comparison. This instruction selector is clearly based on tree covering, but it will fail to find a valid cover for the aforementioned program tree as it will not be able to match and select the necessary chain rules (see Fig. 3.8b).

There are three ways of solving this problem. The simplest method is to simply ignore the incompatibilities during pattern selection, and then—if supported—inject the assembly code for the necessary chain rules afterwards. But this obviously compromises code quality as the cost of the chain rules is not taken into account. A better approach is to consider all chain rule applications during pattern matching, which essentially means that regular patterns are combined with chain rules—this is known as computing the *transitive closure*—to yield new patterns (see Fig. 3.8c). The third and last approach is to augment the program tree by inserting auxiliary nodes, each of which each represents the application of a chain rule (see Fig. 3.8d).

(a) Program tree to cover. Variables A and B are assumed to represent integer values

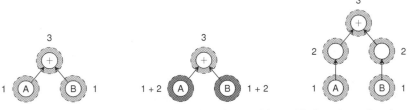

(b) Invalid cover due to in-   (c) Covering using the transitive   (d) Covering using the aug-
compatabilities between the   closure method   mentation method
selected patterns

Fig. 3.8: Examples illustrating how chain rules can be supported by tree covering-based techniques. The numbers next to the shaded areas indicate which rules have been selected

The transitive closure and augmentation methods both come with certain benefits and drawbacks. The former method allows chain rules to be applied in any combination and of any length, but it complicates the tasks of pattern matching and pattern selection. The latter method requires no change in the pattern matcher and pattern selector, but it enlarges the program tree and requires an additional dummy rule to indicate that no chain rule is applied (if more than one chain rule needs to be applied then several auxiliary nodes must be inserted, one after another). As we have seen, several designs ignore this problem by assuming a homogeneous target architecture, and a few techniques apply the inefficient idea of code injection. The transitive closure approach is typically limited to tree covering-based methods, while the augmentation method is mostly applied when covering more general forms such as directed acyclic graphs and graphs (which we will discuss in the coming chapters).

3.6 Separating Pattern Matching from Pattern Selection

In the previously discussed techniques based on tree covering, the tasks of pattern matching and pattern selection are unified into a single step. Although this enables single-pass code generation, it typically also prevents the instruction selector from considering the impact of certain combinations of patterns. By separating these two concerns and allowing the instruction selector to make multiple passes over the program tree, it can gather enough information about all applicable patterns before having to commit to premature decisions.

But the pattern matchers we have seen so far—excluding those based on LR parsing—have all been implementations of algorithms with quadratic time complexity. Fortunately, we can do better.

3.6.1 Algorithms for Linear-Time, Tree-Based Pattern Matching

Over the years many algorithms have been discovered for finding all matches given a subject tree and a set of pattern trees (see for example [74, 81, 103, 179, 197, 286, 287, 306, 334, 345]). For tree covering, most pattern matching algorithms have been derived from methods of string-based pattern matching. This was first discovered by Karp et al. [197] in 1972, and their ideas were later extended by Hoffmann and O'Donnell [179] to form the algorithms most applied by tree-based instruction selection techniques. Hence, in order to understand pattern matching with trees, let us first explore how this is done with strings.

Matching Trees Is Equivalent to Matching Strings

The algorithms most commonly used for string matching were introduced by Aho and Corasick [5] and Knuth et al. [210] (also known as the *Knuth-Morris-Pratt algorithm*) in 1975 and 1977, respectively. Independently discovered from one another, both algorithms operate in the same fashion and are thus nearly identical in their approach.

The intuition is that when a partial match of a pattern with a repetitive substring fails, the pattern matcher does not need to return all the way to the input character where the matching initially started. This is illustrated in the inlined table where the pattern string abcabd is matched against the input string abcabcabd. The arrow indicates the current character under consideration. At first, the pattern matches the beginning of the input string up until the last character (position 5).

	0	1	2	3	4	5	6	7	8
Input string	a	b	c	a	b	c	a	b	d
Pattern string	a	b	c	a	b	d			
						↑			
				a	b	c	a	b	d
									↑

When this fails, instead of returning to position 1 and restarting the matching from scratch, the matcher remembers that the first three characters of the pattern (abc) have already been matched at this point and therefore continues to position 6, attempting to match the fourth character in the pattern. Consequently all occurrences of the pattern can be found in linear time. We continue our discussion with Aho and Corasick's design as it is capable of matching multiple patterns whereas the algorithm of Knuth et al. only considers a single pattern (although it can easily be extended to handle multiple patterns as well).

Aho and Corasick's algorithm relies on three functions—*goto, failure,* and *output*—where the first function is implemented as a state machine and the two latter ones are implemented as simple table lookups. How these are constructed is out of scope

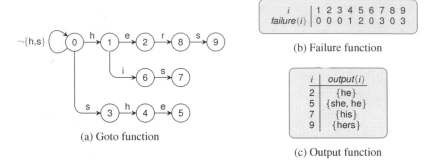

(a) Goto function

(b) Failure function

(c) Output function

Fig. 3.9: A state machine for string matching [5]

for our purpose—the interested reader can consult the referenced paper—and we will instead illustrate how the algorithm works on an example. In Fig. 3.9 we see the corresponding functions for matching the strings he, she, his, and hers. As a character is read from an input string, say shis, it is first given as argument to the *goto* function. Having initialized to state machine to state 0, *goto*(s) first causes a transition to state 3, and *goto*(h) causes a subsequent transition to state 4. For each successful transition to some state i we invoke *output*(i) to check whether some pattern string has been matched, but so far no match has been found. For the next input character i, however, there exists no corresponding edge from the current state (that is, *goto*(i) causes a failure). At this point *failure*(4) is invoked, which dictates that the state machine should fall back to state 1. We then retry *goto*(i), which takes us to state 6. With the last input character, *goto*(s) causes a transition to state 7, where *output*(7) indicates a match with the pattern string his.

The Hoffmann-O'Donnell Algorithm

Hoffmann and O'Donnell [179] developed two algorithms incorporating the ideas of Aho and Corasick and Knuth et al. In a paper from 1982, Hoffmann and O'Donnell first present an $O(np)$ algorithm which matches pattern trees in a top-down fashion, and then an $O(n + m)$ bottom-up algorithm which trades linear-time pattern matching for longer preprocessing times (n is the size of the program tree, p is the number of patterns, and m is the number of matches found).

Pattern matching for the latter—which is the most applied due to its linear runtime behavior—is simple and outlined in Fig. 3.10. Starting at the leaves, each node is labeled with an identifier denoting the set of patterns that match the subtree rooted at that node. We call this set the *matchset*. The label to assign a particular node is retrieved by using the labels of the children as indices in a table that is specific to the type of the current node. For example, label lookups for nodes representing addition are done using one table, while lookups for nodes representing subtraction are done using another table. The dimension of the table is equal to the number of children

```
LABELTREE(program tree rooted at node n):
 1: for each child m_i of n do
 2:     LABELTREE(m_i)
 3: end for
 4: label n with T_n[labels of m_1, ..., m_k]
```

Fig. 3.10: The Hoffmann-O'Donnell algorithm for labeling program trees [179]

that the node may have. For example, binary operation nodes have two-dimensional tables while nodes representing constant values have 0-dimensional tables, which simply consist of a single value. A fully labeled example is shown in Fig. 3.11g, and the matchsets are then retrieved via a subsequent top-down traversal of the labeled tree.

Since the bottom-up algorithm introduced by Hoffmann and O'Donnell has had a historical impact on instruction selection, we will spend some time discussing the details of how the lookup tables are produced.

Definitions

We begin by introducing a few definitions, and to our aid we will use two pattern trees A and B, shown in Figs. 3.11a and 3.11b, respectively. The patterns in our pattern set thus consist of nodes with symbols a, b, c, or v, where an a-node always has exactly two children, and b, c, and v-nodes always have no children. The v-symbol is a special *nullary symbol*, as such nodes represent placeholders that can match any subtree. We say that these symbols collectively constitute the *alphabet* Σ of our pattern set. The alphabet needs to be finite and *ranked*, meaning that each symbol in Σ has a *ranking function* that gives the number of children for a given symbol. Hence, in our case $rank(a) = 2$ and $rank(b) = rank(c) = rank(v) = 0$. Following the terminology used in Hoffmann and O'Donnell's paper, we also introduce the notion of a Σ-*term* and define it as follows:

1. Each $i \in \Sigma$ with $rank(i) = 0$ is a Σ-term.
2. If $i \in \Sigma$ and $rank(i) > 0$, then $i(t_1, \ldots, t_{rank(i)})$ is a Σ-term provided every t_i is a Σ-term.
3. Nothing else is a Σ-term.

A pattern tree is therefore a Σ-term, allowing us to write patterns A and B as $a(a(v,v),b)$ and $a(b,v)$, respectively. Σ-terms are also *ordered*, meaning $a(b,v)$ for example is different from $a(v,b)$. Consequently, commutative operations, such as addition, must be handled through pattern duplication (as in the Graham-Glanville approach).

We continue with some definitions concerning patterns. First, let us denote by $mtrees(p)$ the set of trees that can be matched by the pattern p at the root of any valid tree.[5] Depending on the alphabet, this set could be infinite. Then, a pattern p is said

---

[5] This definition is not used by Hoffmann and O'Donnell in their paper, but having it will simplify the discussion to come.

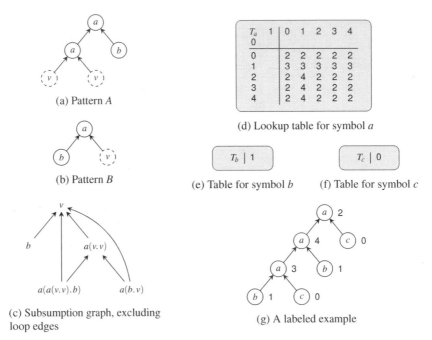

(a) Pattern A

(b) Pattern B

(c) Subsumption graph, excluding
loop edges

(d) Lookup table for symbol a

(e) Table for symbol b

(f) Table for symbol c

(g) A labeled example

Fig. 3.11: Tree pattern matching using Hoffmann-O'Donnell. Nullary nodes v are ac-
centuated with a dashed border. The subpatterns v, b, $a(v,v)$, $a(b,v)$, and $a(a(v,v),b)$
have been labeled 0, 1, 2, 3, and 4, respectively [179]

to *subsume* another pattern q (written $p \geq q$) if and only if any matchset including
p always also includes q (hence $mtrees(q) \subseteq mtrees(p)$). For example, given two
patterns $a(b,b)$ and $a(v,v)$, we have that $a(b,b) \geq a(v,v)$, since the v-nodes must
obviously also match whenever the b-nodes match. By this definition every pattern
also subsumes itself. Furthermore, p *strictly subsumes* q (written $p > q$) iff $p \geq q$
and $p \neq q$, and p *immediately subsumes* q (written $p >_i q$) iff $p > q$ and there exists
no other pattern r such that $p > r$ and $r > q$.

We also say that two patterns p and q are *inconsistent* iff both patterns never
appear in the same matchset (hence $mtrees(q) \cap mtrees(p) = \emptyset$). Lastly, p and q are
independent iff there exist three distinct trees t, t', and t'' (that is, $t \neq t' \neq t''$), such
that (i) t is matched by p but not q (hence $mtrees(p) \not\subseteq mtrees(q)$), (ii) t' is matched
by q but not p (hence $mtrees(q) \not\subseteq mtrees(p)$), and (iii) t'' is matched by both p
and q (hence $mtrees(q) \cap mtrees(p) \neq \emptyset$).

Pattern sets that contain no independent patterns are known as *simple pattern
sets*.[6] For example, the pattern set consisting of patterns A and B is simple as there
exists no tree for which both match. As we will see, simple pattern sets have two
important properties that we will use for generating the lookup tables.

---

[6] In Hoffmann and O'Donnell's paper these are called *simple pattern forests*.

Generating Lookup Tables for Simple Pattern Sets

In general, the size of each lookup table is exponential to the size of the pattern set, as is the time to generate these tables. But Hoffmann and O'Donnell recognized that, for simple pattern sets, the number of possible matchsets is equal to the number of patterns, making it tractable to generate the tables for such sets.

Furthermore, Hoffmann and O'Donnell found that each possible matchset for a simple pattern set can be represented using a single pattern tree. The intuition is as follows. If a pattern p strictly subsumes another pattern q, then by definition it means that q will appear in every matchset where p appears. Consequently, q does not need to be explicitly encoded into the matchset since it can be inferred from the presence of p. Therefore, for every matchset M we can select a subset of patterns in M to encode the entire matchset. Let us call this subset the *base* of M, which we will denote by M_0. It can be proven that different matchsets must have different bases, and that all patterns in M_0 must be pair-wise independent. However, in simple pattern sets we have no such patterns, and therefore the base of every matchset must consist of a single pattern. We will call this pattern the *base pattern* of a matchset, and it is the labels of the base patterns that will appear as entries in the lookup tables.

The key insight behind labeling is that in order to find the matchset for some program tree $T = a(T_1, T_2)$, it is sufficient to only consider the matchsets for T_1 and T_2 in the context of a instead of T in its entirety. If the pattern set is simple, then we know that every matchset has a base pattern. Let p_1 and p_2 denote the base patterns of the matchsets of T_1 and T_2, respectively. With these we can transform T into $T' = a(p_1, p_2)$, and finding the matchset for T' will then be equivalent to finding the matchset for T. Since every entry in a lookup table refers to a matchset (which is represented by its base pattern), and each symbol in Σ has its own table, we can produce the tables simply by finding, for each table entry, the base pattern of the matchset for the tree represented by that entry. For example, if labels 1 and 2 respectively refer to the patterns b and $a(v, v)$, then the table entry $T_c[2, 1]$ will denote the tree $c(a(v, v), b)$, and we are then interested in finding the matchset for that tree.

The next problem is thus to find the base pattern of a given matchset. For simple pattern sets it can be proven that if we have three distinct patterns p, p', and p'', and p subsumes both p' and p'', then it must hold that either $p' > p''$ or $p'' > p'$. Consequently, for every matchset M we can form a *subsumption order* among the patterns appearing in M. In other words, if a matchset M contains m patterns, then we can arrange these patterns such that $p_1 > p_2 > \ldots > p_m$, and the pattern appearing first in this order (in this case, p_1) is the base pattern of M as it strictly subsumes all other patterns in M. Hence, if we know the subsumption order, then we can easily find the base pattern.

For this purpose we first enumerate all unique subtrees, called the *subpatterns*, that appear in the pattern set. In the case of patterns A and B, this includes v, b, $a(v, v)$, $a(b, v)$, and $a(a(v, v), b)$, and we denote the set of all subpatterns as S. We then assign each subpattern in S a sequential number, starting from 0, which will represent the labels (the order in which these are assigned is not important).

Next we form the *subsumption graph* for S, denoted by $\overline{G}_S$, where each node n_i represents a subpattern $s_i \in S$ and each edge $n_i \rightarrow n_j$ indicates that s_i subsumes s_j. For our pattern set, we get the subsumption graph illustrated in Fig. 3.11c,[7] which we produce using the algorithm given in Fig. 3.12a. The algorithm basically works as follows. First, we add a node for every subpattern in S, together with a loop edge, as every pattern always subsumes itself. Next we iterate over all pair-wise combinations of subpatterns and check whether one subsumes the other, and add a corresponding edge to $\overline{G}_S$ if this is the case. To test whether a subpattern q subsumes another pattern q, we check whether the roots of p and q are of the same symbol and whether every subtree of p subsumes the corresponding subtree of q, which can be done by checking whether a corresponding edge exists in $\overline{G}_S$ for each combination of subtrees. Hence, we should iterate this process until $\overline{G}_S$ reaches a fixpoint, but we can minimize the number of checks by first ordering the subpatterns in S by increasing height order and then comparing the subpatterns in that order.

Once we have $\overline{G}_S$ we can generate the lookup tables following the algorithm outlined in Fig. 3.12b. First, we find the subsumption order for all patterns by doing a topological sort of the nodes in $\overline{G}_S$ (see Appendix C for a definition of topological sort). Next, we initialize each entry in the table with the label of the subpattern consisting of a single nullary symbol, and then incrementally update an entry with the label of the next, larger pattern that matches the tree corresponding to that entry. By iterating over the patterns in increasing subsumption order, the last assignment

```
BUILDSUBSUMPTIONGRAPH(set S of subpatterns):
1:  initialize G̅_S with one node and loop edge for every subpattern in S
2:  for each subpattern s = a(s_1,...,s_m) ∈ S in increasing height order do
3:      for each subpattern s' ∈ S s.t. height of s' ≤ height of s do
4:          if s' = v or s' = a(s'_1,...,s'_m) s.t. edge s_i → s'_i ∈ G̅_S, ∀1 ≤ i ≤ m then
5:              add s → s' to G̅_S
6:          end if
7:      end for
8:  end for
```

(a) Algorithm for producing the subsumption graph

```
GENERATETABLE(set S of subpatterns, subsumption graph G̅_S, symbol a ∈ Σ):
1:  do topological sort on G̅_S
2:  initialize all entries in T_a with v ∈ S
3:  for each subpattern s = a(s_1,...,s_m) ∈ S in increasing subsumption order do
4:      for each m-tuple ⟨s'_1,...,s'_m⟩ s.t. s'_i ≥ s_i, ∀1 ≤ i ≤ m, do
5:          T_a[s'_1,...,s'_m] = s
6:      end for
7:  end for
```

(b) Algorithm for producing the lookup tables

Fig. 3.12: The Hoffmann-O'Donnell preprocessing algorithms [179]

---

[7] There is also a corresponding *immediate subsumption graph* G_S. In general, G_S is shaped like a directed acyclic graph, but for simple pattern sets it is always a tree.

to each entry will be that of the largest matching pattern in the pattern set. For our example, this results in the tables shown in Figs. 3.11d, 3.11e, and 3.11f.

As already stated, since patterns are required to be ordered, we need to dupli-cate patterns containing commutative operations by swapping the subtrees of the operands. But doing this yields patterns that are pair-wise independent, destroying the property of the pattern set being simple. In such cases, the algorithm is still able to produce usable lookup tables, but the resulting matchsets will include only one of the commutative patterns and not the other (which one depends on the subpattern last used during table generation). Consequently, not all matches will be found during pattern matching, which may in turn prevent optimal pattern selection.

Compressing the Lookup Tables

Chase [73] further advanced Hoffmann and O'Donnell's table generation technique by developing an algorithm that compresses the final lookup tables. The key insight is that the lookup tables often contain redundant information as many rows and columns are duplicates. For example, this can be seen clearly in T_a from our previous example, which is also shown in Fig. 3.13a. By introducing a set of *index maps*, the duplicates can be removed by mapping identical columns or rows in the index map to the same row or column in the lookup table. The lookup table can then be reduced to contain only the minimal amount of information, as seen in Fig. 3.13b. By denoting the compressed version of T_a by τ_a, and the corresponding index maps by $\mu_{a,0}$ and $\mu_{a,1}$, we replace a previous lookup $T_i[l_0, \ldots, l_m]$ for symbol i with $\tau_i[\mu_{i,0}[l_0], \ldots, \mu_{i,m}[l_m]]$.

Table compression also provides another benefit in that, for some pattern sets, the lookup tables can be so large that they cannot even be constructed in the first place. But Chase discovered that the tables can be compressed as they are generated, thus pushing the limit on how large lookup tables can be produced. Cai et al. [62] later improved the asymptotic bounds of Chase's algorithm.

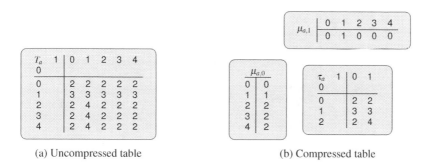

(a) Uncompressed table   (b) Compressed table

Fig. 3.13: An example of compressing the lookup table T_a [73]

3.6.2 Optimal Pattern Selection with Dynamic Programming

Once it became possible to find all matchsets for the entire program tree in linear time, techniques started to appear that also tackled the problem of optimal pattern selection in linear time. According to the literature, Ripken [294] was the first to propose a viable method for optimal linear-time instruction selection, which is described in a 1977 technical report. Ripken based his method on the dynamic programming algorithm by Aho and Johnson—which was mentioned in Chapter 1—and later extended it to handle more realistic instruction sets with multiple register classes and addressing modes. For brevity we will henceforth abbreviate dynamic programming as DP.

Although Ripken appears to have been the first to propose a design of an optimal DP-based instruction selector, it only remained that—a proposal. The first *practical* attempt was instead made in 1986 by Aho et al. [6, 7, 321] with the introduction of a compiler generator called TWIG.

TWIG

As in Ripken's design, TWIG uses a version of Aho and Johnson's DP algorithm for selecting the optimal set of pattern trees to cover a given program tree. The machine description is expressed as an instruction set grammar (see Section 3.3.1) using a language called *Code Generator Language (CGL)*, which as introduced by Aho and Ganapathi [6] in 1985. An excerpt of such a machine description is shown in Fig. 3.14. TWIG takes this machine description and generates an instruction selector that makes three passes over the program tree. The first pass is a top-down

```
node const mem assign plus ind;
label reg no_value;
reg:const                                    /* Rule 1 */
   { cost = 2; }
  ={ NODEPTR regnode = getreg( );
     emit(''MOV'', $1$, regnode, 0);
     return(regnode);
  };
no_value: assign(mem, reg)                   /* Rule 3 */
   { cost = 2+$%1$->cost; }
  ={ emit(''MOV'', $2$, $1$, 0);
     return(NULL);
  };
reg: plus(reg, ind(plus(const, reg)))        /* Rule 6 */
   { cost = 2+$%1$->cost+$%2$->cost; }
  ={ emit(''ADD'', $2$, $1$, 0);
     return($1$);
  };
```

Fig. 3.14: Rule samples for TWIG, written in CGL [7]

labeling pass that finds all matchsets for every node in the program tree[8] using an implementation of the Aho-Corasick string matching algorithm [5]. The second pass is a bottom-up cost computation pass that gives the cost of selecting a particular pattern for a given node. As we will see, the costs are computed using DP and hence the computation constitutes the core of this design. The last pass is a recursive top-down pass that finds the least-cost cover of the program tree. This pass also executes the actions associated with the selected patterns, which in turn emits the corresponding assembly code. As we are already quite familiar with how to do tree-based pattern matching, we will focus on the cost computation and pattern selection algorithms.

The idea behind the cost computation algorithm, outlined in Fig. 3.15a, is as follows. For each node n in the program tree we maintain an array for remembering the lowest cost of reducing n to a particular nonterminal, as well as the rule for making this reduction. These costs are found by iterating over all rules found in the matchset of n and computing the cost of applying a particular rule. This cost is computed as the sum of the cost of the rule itself and the costs of the nonterminals appearing on the rule's pattern tree. Initially, all costs are set to infinity, thus prohibiting reductions using nonterminals which are not available. Once all rules originating from the

```
COMPUTECOSTS(program tree rooted at node n):
 1: for each child nᵢ of n do
 2:     COMPUTECOSTS(nᵢ)
 3: end for
 4: initialize array costsₙ with ∞
 5: R = {rule r : r ∈ matchset of n or r is a chain rule}
 6: for each rule r ∈ R in transitive reduction order do
 7:     c = cost of applying r at n
 8:     l = left-hand nonterminal of r
 9:     if c < costsₙ[l] then
10:         costsₙ[l] = c
11:         rulesₙ[l] = r
12:     end if
13: end for
```

(a) Cost computation algorithm

```
SELECTANDEXECUTE(program tree rooted at node n,
                 goal nonterminal g):
 1: rule r = rulesₙ[g]
 2: for each nonterminal l that appears on the pattern of r do
 3:     SELECTANDEXECUTE(node to reduce to l, l)
 4: end for
 5: execute actions associated with r
```

(b) Pattern selection and code emission algorithm

Fig. 3.15: Algorithms for optimal tree-based pattern selection using dynamic programming [7]

---

[8] Remember that, when using instruction set grammars, a pattern found in the matchset during pattern matching corresponds to the right-hand side of a production.

matchset have been checked, we need to check all applicable chain rules as these may make the current node reducible to additional nonterminals or to the same nonterminals but at a lower cost. However, since one chain rule may depend on another chain rule, it matters in what order the chain rules are checked (at least until a fixpoint is reached). To minimize the number of checks, we sort these chain rules in *transitive reduction order*, meaning for every pair of rules i and j, where i reduces to a nonterminal used by j, i is checked before j.

After the costs have been computed for the root of the program tree, we can find the least-cost cover that reduces the entire program tree to the goal nonterminal simply by consulting the cost arrays (the algorithm is shown in Fig. 3.15b). Starting from the root, we select the rule that reduces this node of the program tree to a particular nonterminal. The same is then done recursively for each nonterminal that appears on the pattern in the selected rule, acting as the goal for the corresponding subtree. Note that since patterns can have arbitrary height, this subtree can appear several levels down from the current node in the program tree. The algorithm also correctly applies the necessary chain rules, as the use of such a rule causes the routine to be reinvoked on the same node but with a different goal nonterminal.

DP Versus LR Parsing

The DP scheme has several advantages over those based on LR parsing. First, reduction conflicts are automatically handled by the cost-computing algorithm, removing the need of ordering the rules which could affect the code quality yielded by LR parsers. Second, rule cycles that cause LR parsers to get stuck in an infinite loop no longer need to be explicitly broken. Third, machine descriptions can be made more concise as rules differing only in cost can be combined into a single rule. Again taking the VAX machine as an example, Aho et al. reported that the entire TWIG specification could be implemented using only 115 rules, which is about half the size of Ganapathi and Fischer's attribute-based instruction set grammar for the same target machine.

However, the DP approach requires that the code generation problem exhibit properties of optimal substructure, meaning that it is possible to generate optimal assembly code by solving each of its subproblems to optimality. As explained in Chapter 1, this is not always the case; some solutions, whose total sum is greater compared to another set of selected patterns, can actually lead to better assembly code in the end.

Further Improvements

Several improvements of TWIG were later made by Yates and Schwartz [348] and Emmelmann et al. [109]. Yates and Schwartz improved the rate of pattern matching by replacing TWIG's top-down approach with the faster bottom-up algorithm proposed by Hoffmann and O'Donnell, and also extended the attribute support for more powerful predicates. Emmelmann et al. modified the DP algorithm to be run as the program trees are built by the frontend, which also inlines the code of auxiliary functions directly into the DP algorithm to reduce the overhead. Emmelmann et al. implemented their improvements in a system called the *Back End Generator (BEG)*, and a modified version of this is currently used in the COSY compiler [89].

Fraser et al. [137] made similar improvements in a system called IBURG that is both simpler and faster than TWIG—IBURG requires only 950 lines of code compared to TWIG's 3,000 lines of C code, and generates assembly code of comparable quality at a rate that is 25 times faster—and has been used in several compilers (such as RECORD [232, 250] and REDACO [215]). Gough and Ledermann [160, 161] later extended the predicate support of IBURG in an implementation called MBURG. Both IBURG and MBURG have later been reimplemented in various programming languages, such as the Java-based JBURG [171], OCAMLBURG [238], which is written in C--, and GPBURG [162], which is written in C#.

According to Leupers and Marwedel [231] and Cao et al. [64], Tjiang [320] later merged the ideas of TWIG and IBURG into a new implementation called OLIVE—the name is a spin-off of TWIG—and made several additional improvements such as rules to use arbitrary cost functions instead of fixed, numeric values. This supports more versatile instruction selection, as rules can be dynamically deactivated by setting infinite costs, which can be controlled from the current context. OLIVE is used in the implementation of SPAM [316]—a fixed-point DSP compiler—and Araujo and Malik [21] employed it in an attempt to integrate instruction selection with scheduling and register allocation.

Code Size-Reducing Instruction Selection

In 2010, Edler von Koch et al. [107] modified the backend in COSY to perform code generation in two stages in order to reduce code size for architectures with mixed 16-bit and 32-bit instructions, where the former is smaller but can only access a reduced set of registers. In the first stage, instruction selection is performed by aggressively selecting 16-bit instructions. Then, during register allocation, whenever a memory spill is required due to the use of a 16-bit instruction, the node "causing" this spill is annotated with a special flag. Once register allocation is finished, another round of instruction selection is performed but this time no nodes which have been annotated are allowed to be covered by patterns originating from 16-bit instructions. Experiments showed that this scheme reduced code size by about 17% on average compared to COSY for the selected target architecture and benchmark suite.

Combining DP with Macro Expansion

After arguing that Glanville and Graham's method attacked the instruction selection problem from the wrong direction (that is, by defining the instructions in terms of IR operations), Horspool [184] developed in 1987 a technique that essentially is

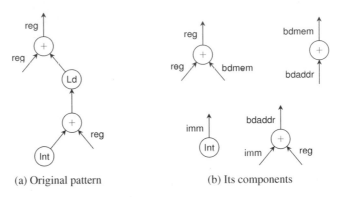

(a) Original pattern   (b) Its components

Fig. 3.16: Breaking down a pattern into single-node components in order for it to be supported by a macro-expanding instruction selector [184]

an enhanced form of macro expansion. As discussed in Chapter 2, because macro-expanding instruction selectors only visit and execute macros one IR node at a time, they do not inherently support instructions where there is an n-to-1 mapping between the IR nodes and the instructions. This limitation can be worked around by incorporating additional logic and bookkeeping into the macro definitions, but doing so by hand often proves to be infeasible. By including an edge labeling step prior to macro expansion, Horspool found a way of supporting such instructions while at the same time simplifying the macro definitions.

The idea is to first break down every pattern into single-node components (see Fig. 3.16). As part of the breakdown process the intermediate edges are labeled with *storage classes* which serve as a form of glue between the components, allowing them to be reconnected during macro expansion. The same storage classes can be used across multiple patterns if this is deemed appropriate, which is akin to refactoring an instruction set grammar in order to reduce the number of rules.

The goal is then to label the edges of the program tree with storage classes such that they correspond to a least-cost cover of the tree, which can be done using dynamic programming (but the paper does not go into detail about how the component costs should be assigned). Once the program tree has been labeled, the assembly code can be emitted using a straightforward macro expander that uses the current node's type and the storage classes of its edges as indices to a macro table. Since the bookkeeping is essentially lifted into the storage classes, the macro definitions become much simpler compared to those of traditional macro-expanding techniques. Moreover, there is no need to handle backtracking, as such a combination of edge labels would imply an illegal cover of the program tree.

In principle, Horspool's design is comparable to that of Aho et al., and should yield similar code quality. However, Horspool appears to have had to implement his instruction selection tables by hand whereas Aho et al. built a tool to do it for them.

3.6.3 Faster Pattern Selection with Offline Cost Analysis

In the DP approach just discussed, the rule costs needed for selecting the patterns are dynamically computed while the pattern matcher is completely table-driven. It was later discovered that these calculations can also be done beforehand and represented as tables, improving the speed of the pattern selector as it did for pattern matching. We will refer to this aspect as *offline cost analysis*, which means that the costs of covering any given program tree are precomputed as part of generating the compiler instead at compilation time.

Extending Matchset Labels with Costs

To make use of offline cost analysis, we need to extend the labels to not only represent matchsets, but also incorporate the information about which pattern will lead to the lowest covering cost given a specific goal. To distinguish between the two, we refer to this extended form of label as a *state*. A state is essentially a representation of a specific combination of goals, patterns, and costs, where each possible goal g is associated with a pattern p and a relative cost c. A goal in this context typically dictates where the result of an expression must appear, like a particular register class or memory, and in grammar terms this means that each nonterminal is associated with a rule and a cost. This combination is such that

1. for any program tree whose root has been labeled with a particular state,
2. if the goal of the root must be g,
3. then the entire program tree can be covered with minimal cost by selecting pattern p at the root. The relative cost of this covering, compared to the scenario in which the goal is something else, is equal to c.

A key point to understand here is that a state does not necessarily need to carry information about how to optimally cover the *entire* program tree—indeed, such attempts would require an infinite number of states. Instead, the states only convey enough information about how to cover the distinct key shapes that can appear in any program tree. To explain this further, let us observe how most (if not all) target machines operate: between the execution of two instructions, the data is synchronized by storing it in registers or in memory. The manner in which some data came to appear in a particular location has in general no impact on the execution of the subsequent instructions. Consequently, depending on the available instructions, one can often break a program tree at certain key places without compromising code quality. This yields a set of many, smaller program trees, each with a specific goal at the root, which then can be optimally covered in isolation. In other words, the set of states only needs to collectively represent enough information to communicate where these cuts can be made for all possible program trees. This does not mean that the program tree is *actually* partitioned into smaller pieces before pattern selection, but thinking about it in this way helps us understand why we can restrict ourselves to a finite number of states and still get optimal pattern selection.

```
SELECTANDEXECUTE(program tree rooted at node n,
                 goal-nonterminal g):
 1: rule r = RT[state assigned to n, g]
 2: for each nonterminal l that appears on the pattern of r do
 3:     SELECTANDEXECUTE(node to reduce to l, l)
 4: end for
 5: execute actions associated with r
```

Fig. 3.17: Table-driven algorithm for performing optimal tree-based pattern selection and code emission. *RT* stands for *rule table* and specifies the rule to select for optimal covering given a certain state and goal [281]

Since a state is simply an extended form of a label, the process of labeling a program tree with states is exactly the same as before (see Fig. 3.10 on p. 53), as we simply need to replace the lookup tables. Pattern selection and assembly code emission is then done as described in Fig. 3.17, more or less identically to the algorithm used in conjunction with dynamic programming (compare with Fig. 3.15b on p. 59). However, we have yet to describe how to compute the states.

First Technique to Apply Offline Cost Analysis

Due to a 1986 paper, Hatcher and Christopher [172] appear to have been pioneers in applying offline cost analysis to pattern selection. Hatcher and Christopher's design is an extension of the work by Hoffmann and O'Donnell, and their intuition is to find which rule to apply for some program tree, whose root has been assigned a label l, such that the entire tree can be reduced to a given nonterminal at lowest cost. Hatcher and Christopher argued that for optimal pattern selection we can consider each pair of a label l and nonterminal nt, and then always apply the rule that will reduce the largest program tree T_l, which is representative of l, to nt at the lowest cost. In Hoffmann and O'Donnell's design, where there is only one nullary symbol that may match any subtree, T_l is equal to the largest pattern appearing in the matchset, but to accommodate instruction set grammars, Hatcher and Christopher's version includes one nullary symbol per nonterminal. This means that T_l has to be found by overlapping all patterns appearing in the matchset. We then calculate the cost of transforming a larger pattern p into a subsuming, smaller pattern q (hence $p > q$) for every pair of patterns. This cost, which is later annotated to the subsumption graph, is calculated by recursively rewriting p using other patterns until it is equal to q, making the cost of this transformation equal to the sum of all applied patterns. We represent this cost with a function $reducecost(p \xrightarrow{*} q)$. With this information we retrieve the rule that leads to the lowest-cost reduction of T_l to a goal g by finding the rule r for which

$$reducecost(T_l \xrightarrow{*} g) = reducecost(T_l \xrightarrow{*} \text{pattern tree of } r) + \text{cost of } r.$$

This will select either the largest pattern appearing in the matchset of l, or, if one exists, a smaller pattern that in combination with others has a lower cost. We have of course glossed over many details, but this covers the main idea of Hatcher and Christopher's design.

By encoding the selected rules into an additional table to be used during pattern matching, we achieve a completely table-driven instruction selector which also performs optimal pattern selection. Hatcher and Christopher also augmented the original algorithm so that the returned matchsets contain all patterns that were duplicated due commutative operations. However, if the pattern set contains patterns which are truly independent, then Hatcher and Christopher's design does not always guarantee that the program trees can be optimally covered. It is also not clear whether optimal pattern selection for the largest program trees representative of the labels is an accurate approximation for optimal pattern selection for all possible program trees.

Generating the States Using BURS Theory

A different and more well-known method for generating the states was developed by Pelegrí-Llopart and Graham [278]. In a seminal paper from 1988, Pelegrí-Llopart and Graham prove that the methods of tree rewriting can always arranged such that all rewrites occur at the leaves of the tree, resulting in a *bottom-up rewriting system (BURS)*. We say that a collection of such rules constitute a *BURS grammar*, which is similar to the grammars already seen, with the exception that BURS grammars allow multiple symbols—including terminals—to appear on the left-hand side of a production. An example of such a grammar is given in Fig. 3.18a, and Dold et al. [99], as

	PATTERN
1	r → op a a
2	r → R
3	r → a
4	a → r
5	a → C
6	a → + C r
7	C → 0
8	x → + x 0
9	+ y x → + x y
10	op x y → + x y

(a) BURS grammar

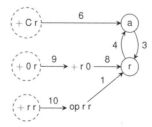

(b) Example of an LR graph based on the program tree + 0 + C C and the grammar shown in (a). Dashed nodes represent subtrees of the program tree and fully drawn nodes represent goals. Edges indicate rule applications, with the number of the applied rule appearing next to the edge

Fig. 3.18: BURS example [278]

an extension to the work of Zimmermann and Gaul [355], later developed a method
for proving the correctness of BURS grammars using abstract state machines.

Using BURS theory Pelegrí-Llopart and Graham developed an algorithm that
computes the tables needed for optimal pattern selection based on a given BURS
grammar. The idea is as follows: for a given program tree T, a *local rewrite (LR)*
graph is formed where each node represents a specific subtree appearing in T and
each edge indicates the application of a particular rewrite rule on that subtree (an
example is shown in Fig. 3.18b). Setting some nodes as goals (that is, the desired
results of tree rewriting), a subgraph called the *uniquely invertible (UI) LR graph*
is then selected from the LR graph such that the number of rewrite possibilities is
minimized. Each UI LR graph then corresponds to a state, and by generating all
LR graphs for all possible program trees that can be given as input, we can find
all the necessary states. Since finding a UI LR graph is an NP-complete problem,
Pelegrí-Llopart and Graham applied a heuristic that iteratively removes nodes which
are deemed "useless" until a UI LR graph is achieved.

Achieving a Bounded Number of States

To achieve optimal pattern selection, the LR graphs are augmented such that each
node no longer represents a pattern tree but a (p,c) pair, where c denotes the minimal
cost of covering the corresponding subtree with pattern p. This is the information
embodied by the states as discussed earlier. A naïve approach would be to include the
full cost of reaching a particular pattern into the state, but depending on the rewrite
system this may require an infinite number of states. An example where this occurs
is given in Fig. 3.19b. A better method is to instead account for the *relative* cost of
a selected pattern. This is achieved by computing c as the difference between the
cost of p and the smallest cost associated with any other pattern appearing in the
LR graph. This yields the same optimal pattern selection but the number of needed

 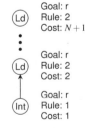 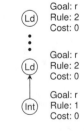

(a) A rewrite system that may lead to an unbounded number of states. Ld stands for "load"

(b) Input tree labeled with states that incorporate the full cost (requires $N+1$ states)

(c) Input tree labeled with states that incorporate the delta costs (requires only two states)

Fig. 3.19: An example illustrating how incorporating costs into states can result in an infinite number of states [278]

states is bounded, as seen in Fig. 3.19c. This cost is called the *delta cost* and the augmented LR graph is thus known as a δ-*LR graph*. To limit the memory footprint when generating the δ-LR graphs, Pelegrí-Llopart and Graham used an extension of Chase's table compression algorithm [73] (which we discussed on p. 57).

During testing, Pelegrí-Llopart and Graham reported that their implementation yielded state tables only slightly larger than those produced by LR parsing, and generated assembly code of quality comparable to TWIG's but at a rate that was about five times faster.

BURS ⇎ Offline Cost Analysis

Since Pelegrí-Llopart and Graham's 1988 paper, many later publications mistakenly associate to the idea of offline cost analysis with BURS theory, typically using terms like *BURS states*, when these two aspects are in fact orthogonal to each other. Although the work by Pelegrí-Llopart and Graham undoubtedly led to making offline cost analysis an established aspect of modern instruction selection, the application of BURS theory is only *one* means to achieving optimal pattern selection using tables.

For example, in 1990 Balachandran et al. [35] introduced an alternative method for generating the states that is both simpler and more efficient than that of Pelegrí-Llopart and Graham. At its heart their algorithm iteratively creates new states using those already committed to appear in the state tables. Remember that each state represents a combination of nonterminals, rules, and costs, where the costs have been normalized such that the lowest cost of any rule appearing in that state is 0. Hence two states are identical if the rules selected for all nonterminals and costs are the same. Before a new state is created it is first checked whether it has already been seen—if not, then it is added to the set of committed states—and the process repeats until no new states can be created. We will go into more detail shortly.

Compared to Pelegrí-Llopart and Graham, this algorithm is less complicated and also faster as it directly generates a smaller set of states instead of first enumerating all possible states and then reducing them. In addition, Balachandran et al. expressed the instructions as a more traditional instruction set grammar—like those used in the Graham-Glanville approach—instead of as a BURS grammar.

Linear-Form Grammars

In the same paper, Balachandran et al. also introduce the idea of grammars being in *linear form*, which means that the pattern of every production in the grammar is restricted to one of the following forms:

1. lhs $\rightarrow$ Op $n_1 \ldots n_k$, where Op is a terminal representing an operator for which $rank(\text{Op}) > 0$ and n_i are all nonterminals. Rules with such productions are called *base rules*.
2. lhs $\rightarrow$ T, where T is a terminal. Such rules are also called base rules.
3. lhs $\rightarrow$ nt, where nt is a nonterminal. As before, such rules are called chain rules.

A nonlinear-form grammar can easily be rewritten into linear form by introducing new nonterminals and rules for making the necessary transitions. An example is shown below:

PRODUCTION	COST		PRODUCTION	COST
reg → Ld + Const Const	2		reg → Ld n_1	2
			n_1 → + n_2 n_2	0
			n_2 → Const	0
Original grammar		⇒	Linear-form grammar	

The advantage of this kind of grammar is that the pattern matching problem is reduced to simply comparing the operator of the root in the pattern with the operator of a node in the program tree. This also means that the productions appearing in the rules become more uniform, which greatly simplifies the task of generating the states.

A Work Queue Approach for State Table Generation

Another state-generating algorithm similar to the one by Balachandran et al. was proposed by Proebsting [281, 284]. This algorithm was also implemented by Fraser et al. [138] in a renowned code generation system called BURG,[9] which since its publication in 1992 has sparked a naming convention within the compiler community that I have chosen to call the BURG*er phenomenon*.[10] Although Balachandran et al. were first, we will continue with studying Proebsting's algorithm as it is better documented. More details are also available in Proebsting's doctoral dissertation [282].

The algorithm is centered around a work queue that contains a backlog of states under consideration. Again, it is assumed that the instruction set grammar is in linear form. The queue is first initialized with the states that can be generated from all possible leaves. A state is then popped from the queue and used in combination with other already-visited states in an attempt to produce new states. This is done by effectively simulating what would happen if a set of nodes, appearing as children to some node *n*, were labeled with

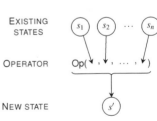

EXISTING STATES

OPERATOR

NEW STATE

---

[9] The keen reader will notice that Fraser et al. also implemented the DP-based system IBURG which was introduced on p. 61. The connection between the two is that IBURG began as a testbench for the grammar specification to be used as input to BURG. Fraser et al. later recognized that some of the ideas for the testbench showed some merit in themselves, and therefore improved and extended them into a stand-alone generator. Unfortunately the authors neglected to say in their papers what these acronyms stand for. My tentative guess is that BURG was derived from the BURS acronym and stands for *Bottom-Up Rewrite Generator*.

[10] During my research for this book, I came across the following systems, all with equally creative naming schemes: BURG [138], CBURG [303], DBURG [117], GBURG [139], GPBURG [162], HBURG [48], IBURG [137], JBURG [171], LBURG [169], MBURG [160, 161], WBURG [285], and OCAMLBURG [238].

some combination of states, including the state that was just popped. If n can be labeled using an already existing state, then nothing happens; if not, then a new appropriate state is created and appended to the queue, making sure that all applicable chain rules have been applied to the state, as this can affect costs. This is checked for every possible combination of states and operator symbols, and the algorithm terminates when the queue becomes empty, indicating that all states necessary for the instruction set grammar have been generated.

Further Improvements

The time required to generate the state tables can be decreased if the number of committed states can be minimized. According to Proebsting [284], the first attempts to do this were made by Henry [176], whose methods were later improved and generalized by Proebsting [281, 284]. Proebsting developed two methods for reducing the number of generated states: *state trimming*, which extends and generalizes Henry's ideas; and a new technique called *chain rule trimming*. Without going into details, state trimming increases the likelihood that two created states will be identical by removing the information about nonterminals that can be proven to never take part in a least-cost covering. Chain rule trimming then further minimizes the number of states by attempting to use the same rules whenever possible. This technique was later improved by Kang and Choe [195, 196], who exploited properties of common machine descriptions to decrease the amount of redundant state testing.

More Applications

The approach of extending pattern selection with offline cost analysis has been applied in numerous compiler-related systems. Some notable applications that we have not already mentioned include UNH-CODEGEN [174], DCG [114], LBURG [169], and WBURG [285]. BURG is also available as a Haskell clone called HBURG [48], and has been adapted by Boulytchev [52] to assist instruction set selection. LBURG was developed to be used in the *Little C Compiler (LCC)* [169], and was adopted by Brandner et al. [55] in designing an architecture description language from which the instructions can automatically be inferred. LBURG was also extended by Farfeleder et al. [121] to support certain multi-output instructions by adding an additional, handwritten pass in the pattern matcher.

3.6.4 Generating States Lazily

The two main approaches achieving optimal pattern selection—those that dynamically compute the costs as the program is compiled, and those that rely on statically computed costs via state tables—both have their respective advantages and drawbacks.

The former have the advantage of being able to support dynamic costs (meaning the pattern cost is not fixed but depends on the context), but they are also considerably slower than their purely table-driven counterparts. The latter yield faster but larger instruction selectors due to the use of state tables, which are also very time-consuming to generate—for pathological grammars this may even be infeasible—and they only support grammar rules with fixed costs.

Combining the Best of State Tables and DP

In 2006, Ertl et al. [118] introduced a method that allows the state tables to be generated lazily and on demand. The intuition is that instead of generating the states for *all* possible program trees in advance, one can get away with only generating the states needed for the program trees that actually appear in the program.

The scheme can be outlined as follows. As the instruction selector traverses a program tree, the states required for covering its subtrees are created using dynamic programming. Once the states have been generated, the subtree is labeled and patterns are selected using the familiar table-driven techniques. Then, if an identical subtree is encountered elsewhere—either in the same program tree or in another tree of the program—the same states can be reused. This allows the cost of state generation to be amortized as the subtree can now be optimally covered faster than if it had been processed using a purely DP-based pattern selector. Ertl et al. reported the overhead of state reuse was minimal compared to purely table-driven implementations, and the time required to first compute the states and then label the program trees was on par with selecting patterns using ordinary DP-based techniques. Moreover, by generating the states lazily it is possible to handle larger and more complex instruction set grammars which otherwise would require an intractable number of states.

Ertl et al. also extended this design to support dynamic costs by recomputing and storing the states in hash tables whenever the costs at the program tree roots differ. The authors noted that while this incurs an additional overhead, their instruction selector was still faster than a purely DP-based instruction selector.

3.7 Other Tree-Based Approaches

So far we have discussed the conventional methods of covering trees: LR parsing, top-down recursion, dynamic programming, and the use of state tables. In this section we will look at other designs which also rely on trees, but solve the instruction selection problem using alternative methods.

3.7.1 Techniques Based on Formal Frameworks

Homomorphisms and Inversion of Derivors

In order to simplify the machine descriptions and enable formal verification, Giegerich and Schmal [157] proposed in 1988 an algebraic framework intended to support all aspects of code generation, including instruction scheduling and register allocation. In brief terms Giegerich and Schmal reformulated the instruction selection problem into a "problem of a hierarchic derivor," which essentially entails the specification and implementation of a mechanism

$$\gamma : T(Q) \to T(Z),$$

where $T(Q)$ and $T(Z)$ denote the term algebras for expressing programs in an intermediate language and target machine language, respectively. Hence γ can be viewed as the resulting instruction selector. Most machine descriptions, however, are typically expressed in terms of Z rather than Q. We therefore view the machine specification as a *homomorphism*

$$\delta : T(Z) \to T(Q),$$

and the task of an instruction selection-generator is thus to derive γ by inverting δ. Usually this is achieved by resorting to pattern matching, but for optimal instruction selection the generator must also interleave the construction of the inverse δ^{-1} with a *choice function* ξ whenever some $q \in T(Q)$ has several $z \in T(Z)$ such that $\delta(q) = z$. Conceptually this gives us the following functionality:

$$T(Q) \xrightarrow{\delta^{-1}} 2^{T(Z)} \xrightarrow{\xi} T(Z).$$

In the same paper, Giegerich and Schmal also demonstrate how some other methods, such as tree parsing, can be expressed using this framework. A similar scheme based on rewriting techniques was later proposed by Despland et al. [94, 95] in an implementation called PAGODE [63].

Equational Logic

Shortly after Giegerich and Schmal, Hatcher [173] developed a design similar to that of Pelegrí-Llopart and Graham that relies on *equational logic* [272] instead of BURS theory. The two are closely related in that both apply a set of predefined rules to rewrite the program tree into a single goal term, but an equational specification has the advantage that all such rules—which are derived from the instructions and axiomatic transformations—are based on a set of so-called *built-in operations*. Each built-in operation has a cost and implicit semantics, expressed as assembly code emission. The cost of a rule is then equal to the sum of all built-in operations it applies, removing the need to set the rule costs manually. In addition, no built-in operations are predefined, but are instead given as part of the equational specification, providing a very general mechanism for describing target machines. Experimental results with an implementation called UCG—the paper does not say what this acronym stands for—indicated that UCG could, for a selected set of problems, generate assembly code of comparable quality to that of contemporary techniques but in less time.

3.7.2 More Tree Rewriting-Based Methods

We have already discussed numerous techniques which perform instruction selection by rewriting the program tree such that it finally reaches a particular goal. For completeness we will in this section examine the remaining such designs, but without going into much detail.

Using Finite Tree Automata, Series Transducers, and Pushdown Automata

Emmelmann [110] introduced in 1992 a technique that relies on the theories of *finite tree automata* (see for example [154] for an overview), which was later extended by Ferdinand et al. [127]. In their 1994 paper, Ferdinand et al. demonstrate how finite tree automata can be used to solve both pattern matching and pattern selection—greedily as well as optimally—and also present algorithms for how to produce these automata. An experimental implementation demonstrated the feasibility of this technique, but the results were not compared to those of other techniques. Similar designs were later proposed by Borchardt [50] and Janoušek and Málek [187], who made use of *tree series transducers* (see for example [112] for an overview) and *pushdown automata*, respectively.

Rewriting Strategies

In 2002, Bravenboer and Visser presented a design where rule-based program transformation systems [329] are adapted to instruction selection. Through a system called STRATEGO [330], a machine description can be augmented by pattern selection strategies, allowing the pattern selector to be tailored to that particular target machine. Bravenboer and Visser refer to this as providing a *rewriting strategy*, and their system supports modeling of several strategies such as exhaustive search, maximum munch, and dynamic programming. Purely table-driven techniques, however, do not seem to be supported at the time of writing, which excludes the application of offline cost analysis. In their paper, Bravenboer and Visser argue that this setup allows several pattern selection techniques to be combined, but they do not provide an example of where this would be beneficial.

3.7.3 Techniques Based on Genetic Algorithms

To solve the pattern selection problem, Shu et al. [308] employed the theories of
genetic algorithms (GAs), which mimic the process of natural selection (see for
example [292] for an overview).[11] The idea is to formulate a solution as a string,
called a *chromosome* or *gene*, and then mutate it in order to hopefully end up with a
better solution. For a given program tree whose matchsets have been found using an
$O(nm)$ pattern matcher, Shu et al. formulated each chromosome as a binary bit string
where a 1 indicates the selection of a particular pattern. Likewise, a 0 indicates that
the pattern is not used in the tree covering. The length of a chromosome is therefore
equal to the sum of the number of patterns appearing in all matchsets. The objective
is then to find the chromosome which maximizes a *fitness function* f, which Shu et al.
defined as

$$f(c) = \frac{1}{k * p_c + n_c},$$

where k is a tweakable constant greater than 1, p_c is the number of selected patterns
in the chromosome c, and n_c is the number of nodes in c which are covered by more
than one pattern. Hence patterns are allowed to overlap in covering the program tree.
First, a fixed number of chromosomes is randomly generated and evaluated. The best
ones are kept and subjected to standard GA operations—such as fitness-proportionate
reproduction, single-point crossover, and one-bit mutations—in order to produce
new chromosomes, and the process repeats until a termination criterion is reached.
The authors claim to be able to find optimal tree covers in "reasonable" time for
medium-sized program trees, but these include at most 50 nodes. Moreover, due to
the nature of GAs, optimality cannot be guaranteed for all program trees. A similar
technique was devised by Eriksson et al. [115], which also incorporates instruction
scheduling, for generating assembly code for clustered *very long instruction word
(VLIW)* architectures.

3.7.4 Techniques Based on Trellis Diagrams

The last instruction selection technique that we will examine in this chapter is a rather
unusual design by Wess [336, 337]. Specifically targeting digital signal processors,
Wess's design integrates instruction selection with register allocation through the use
of *trellis diagrams*.

A trellis diagram is a graph where each node consists of an *optimal value array
(OVA)*. An element in an OVA represents that the data is stored either in memory (m)
or in a particular register (r_x), and its value indicates the lowest accumulated cost
from the leaves to the node. The cost is computed similarly as in the DP-based

---

[11] On a related note, Wu and Li [343] applied *ant colony optimization*—a meta-heuristic inspired
by the shortest-path searching behavior of various ant species [102]—to improve overall code size
by alternating between instruction sets on a per-function basis.

techniques. For example, let us assume a target machine with two registers r_1 and r_2 yields the following OVA

i	0	1	2	3	4
OVA					
TL	m	r_1	r_1	r_2	r_2
RA	$\{r_1,r_2\}$	$\{r_1\}$	$\{r_1,r_2\}$	$\{r_2\}$	$\{r_1,r_2\}$

where TL denotes the target location of the data produced at this node, and RA denotes the set of registers that may be used when producing the data. To facilitate the following discussion, let us denote by $TL(i,n)$ and $RA(i,n)$ the target location and set of available registers, respectively, for the ith element in the OVA of node n.

We create the trellis diagram using the following scheme. For each node in the program tree, a new node representing an OVA is added to the trellis diagram. For the leaves an additional node is added in order to handle situations where the values first need to be transferred to another location before being used (this is needed for example if the value resides in memory). Next we add the edges. Let us denote by $e(i,n)$ the ith element in the OVA of a node n. For a unary operation node n, with a child m, we add an edge between $e(i,n)$ and $e(j,m)$ if there exists a sequence of instructions that implements the operation of n, stores the result in $TL(i,n)$, takes as input the value stored in $TL(j,m)$, and exclusively uses the registers in $RA(i,n)$. Similarly, for a binary operation node o and two children n and m, we add an edge pair from $e(i,n)$ and $e(j,m)$ to $e(k,o)$ if there exists a sequence of instructions that implements the operation of o, stores the result in $TL(k,o)$, takes as input the two values stored in $TL(i,n)$ and $TL(j,m)$, and exclusively uses the registers in $RA(k,o)$. This can be generalized to n-ary operations, and a complete example is given in Fig. 3.20.

The edges in the trellis diagram thus correspond to the possible combinations of instructions and registers that implement a particular operation in the program tree, and a path from every leaf in the trellis diagram to its root represents a selection of such combinations. By keeping track of the costs, we can get the optimal instruction sequence by selecting the path which ends at the OVA element with the lowest cost in the root of the trellis diagram.

The strength of Wess's design is that target machines with asymmetric register classes—where different instructions are needed for accessing different registers—are easily handled, as instruction selection and register allocation is done simultaneously. The drawback is that the number of nodes in the trellis diagram is exponential in the number of registers. This problem was mitigated by Fröhlich et al. [142], who augmented the algorithm to build the trellis diagram in a lazy fashion, but both schemes nonetheless require a 1-to-1 mapping between the nodes in a trellis diagram and the instructions in order to be effective.[12]

---

[12] This, in combination of how instructions are selected, makes one wonder whether these techniques actually conform to the principles of tree and DAG covering. I certainly struggled with deciding how to categorize them, and finally I opted against creating a separate principle, as that would indeed be a very short chapter.

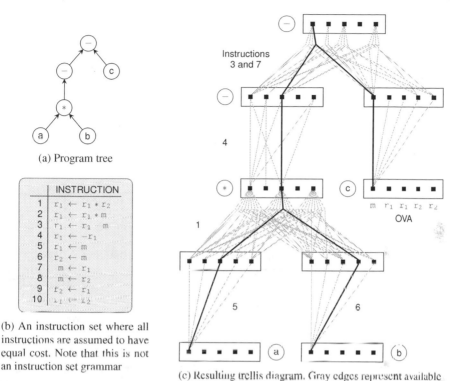

(a) Program tree

	INSTRUCTION
1	$r_1 \leftarrow r_1 * r_2$
2	$r_1 \leftarrow r_1 * m$
3	$r_1 \leftarrow r_1 - m$
4	$r_1 \leftarrow -r_1$
5	$r_1 \leftarrow m$
6	$r_2 \leftarrow m$
7	$m \leftarrow r_1$
8	$m \leftarrow r_2$
9	$r_2 \leftarrow r_1$
10	$r_1 \leftarrow r_2$

(b) An instruction set where all instructions are assumed to have equal cost. Note that this is not an instruction set grammar

(c) Resulting trellis diagram. Gray edges represent available paths, and black edges indicate the (selected) optimal path

Fig. 3.20: A trellis diagram corresponding to an expression $-(a * b) - c$ and a two-register target machine. The variables a, b, and c are assumed to be initially stored in memory. Note that two instructions are selected for the root as the result is required to be stored in memory [336]

3.8 Summary

In this chapter we have looked at numerous techniques that are based on the principle of tree covering. In contrast to macro expansion, tree covering enables use of more complex patterns, allowing a wider range of instructions to be selected. By applying dynamic programming, optimal covers can be found in linear time, which further improve the quality of the generated assembly code, and several techniques also incorporate offline cost analysis into the instruction selector generator to reduce compilation time. In other words, this kind of implementation is very fast and efficient while also supporting a wide array of target machines. Consequently, tree covering has become the most known—although perhaps no longer the most applied— principle of instruction selection. However, restricting oneself to trees has several inherent disadvantages.

3.8.1 Restrictions That Come with Trees

The first disadvantage of trees has to do with expression
modeling. Due to the definitions of trees, common subexpressions cannot be properly modeled in a program tree.

```
x = a + b;
y - x + x;
```

For example, the inlined code cannot be modeled directly without applying one of
the following workarounds:

1. Repeating the shared operations, which in Polish notation results in

   $$= y + + a b + a b.$$

2. Splitting the expression, which results in

   $$= x + a b$$
   $$= y + x x.$$

The first approach leads to additional instructions in the assembly code, while
the second hinders the use of more complex instructions. Hence code quality is
compromised in both cases.

   The second disadvantage is limited instruction set support. For example, since
trees only allow a single root, multi-output instructions cannot be represented as
pattern trees as such instructions would require multiple roots. Even disjoint-output
instructions, where each individual operation can be modeled as trees, cannot be
selected because tree covering-based instruction selectors can only consider a single
pattern tree at a time.

   The third disadvantage is that program trees typically cannot model control flow.
For example, a *for* loop statement requires a cyclic edge between blocks, which
violates the definition of trees. For this reason, tree-based instruction selectors are
limited to selecting instructions for a single program tree at a time—this is called *local
instruction selection*—and handle assembly code emission for control flow using
a separate component. This in turn excludes matching and selection of inter-block
instructions, whose behavior incorporates control flow.

   To summarize, although the principle of tree covering greatly improves code
quality over the principle of pure macro expansion (ignoring peephole optimization,
that is), the inherent restrictions of trees prevent exploitation of many instructions
provided by modern target machines. In the next chapter we will look at a more
general principle that addresses some of these issues.

Chapter 4
DAG Covering

As we saw in Chapter 3, the principle of tree covering has two significant disadvantages. The first is that common subexpressions cannot be properly expressed in program trees, and the second is that many machine instruction characteristics—such as multi-output instructions—cannot be modeled as pattern trees. As these shortcomings are primarily due to the restricted use of trees, we can achieve a more powerful approach to instruction selection by extending tree covering to *DAG covering*.

4.1 The Principle

By lifting the restriction that every node in the tree have exactly one parent, we get a new shape called a *directed acyclic graph (DAG)*. Because DAGs permit nodes to have multiple parents, the intermediate values in an expression can be shared and reused within the same *program DAG*. This also enables *pattern DAGs* to contain multiple root nodes, which signify the production of multiple output values and thus extend the instruction support to include multi-output instructions.

Since DAGs are less restrictive compared to trees, transitioning from tree covering to DAG covering requires new methods for solving the problems of pattern matching and pattern selection. Pattern matching is typically addressed using one of the following methods:

- First split the pattern DAGs into trees, then match these individually, and then recombine the matched pattern trees into their original DAG form. In general, matching trees on DAGs is NP-complete [151], but designs applying this technique typically sacrifice completeness to retain linear time complexity.
- Match the pattern DAGs directly using a generic subgraph isomorphism algorithm. Although such algorithms exhibit exponential worst-case time complexity, in the average case they often finish in polynomial time and are therefore used by several DAG covering-based designs discussed in this chapter.

© Springer International Publishing Switzerland 2016
G. Hjort Blindell, *Instruction Selection*,
DOI 10.1007/978-3-319-34019-7_4

Optimal pattern selection on program DAGs, however, does not offer the same range of choices in terms of complexity.

4.2 Optimal Pattern Selection on DAGs Is NP-Complete

The cost of the gain in generality and modeling capabilities that DAGs give us is a substantial increase in complexity. As we saw in Chapter 3, selecting an optimal set of patterns to cover a program tree can be done in linear time, but doing the same for program DAGs is an NP-complete problem. Proofs were given in 1976 by Bruno and Sethi [60] and Aho et al. [4], but these were most concerned with the optimality of instruction scheduling and register allocation. In 1995, Proebsting [283] gave a very concise proof for optimal instruction selection, and a longer, more detailed proof was given by Koes and Goldstein [212] in 2008. In this book, we will paraphrase the longer proof.

4.2.1 The Proof

The idea behind the proof is to transform the *Boolean satisfiability (SAT) problem* to an optimal—that is, least-cost—DAG covering problem. The SAT problem is the task of deciding whether a Boolean formula, written in *conjunctive normal form (CNF)*, can be satisfied. A CNF formula is an expression consisting of Boolean variables and the Boolean operations $\lor$ *(or)* and $\land$ *(and)* with the following structure:

$$(x_{1,1} \lor x_{1,2} \lor \ldots) \land (x_{2,1} \lor x_{2,2} \lor \ldots) \land \ldots$$

A variable x can also be negated, written as $\neg x$.

Since the SAT problem is NP-complete, all polynomial-time transformations from SAT to any other problem $\mathscr{P}$ must also render $\mathscr{P}$ NP-complete.

Modeling SAT as a Covering Problem

First, we transform an instance S of the SAT problem into a program DAG. The goal is then to find an exact cover for the DAG in order to deduce the truth assignment for the Boolean variables from the set of selected patterns. For this purpose we will use $\lor$, $\land$, $\neg$, v, $\square$, and $\bigcirc$ as node types, and define $type(n)$ as the type of a node n. Nodes of type $\square$ and $\bigcirc$ will be referred to as *box nodes* and *stop nodes*, respectively. Now, for each Boolean variable $x \in S$ we create two nodes n_1 and n_2 such that $type(n_1) = v$ and $type(n_2) = \square$, and add these to the program DAG. At the same time we also add an edge $n_1 \to n_2$. The same is done for each binary Boolean operator $op \in S$ by creating two nodes n'_1 and n'_2 such that $type(n'_1) = op$

and $type(n'_2) = \square$, along with an edge $n'_1 \rightarrow n'_2$. To model the connection between the op operation and its two input operands x and y, we add two edges $n_x \rightarrow n'_1$ and $n_y \rightarrow n'_1$ such that $type(n_x) = type(n_y) = \square$. For the unary operation $\neg$ we obviously only need one such edge, and since $\vee$ and $\wedge$ are commutative it does not matter in what order the edges are arranged with respect to the operator node. Hence, in the resulting program DAG, only box nodes will have more than one outgoing edge. An example of such a DAG is shown in Fig. 4.1b, which can be constructed in linear time simply by traversing the Boolean formula.

Boolean Operations as Patterns

To cover the program DAG, we will use the pattern trees given in Fig. 4.1a, and we will refer to this pattern set as P_{SAT}. Every pattern in P_{SAT} adheres to the following invariant:

1. If a variable x is set to T (*true*), then the selected pattern covering the x node will also cover the corresponding box node of x
2. If the result of an operation op evaluates to F (*false*), then that pattern will not cover the corresponding box node of op.

Another way of looking at it is that an operator in a pattern *consumes* a box node if its corresponding value must be set to T, and *produces* a box node if the result

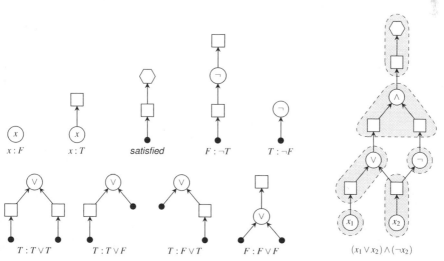

(a) The SAT patterns. For brevity, the patterns for the $\wedge$ operation are omitted (but these can be easily inferred from the $\vee$ patterns) All patterns are assumed to have the same unit cost

(b) Example of a SAT problem represented as a DAG covering problem

Fig. 4.1: Transforming SAT to DAG covering [212]

must evaluate to F. Using this scheme, we can easily deduce the truth assignments to the variables by inspecting whether the patterns selected to cover the DAG consume the box nodes of the variables. Since the only pattern to contain a stop node also consumes a box node, the entire expression will be forced to evaluate to T.

In addition to the node types that can appear in the program DAG, the patterns can also contain nodes of an additional type, •, which we will refer to as *anchor nodes*. Let $numch(n)$ denote the number of children of n, and $child(i,n)$ the ith child of n. We now say that a pattern p, with root node p_r, *matches* the part of a program DAG (N,E) which is rooted at a node $n \in N$ if and only if:

1. $type(n) = type(p_r)$,
2. $numch(n) = numch(p_r)$, and
3. $type(child(i,n)) = • \lor child(i,n)$ matches $child(i,p_r)$, $\forall 1 \leq i \leq numch(n)$.

In other words, the structure of the pattern tree—which includes the node types and edges—must correspond to the structure of the matched subgraph, with the exception of anchor nodes, which match any node in the program DAG.

We also introduce two new definitions, $matchset(n)$ and $matched(p,n_p)$: for a node $n \in N$ in the program DAG $G = (N,E)$, $matchset(n)$ is the set of patterns in P_{SAT} that match at n; and for a node $n_p \in N_p$ in the selected match of pattern (N_p,E_p), $matched(n,n_p)$ is the node $n \in N$ that is matched by n_p. Lastly, we say that G is *covered* by a function $f: N \to 2^{P_{SAT}}$, which maps nodes in the program DAG to a set of patterns, if and only if, for each $n \in N$,

1. p matches n, $\forall p \in f(n)$,
2. $type(n) = \bigcirc \Rightarrow f(n) \neq \emptyset$, and
3. $type(n_p) = • \Rightarrow f(matched(n,n_p)) \neq \emptyset$, $\forall p = (N_p,E_p) \in f(v), n_p \in N_p$.

The first constraint enforces that only valid matches are selected. The second constraint enforces that some match has been selected to cover the stop node, and the third constraint enforces that matches have been selected to cover the rest of the DAG. An optimal cover is thus a mapping f which covers the program DAG (N,E) and also minimize

$$\sum_{n \in N} \sum_{p \in f(n)} cost(p),$$

where $cost(p)$ is the cost of pattern p.

Optimal Solution to DAG Covering $\Rightarrow$ Solution to SAT

We now postulate that if the optimal cover has a total cost equal to the number of non-box nodes in the program DAG, then the corresponding SAT problem is satisfiable. Since all patterns in P_{SAT} cover exactly one non-box node and have equal unit cost, the condition above means that every node in the DAG is covered by exactly one pattern. This in turn means that exactly one value will be assumed for every Boolean variable and operator result, which is easy to deduce through inspection of the selected matches.

We have thereby shown that an instance of the SAT problem can be solved by transforming it, in polynomial time, to an instance of the optimal DAG covering problem. Hence optimal DAG covering—and therefore also optimal instruction selection based on DAG covering—is NP-complete.   □

4.3 Straightforward, Greedy Techniques

Since instruction selection on DAGs with optimal pattern selection is computationally difficult, most instruction selectors based on this principle are suboptimal. One of the first code generators to operate on DAGs was developed by Aho et al. [4]. In a paper from 1976, Aho et al. introduce some simple greedy heuristics for producing assembly code for a commutative one-register target machine, but these methods assume a one-to-one mapping between the nodes in a program DAG and the instructions and thus effectively ignore the instruction selection problem.

4.3.1 LLVM

A more flexible, but still greedy, heuristic is applied in the well-known LLVM compiler infrastructure [224]. According to a blog entry by Bendersky [46]—which at the time of writing provides the only documentation, except for the source code itself—the instruction selector is basically a greedy DAG-to-DAG rewriter.[1]

The patterns—which are limited to trees—are expressed in a machine description that allows common features to be factored out into abstract instructions. A tool called TABLEGEN expands the abstract instructions into pattern trees, which are then processed by a matcher generator. To ensure a partial order among all patterns, the matcher generator first performs a lexicographical sort on the pattern set: first by decreasing complexity, which is the sum of the pattern's size and a constant that can be tweaked to give higher priority for particular instructions; then by increasing cost; and lastly by increasing the size of the subgraph that replaces the covered part in the program DAG if the corresponding pattern is selected. Once sorted, the patterns are converted into small recursive programs which essentially check whether the corresponding pattern matches at a given node in the program DAG. These programs are then compiled into a form of byte code and assembled into a matcher table, arranged such that the lexicographical sort is preserved. The instruction selector applies this table by simply executing the byte code, starting with the first element. When a match is found, the pattern is greedily selected and the matched subgraph is replaced with the output (usually a single node) of the selected pattern. This process repeats until there are no nodes remaining in the original program DAG.

---

[1] LLVM is also equipped with a "fast" instruction selector, but it is implemented as a typical macro expander and is only intended to be used when compiling without extensive program optimization.

Although in extensive use (as of version 3.4), LLVM's instruction selector has several drawbacks. The main disadvantage is that any pattern that is not supported by TABLEGEN has to be handled manually through custom C functions. Unlike GCC—which applies macro expansion combined with peephole optimization (see Section 2.3.2)—this includes all multi-output instructions, since LLVM is restricted to pattern trees only. In addition, the greedy scheme compromises code quality.

4.4 Techniques Based on Exhaustive Search

Although optimal pattern selection can be achieved through exhaustive search, in practice this is typically infeasible due to the exponential number of possible combinations. Nonetheless, there do exist a few techniques that do exactly this, but they apply various techniques to prune the search space.

4.4.1 Extending Means-End Analysis to DAGs

Twenty years after Newcomer and Cattell et al. (see Section 3.4.1), Yu and Hu [351, 352] rediscovered means-end analysis as a method for instruction selection and also made two major improvements. First, Yu and Hu's design supports and pattern DAGs whereas those by Newcomer and Cattell et al. are both limited to trees. Second, it combines means-end analysis with *hierarchical planning* [298], which is a search strategy that relies on the fact that many problems can be arranged in a hierarchical manner for handling larger and more complex problem instances. Using hierarchical planning enables exhaustive exploration of the search space while at the same time avoiding the situations of dead ends and infinite looping that may occur in straightforward implementations of means-end analysis (Newcomer and Cattell et al. both circumvented this problem by enforcing a cut-off when a certain depth in the search space had been reached).

Although this technique exhibits a worst time execution that is exponential in the depth of the search, Yu and Hu assert that a depth of 3 is sufficient to yield results of equal quality to that of handwritten assembly code. This claim notwithstanding, it is unclear whether it can be extended to support complex instructions such as inter-block and interdependent instructions.

4.4.2 Relying on Semantic-Preserving Transformations

In 1996, Hoover and Zadeck [182] developed a system called TOAST with the goal of automating the generation of entire compiler frameworks—including instruction scheduling and register allocation—from a declarative machine description. In

TOAST the instruction selection is done by applying semantic-preserving transformations during pattern selection to make better use of the instruction set. For example, although $x * 2$ is semantically equivalent to $x \ll 1$—meaning that x is arithmetically shifted one bit to the right, which is faster than executing a multiplication—most instruction selectors will fail to select instructions implementing the latter when the former appears in the program DAG, as the patterns are syntactically different from one another.

Their design works as follows. First, the frontend emits program DAGs consisting of *semantic primitives*, a kind of IR code also used for describing the instructions. The program DAG is then semantically matched using single-output patterns derived from the instructions. Semantic matches—which Hoover and Zadeck call *toe prints*—and are found by a *semantic comparator*. The semantic comparator first performs syntactic matching—that is, checking that the nodes are of the same type, which is done using a straightforward $O(nm)$ algorithm— and then resorts to semantic-preserving transformations for when syntactic matching fails. To bound the exhaustive search for all possible toe prints, a transformation is only applied if it will lead to a syntactic match later on. Once all toe prints have been found, they are combined into *foot prints*, which correspond to the full effects of an instruction. A foot print can consist of just a single toe print (as with single-output instructions) or several (as with multi-output instructions), but the paper lacks details on how this is done exactly. Lastly, all combinations of foot prints are considered in pursuit of the one leading to the most effective implementation of the program DAG. To further prune the search space, this process only considers combinations where each selected foot print syntactically matches at least one semantic primitive in the program DAG, and only "trivial amounts" of the program DAG (for example constants) may be included in more than one foot print.

Using a prototype implementation, Hoover and Zadeck reported that almost 10^{70} "implied instruction matches" were found for one of the test cases, but it is unclear how many of them were actually useful. Moreover, in its current form the design appears to be unpractical for generating assembly code for all but very small programs.

4.5 Extending Tree Covering Techniques to DAGs

Another common approach to DAG covering is to reuse already-known, linear-time methods from tree covering. This can be achieved either by transforming the program DAGs into trees, or by generalizing the tree-based algorithms for pattern matching and pattern selection. We begin by discussing designs that apply the first technique.

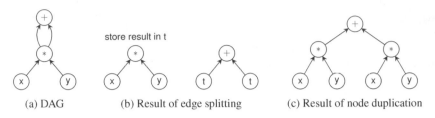

(a) DAG   (b) Result of edge splitting   (c) Result of node duplication

Fig. 4.2: Undagging a program DAG with a common subexpression

4.5.1 Undagging Program DAGs

The simplest approach for reusing tree covering techniques is to transform the program DAG into several program trees. We will refer to this idea as *undagging*.

As illustrated in Fig. 4.2, a program DAG can be undagged into program trees in two ways. The first approach is to split the edges involving *shared nodes*—these are nodes where reuse occurs due to the presence of common subexpressions—which results in a set of disconnected program trees that can then be covered individually. Not surprisingly, this approach is called *edge splitting*. An implicit connection between the program trees is maintained by forcing the values computed at the shared nodes to be stored and read from a specific location, typically in memory. An example of such an implementation is DAGON, a technology binder developed by Keutzer [203], which maps technology-independent descriptions onto circuits. The second approach is to duplicate the nodes involved in computing the shared value, which is known as *node duplication*. This results in a single but larger program tree compared to those produced with edge splitting.

Common for both schemes is that they compromise code quality: too aggressive edge splitting produces many small trees that cannot be covered using larger patterns, inhibiting use of more efficient instructions; and too aggressive node duplication incurs a larger computational workload where many operations are needlessly re-executed in the final assembly code. Moreover, the intermediate results of an edge-split program DAG must be forcibly stored in specific locations, which can be troublesome for heterogeneous memory-register architectures (this particular problem was studied by Araujo et al. [22]).

Balancing Splitting and Duplication

In 1994, Fauth et al. [125, 258] developed a technique that tries to mitigate the deficiencies of undagging by balancing the use of node duplication and edge splitting. Implemented in the *Common Bus Compiler (CBC)*, the instruction selector applies a heuristic algorithm that first favors node duplication, and resorts to edge splitting when the former is deemed too costly. The decision about whether to duplicate or to split is taken by comparing the cost of the two solutions and selecting the cheapest one. The cost is calculated as a weighted sum $w_1 n_{dup} + w_2 n_{split}$, where n_{dup} is the number of nodes in the program DAG (a rough estimate of code size), and n_{split} is the expected number of nodes executed along each execution path (a rough estimate of execution time). Once this is done, each resulting program tree is covered by an improved version of IBURG (see Section 3.6.2) with extended match condition support. However, the experimental data is too limited for us to judge how efficient this technique is compared to a design where the program DAGs have been transformed into program trees using just one method.

Register-Sensitive Instruction Selection

In 2001, Sarkar et al. [300] developed an instruction selection technique that attempts to reduce the *register pressure*—that is, the number of registers needed by the program—in order to facilitate register allocation.[2]

The design works as follows. The program DAG is first augmented with additional edges to signify scheduling dependencies between memory operations, and then it is split into a several program trees using a heuristic to decide which edges to break. The program trees are then covered individually using conventional methods based on tree covering, but instead of being the usual number of execution cycles, the cost of each instruction is set so as to reflect the amount of register pressure incurred by that instruction (unfortunately, the paper lacks details on how these costs are computed exactly). Once patterns have been selected, the nodes which are covered by the same pattern are merged into *super nodes*. The resulting graph is then checked for whether it contains any cycles, which may appear due to the extra data dependencies that were added at the earlier stage. If it does, it means that there exist cyclic scheduling dependencies between two or more memory operations, making it an illegal cover. The splits are then reverted and the process repeats until a legal cover is found.

Sarkar et al. implemented their register-sensitive design in JALAPEÑO, a register-based Java virtual machine developed by IBM. For a small set of problems the performance increased by about 10%, which Sarkar et al. claim to be due to fewer instructions needed for register spilling compared to the default instruction selector. Although innovative, it is doubtful that the technique can be extended much further.

4.5.2 Extending the Dynamic Programming Approach to DAGs

To avoid the application of ad hoc heuristics, several DAG-based instruction selectors perform pattern selection by applying an extension of the tree-based DP algorithm originally developed by Aho and Johnson [3] (see Section 1.3). According to the literature, Liem et al. [237, 276, 277] appear to have been the first to have done so.

---

[2] Another register-aware instruction selection technique was developed in 2014 by Xie et al. [346], with the aim of reducing the number of writes to a nonvolatile register file. However, the instructions are selected using a proprietary and greedy heuristic hat does not warrant in-depth discussion.

In a seminal paper from 1994, Liem et al. introduce a design which is part of CODESYN, a well-known code synthesis system, which in turn is part of a development environment for embedded systems called FLEXWARE. For pattern matching, Liem et al. applied the same technique as Weingart [332] (see Section 3.2) by combining all available pattern trees into a single tree of patterns. This pattern tree is traversed in tandem with the program DAG, and for each node an $O(nm)$ pattern matcher is used to find all matchsets. Pattern selection is then performed using an extended version of the DP algorithm, but the paper does not explain how this is done exactly. Moreover, the algorithm is only applied on the data flow of the program DAG—control flow is covered separately using a simple heuristic—and no guarantees are made that the pattern selection is optimal, as that is an NP-complete problem.

Potentially Optimal Pattern Selection

In a paper from 1999, Ertl [117] introduces a design which guarantees optimal pattern selection on program DAGs for certain instruction set grammars. The idea is to first make a bottom-up pass over the program DAG and compute the costs using the conventional DP algorithm as discussed in Chapter 3. Each node is thus labeled with the same costs, as if the program DAG had first been transformed into a tree through node duplication; but Ertl recognized that if several patterns reduce the same node to the same nonterminal, then the reduction to that nonterminal can be shared between several rules whose patterns contain the nonterminal. Hence the instructions for implementing shared nonterminals only need to be emitted once, decreasing code size and also improving performance, since the amount of redundant computation is reduced. With appropriate data structures, a linear-time implementation can be achieved.

An example illustrating such a situation is given in Fig. 4.3, where we see an addition that will have to be implemented twice, as its node is covered by two separate patterns each of which reduces the subtree to a different nonterminal. The

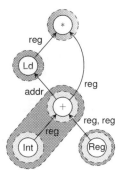

Fig. 4.3: A tree covering of a program DAG where the patterns have been selected optimally. The two shades indicate the relation between rules, and the text along the edges indicates the nonterminals to which each pattern is reduced. Note that the Reg node is covered by two patterns (as indicated by the double dash pattern) which both reduce to the same nonterminal and can thus be shared [117]

Reg node, on the other hand, is reduced twice to the same nonterminal (reg), and can thus be shared between the rules that use this nonterminal in the patterns.

As said earlier, however, this technique yields optimal pattern selection only for certain instruction set grammars. Ertl therefore devised a checker, called DBURG, that detects when the grammar does not belong into this category and thus cannot guarantee optimality. The basic idea is to check whether every locally optimal decision is also globally optimal by performing inductive proofs over the set of all possible program DAGs. To do this efficiently, Ertl implemented DBURG using the ideas behind BURG (hence the name).

Combining DP and Edge Splitting

Koes and Goldstein [212] extended Ertl's ideas by providing a heuristic that splits the program DAG at points where node duplication is estimated to have a detrimental effect on code quality. Like Ertl's algorithm, Koes and Goldstein's first selects patterns optimally by performing a tree-like, bottom-up DP pass which ignores the fact that the input is a DAG. Then, at points where multiple patterns overlap, two costs are calculated: an *overlap-cost* and a *cse-cost*. The overlap-cost is an estimate of the cost of letting the patterns overlap and thus incur duplication of operations in the final assembly code. The cse-cost is an estimate of the cost of splitting the edges at such points. If cse-cost is lower than overlap-cost, then the node where overlapping occurs is marked as *fixed*. Once all such nodes have been processed, a second bottom-up DP pass is performed on the program DAG, but this time no patterns are allowed to span across fixed nodes, which can only be matched at the root of a pattern. Lastly, a top-down pass emits the assembly code.

For evaluation purposes Koes and Goldstein compared their own implementation, called NOLTIS, against an implementation based on integer programming—we will discuss such techniques later in this chapter—and found that NOLTIS achieved optimal pattern selection in 99.7% of the test cases. More details are given in Koes's doctoral dissertation [211]. But like Ertl's design, Koes and Goldstein's is limited to pattern trees and thus cannot support more complex instructions such as multi-output instructions.

Supporting Multi-output Instructions

In most instruction selection techniques based on DAG covering, it is assumed that the outputs of a pattern DAG always occur at the root nodes. But in a design by Arnold and Corporaal [26, 27] (originally introduced in a technical report by Arnold [25]), the nodes representing output can be marked explicitly. The advantage of this is that it allows the pattern DAGs to be fully decomposed into trees such that each output value receives its own pattern tree, which Arnold and Corporaal call *partial patterns*. An example is given in Fig. 4.4.

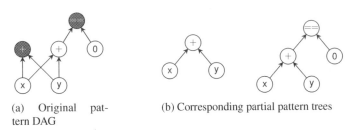

(a)   Original   pattern DAG

(b) Corresponding partial pattern trees

Fig. 4.4: Converting a pattern DAG, which represents an add instruction that also sets a status flag if the result is equal to 0, into partial pattern trees. The darkly shaded nodes indicate the output nodes

The partial patterns are then matched over the program DAG using an $O(nm)$ algorithm. After matching, another algorithm attempts to merge appropriate combinations of partial matches into matches of the original pattern DAG. This is done in a straightforward manner by maintaining, for each match, an array that maps the nodes in the pattern DAG to the covered nodes in the program DAG, and then checking whether two partial patterns belong to the same original pattern DAG and have compatible mappings. This means that no pair of pattern nodes belonging to different partial patterns but corresponding to the same node in the original pattern DAG may cover different nodes in the program DAG. For pattern selection Arnold and Corporaal applied a variant of the DP scheme but combined it with a greedy heuristic in order to enforce that each node is covered exactly once. Hence code quality is compromised.

4.6 Transforming Pattern Selection to an M(W)IS Problem

In the techniques discussed so far, the instruction selector operates directly on the program DAG when performing pattern selection. The same applies for most designs based on tree covering. But another approach is to indirectly solve the pattern selection problem by first transforming it into an instance of some other problem for which there already exist efficient solving methods. When that problem has been solved, the answer can be translated back into a solution for the original pattern selection problem.

One such problem is the *maximum independent set (MIS) problem*, where the task is to select the largest set of nodes from a graph such that no pairs of selected nodes have an edge between them. In the general case, finding such a solution is NP-complete [151], and the pattern selection problem is transformed into an MIS problem as follows. From the matchsets found by pattern matching, a corresponding *conflict graph*—or *interference graph*, as it is sometimes called—is formed. Each node in the conflict graph represents a match, and there exists an edge between two

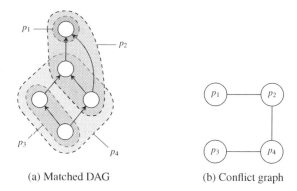

(a) Matched DAG   (b) Conflict graph

Fig. 4.5: Example of a pattern-matched program DAG and its corresponding conflict graph

nodes if and only if the corresponding matches overlap. An example of this is given in Fig. 4.5. By solving the MIS problem for the conflict graph, we obtain a selection of matches such that every node in the program DAG is covered by exactly one match.

But a solution to the MIS problem does not necessarily yield an optimal solution to the pattern selection problem, as the former does not incorporate costs. We address this limitation by transforming the MIS problem into a *maximum weighted independent set (MWIS) problem*, where the task is to find a solution to the MIS problem that maximizes $\sum_p weight(p)$, and assign as weights the costs of the patterns. We can get the solution with minimal total cost simply by negating the weights. Note that although the MWIS-based techniques discussed in this book have all been limited to program DAGs, the approach can just as well be applied in graph covering, which will be introduced in Chapter 5.

4.6.1 Applications

In 2007, Scharwaechter et al. [303] introduced what appears to be the first instruction selection technique to use the MWIS approach for selecting patterns. But despite this novelty, the most cited contribution of their design is its extensions to instruction set grammars to support multi-output instructions.

Instruction Set Grammars with Multiple Left-Hand Side Nonterminals

To begin with, Scharwaechter et al. distinguishes between rules having only one left-hand side nonterminal in their productions from rules containing multiple left-hand side nonterminals by referring to them as *rules* and *complex rules*, respectively. In addition, we will refer to the right-hand side symbols appearing in rules as *simple patterns*, and to the right-hand side symbols appearing in complex rules as *split patterns*.[3] A combination of split patterns is thus known as a *complex pattern*. The aforementioned terms are illustrated more clearly below:

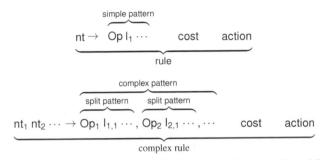

Pattern matching is a two-step process. First, the matchsets are found for the simple and split patterns, using conventional tree-based pattern matching techniques. Second, the matchsets for the complex patterns are found by combining the matches of split patterns into matches of complex patterns where appropriate. The pattern selector then checks whether it is worth applying a complex pattern for covering a certain set of nodes, or if they should be covered using the simple patterns instead. Since the intermediate results of nodes within complex patterns cannot be reused for other patterns, selecting a complex pattern can incur an additional overhead cost as nodes in the program DAG may need to be covered using multiple patterns. Consequently, a complex pattern will only be selected if the cost reduced by replacing a set of simple patterns with this pattern is greater than the cost incurred by code duplication. After these decisions have been taken, the next step is to perform pattern selection. For this, Scharwaechter et al. solve the corresponding MWIS problem in order to limit solutions to those of exact covering only. The weights are calculated as the negated sum of the split pattern costs, but the paper is ambiguous on how these costs are calculated. Since the MWIS problem is known to be NP-complete, Scharwaechter et al. employed a greedy heuristic called GWMIN2 by Sakai et al. [299]. Lastly, split patterns which have not been merged into complex patterns are replaced by corresponding simple patterns before assembly code emission.

Scharwaechter et al. implemented a prototype called CBURG as an extension of OLIVE (see Section 3.6.2), and then ran some experiments by targeting a MIPS-like architecture. In these experiments CBURG generated assembly code which improved performance by almost 25%, and reduced code size by nearly 22%, compared to assembly code which was only allowed to make use of single-output instructions. Measurements of CBURG also indicate that this technique exhibits near-linear time complexity. Ahn et al. [2] later broadened this work by including scheduling dependency conflicts between complex patterns, and incorporating a feedback loop with the register allocator to facilitate register allocation.

---

[3] In their paper, Scharwaechter et al. call these *simple rules* and *split rules*, respectively, but to conform with the terminology established on p. 37, I chose to refer to them as patterns.

A shortcoming of both designs by Scharwaechter et al. and Ahn et al. is that complex rules can only consist of disconnected pattern trees (hence there can be no sharing of nodes between the split patterns). Youn et al. [349] address this problem in a 2011 paper—which is a revised and extended version of the original paper by Scharwaechter et al.—by introducing index subscripts for the operand specification of the complex rules; but the subscripts are restricted to the input nodes of the pattern, still hindering support for completely arbitrary pattern DAGs.

Targeting Machines with Echo Instructions

In 2004, Brisk et al. [58] introduced a technique to perform instruction selection for target machines with special *echo instructions*, which are small markers that refer back to an earlier portion in the assembly code for re-execution. This allows the assembly code to be compressed by basically using the same idea that is applied in the LZ77 algorithm [356].[4] Since echo instructions do not incur a branch or a procedure call, the assembly code can be reduced in size without sacrificing performance. Consequently, unlike for traditional target machines, the pattern set is not fixed in this case but must be determined as a precursor to pattern matching (this is closely related to the ISE problem, which we will discuss in Chapter 6).

The intuition behind this design is to use echo instructions where code duplication is most prominent. To find these cases in a given program, Brisk et al. first enumerate all subgraphs from the program DAGs, and then match each subgraph over the program DAGs. Pattern matching is done using VF2, which is a generic subgraph isomorphism algorithm that we will describe in Chapter 5. Summing the sizes of the resulting matchsets gives a measure of code duplication for each subgraph, but this value will be an overestimation as the matchsets may contain overlapping matches. Brisk et al. addressed this by first solving the MIS problem on the conflict graph for each matchset, and then adding up the sizes of *these* sets. After selecting the most beneficial subgraph, the covered nodes in the program DAGs are collapsed into single nodes to reflect the use of echo instructions. This process of matching and collapsing is then repeated until no new subgraph better than some user-defined value criterion can be found. Brisk et al. performed experiments on a prototype using a selected set of benchmark applications, which showed code size reductions of 25% to 36% on average.

---

[4] The algorithm performs string compression by replacing recurring substrings that appear earlier in the string with pointers, allowing the original string to be reconstructed by "copy-pasting."

4.7 Transforming Pattern Selection to a Unate/Binate Covering Problem

Another approach to solving pattern selection is to translate it to a corresponding *unate* or *binate covering* problem. The concepts behind the two are identical with the exception of one detail, and both unate and binate covering can be used directly for covering graphs even though the designs discussed in this book have only been applied on program DAGs.

Although binate covering-based techniques actually appeared first, we will begin with explaining unate covering, as binate covering is an extension of unate covering.

Unate Covering

The idea of unate covering is to create a Boolean matrix $\mathbf{M}$, where each row represents a node in the program DAG and each column represents a match covering one or more nodes in the program DAG. If we denote m_{ij} as row i and column j in $\mathbf{M}$, then $m_{ij} = 1$ indicates that node i is covered by pattern j. Hence the pattern selection problem is equivalent to finding a valid configuration of $\mathbf{M}$ such that the sum of every row is at least 1. An example is given in Fig. 4.6. Unate covering is an NP-complete problem, but as with the MIS and MWIS problems there exist several efficient techniques for solving it heuristically (see for example [87, 159] for an overview).

Unate covering alone, however, does not incorporate all necessary constraints of pattern selection since some patterns require—and prevent—the selection of other patterns in order to yield correct assembly code. For example, assume that pattern p_3 in Fig. 4.6a requires that pattern p_6 be selected to cover n_4 instead of pattern p_5. Using instruction set grammars this can be enforced with the appropriate use of

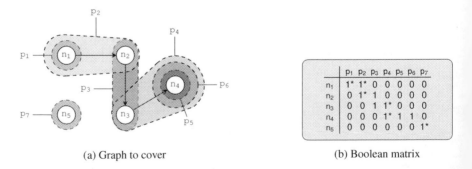

(a) Graph to cover   (b) Boolean matrix

Fig. 4.6: Example of unate covering. Unmarked 1s in the matrix represent potential but not selected covers, while the 1s marked with a star (1*) indicate a selection that is optimal (assuming all patterns have the same cost)

nonterminals, but for unate covering we have no means of expressing this constraint. We therefore turn to binate covering, where this is possible.

Binate Covering

We first rewrite the Boolean matrix from the unate covering problem into Boolean formulas consisting of conjunctions of non-negated disjunctions. The Boolean matrix in Fig. 4.6b can thus be rewritten as

$$ f = (p_1 \lor p_2) \land (p_2 \lor p_3) \land (p_3 \lor p_4) \land (p_4 \lor p_5 \lor p_6) \land p_7. $$

Now, the difference between unate covering and binate covering is that all variables must be non-negated in the former, but may be negated in the latter. Hence, the aforementioned constraint regarding the compulsory selection of p_6 if p_4 is selected can now be expressed as

$$ \neg p_4 \lor p_6, $$

which is called an *implication clause* as it is logically equivalent to $p_4 \to p_6$. This is then simply appended to the Boolean formula f using the $\land$ operator.

Applications

According to Liao et al. [235, 236] and Cong et al. [82], the pioneering use of binate covering to solve DAG covering was done by Rudell [296] in 1989 as a part of a *very large scale integration (VLSI)* synthesis design. Liao et al. [235, 236] later adapted it to instruction selection in a method that optimizes code size for one-register target machines. To prune the search space, Liao et al. perform pattern selection in two iterations. In the first iteration, patterns are selected such that the program DAG is covered but the costs of necessary data transfers are ignored. After this step the nodes covered by the same pattern are collapsed into single nodes, and a second binate covering problem is constructed to minimize the costs of data transfers. Although these two problems can be solved simultaneously, Liao et al. chose not to do so as the number of necessary implication clauses would become very large. Recently, Cong et al. [82] also applied binate covering as part of generating application-specific instructions for configurable processor architectures.

Unate covering was applied by Clark et al. [77] in generating assembly code for acyclic computation accelerators, which can be partially customized in order to increase performance of the currently executed program. Described in a paper from 2006, the target machines are presumably homogeneous enough that implication clauses are unnecessary. The work by Clark et al. was later expanded by Hormati et al. [183] to reduce the number of interconnects as well as data-centered latencies in accelerator designs. Martin et al. [248, 249] also applied unate covering to solve a similar problem concerning reconfigurable processor extensions, but combined the instruction selection problem with instruction scheduling and solved both in tandem using a method called constraint programming—we will discuss this approach later in this chapter—which they also applied for solving the pattern matching problem. Unlike in the cases of Clark et al. and Hormati et al., who solved their unate covering problems using heuristics, the assembly code generated by Martin et al. is potentially optimal.

4.8 Modeling Instruction Selection with IP

As explained in Chapter 1, performing instruction selection, instruction scheduling, or register allocation in isolation will typically always yield suboptimal assembly code. But since each subproblem is already NP-complete on its own, attaining *integrated code generation*—where all these problems are solved simultaneously—is an even more difficult problem.

These challenges notwithstanding, Wilson et al. [340] introduced in 1994 what appears to be the first design that could be said to yield truly optimal assembly code. Wilson et al. accomplished this by using *integer programming (IP)*, which is a method for solving combinatorial optimization problems (sometimes IP is also called *integer linear programming (ILP)*). In IP a problem is expressed using sets of integer variables and linear equations (see for example [341] for an overview), and a solution to an IP model is an assignment to all variables such that all equations are fulfilled. In general, solving an IP model is NP-complete, but extensive research in this field has made many problem instances tractable.

In their seminal paper, Wilson et al. describe that the pattern selection problem can be expressed as the following linear inequality:

$$\sum_{p\in P_n} x_p \leq 1, \ \forall n \in N.$$

This reads: for every node n in the program DAG (N,E), at most one pattern p from the matchset involving n (represented by P_n) may be selected. The decision is represented by x_p, which is a Boolean 0/1 variable.[5] Similar linear equations can be formulated for modeling instruction scheduling and register allocation—which Wilson et al. also included in their model—but these are out of scope for this book. In fact, any constraint that can be formulated in this way can be added to an existing IP model, making this approach a suitable code generation method for targeting irregular architectures. Furthermore, this is the first design we have seen that could potentially support interdependent instructions (although this was not the main focus of Wilson et al.).

Solving this monolithic IP model, however, typically requires considerably more time compared to the previously discussed techniques of instruction selection. But the trade-off for longer compilation times is higher code quality; Wilson et al. reported

---

[5] The more common constraint is that *exactly one* pattern must be selected, but in the design by Wilson et al., nodes are allowed to become *inactive* and thus need not be covered.

that experiments showed that the generated assembly code was of comparable code quality to that of manually optimized assembly code. In theory, optimal assembly code can be generated, although this is in practice only feasible for small enough programs. Another much-valued feature is the ability to extend the model with additional constraints in order to support complicated target machines, which cannot be properly handled by the conventional designs as that typically violates assumptions made by the underlying heuristics.

4.8.1 Approaching Linear Solving Time with Horn Clauses

Although IP models are NP-complete to solve in general, it was discovered that for a certain class of problem instances—namely those based on *Horn clauses*—an optimal solution can be found in linear time [181]. A Horn clause is a disjunctive Boolean formula which contains at most one non-negated term. This can also be phrased as a logical statement that has at most one conclusion. For example, the statement

$$\text{if } p_1 \text{ and } p_2 \text{ then } p_3$$

can be expressed as $\neg p_1 \vee \neg p_2 \vee p_3$, which is a Horn clause, as only p_3 is not negated. This can then easily be rewritten into the linear inequality

$$(1 - x_1) + (1 - x_2) + x_3 \geq 1,$$

where x_i is a Boolean variable corresponding to literal p_i. Moreover, statements that do not yield Horn clauses in their current form can often be rewritten so that they do. For example,

$$\text{if } a \text{ then } b \text{ and } c$$

can be expressed as $\neg a \vee b \vee c$ and is thus not a Horn clause because it has more than one non-negated term. But by rewriting it into

$$\text{if } a \text{ then } b$$
$$\text{if } a \text{ then } c$$

the statement can now be expressed as $\neg a \vee b$ and $\neg a \vee c$, which are two valid Horn clauses.

Gebotys [152] exploited this property in 1997 by developing an IP model for TMS320C2x—a typical DSP at the time—where many of the target architecture, instruction selection, and register allocation constraints, and a part of the instruction scheduling constraints, are expressed as Horn clauses. Using only Horn clauses may require a larger number of constraints than are otherwise needed, but Gebotys claims that the number is still manageable. When compared against a then-contemporary industrial DSP compiler, Gebotys demonstrated that an implementation based on IP yielded a performance improvement mean of 44% for a select set of functions, while attaining reasonable compilation times. However, the solving time increased

by orders of magnitude when Gebotys augmented the IP model with the complete
set of constraints for instruction scheduling, which cannot be expressed entirely as
Horn clauses.

4.8.2 IP-Based Designs with Multi-output Instruction Support

Leupers and Marwedel [226, 233] expanded the work of Wilson et al.—whose design
is restricted to pattern trees—by developing an IP-based instruction selector which
also supports multi-output instructions. In a paper from 1996, Leupers and Marwedel
describe a scheme where the pattern DAGs of multi-output instructions—Leupers
and Marwedel refer to these as *complex patterns*—are first decomposed into multiple
pattern trees according to their *register transfers (RTs)*. RTs are akin to Fraser's
RTLs [136] (see Section 2.3.1), and essentially mean that each observable effect
gets its own pattern tree. Each individual RT may in turn correspond to one or more
instructions, but unlike in Fraser's design this is not strictly required.

Assuming the program DAG has already been undagged, each program tree is first
optimally covered using IBURG. The RTs are expressed as rules in an instruction set
grammar that has been automatically generated from a machine description written
in MIMOLA (we will come back to this in Section 4.10.3). Once RTs have been
selected, the program tree is reduced to a tree of *super nodes*, where each super
node represents a set of nodes covered by some RT that have been collapsed into a
single node. Since multi-output and disjoint-output instructions implement more than
one RT, the goal is now to cover the super node graph using the patterns which are
formed when the instructions are modeled as RTs. Leupers and Marwedel addressed
this problem by applying a modified version of the IP model by Wilson et al.

But because the step of selecting RTs to cover the program tree is separate from
the step which implements them with instructions, the generated assembly code is
not necessarily optimal for the whole program tree. To achieve this property, the
covering of RTs and selection of instructions must be done in tandem.

4.8.3 IP-Based Designs with Disjoint-output Instruction Support

Leupers [228] later made a more direct extension of the IP model by Wilson et al.
in order to support SIMD instructions, which belong to the class of disjoint-output
instructions. Described in a paper from 2000, Leupers's design assumes every SIMD
instruction performs two operations, each of which takes a disjoint set of input
operands. This is collectively called a *SIMD pair*, and Leupers then extended the
IP model with linear equations for combining SIMD pairs into SIMD instructions
and defined the objective function so as to maximize the use of SIMD instructions.

In the paper, Leupers reports experiments where the use of SIMD instructions
reduced code size by up to 75% for the selected test cases and target machines. But

since this technique assumes that each individual operation of the SIMD instructions is expressed as a single node in the program DAG, it is unclear whether the method can be extended to more complex SIMD instructions, and whether it scales to larger programs. Tanaka et al. [317] later expanded Leupers's work for selecting SIMD instructions while also taking the cost of data transfers into account by introducing auxiliary transfer nodes and transfer patterns into the program DAG.

4.8.4 Modeling the Pattern Matching Problem with IP

In 2006, Bednarski and Kessler [43] developed an integrated code generation design where both pattern matching and pattern selection are solved using integer programming. The scheme—which later was applied by Eriksson et al. [115], and is also described in an article by Eriksson and Kessler [116]—is an extension of their earlier work where instruction selection had previously more or less been ignored (see [199, 200]).

In broad outline, the IP model assumes that a sufficient number of matches has been generated for a given program DAG G. This is done using a pattern matching heuristic that computes an upper bound. For each match m, the IP model contains integer variables that:

- map a pattern node in m to a node in G;
- map a pattern edge in m to an edge in G; and
- decide whether m is used in the solution. Remember that we may have an excess of matches, so they cannot all be selected.

Hence, in addition to the typical linear equations we have seen previously for enforcing coverage, this IP model also includes equations to ensure that the selected matches are valid matches.

Implemented in a framework called OPTIMIST, Bednarski and Kessler compared their IP model against another integrated code generation design based on dynamic programming, which was developed by the same authors (see [199]) and has nothing to do with the conventional DP algorithm by Aho et al. [7]). Bednarski and Kessler found that OPTIMIST substantially reduced compilation times while retaining code quality, but for several test cases—the largest program DAG containing only 33 nodes—OPTIMIST failed to generate any assembly code whatsoever within the set time limit. One reasonable cause could be that the IP model also attempts to solve pattern matching—a problem which we have seen can be solved externally—and thus further exacerbates an already computationally difficult problem.

4.9 Modeling Instruction Selection with CP

Although integer programming allows auxiliary constraints to be included into the
IP model, they may be cumbersome to express as linear equations. This issue can
be alleviated by using *constraint programming (CP)*, which is another method for
solving combinatorial optimization problems (see for example [295] for an overview)
but has more flexible modeling capabilities compared to IP. In brief terms, a CP model
consists of a set of *domain variables*, each of which has an initial set of values that it
can assume, and a set of constraints that essentially specify the valid combinations
of values for a subset of the domain variables. A solution to the CP model is thus
an assignment for all domain variables—meaning that each domain variable takes
exactly one value—such that all constraints are fulfilled.

In 1990, Bashford and Leupers [40] pioneered the use of constraint programming in code generation by developing a CP model for integrated code generation
that targets DSPs with highly irregular architectures (the work is also discussed
in [228, 229]). Like Leupers and Marwedel's IP-based design, Bashford and Leupers's first breaks down the instruction set of the target machine into a set of RTs
which are used to cover individual nodes in the program DAG. As each RT concerns
specific registers on the target machine, the covering problem essentially also incorporates register allocation. The goal is then to minimize the cost of covering by
combining multiple RTs that can be executed in parallel as part of some instruction.

For each node in the program DAG a *factorized register transfer (FRT)* is introduced, which basically embodies all RTs that match a particular node and is formally
defined as the following tuple:

$$\langle Op, D, [U_1, \ldots, U_n], F, C, T, CS \rangle.$$

Op is the operation of the node. D and $U_1, \ldots, U_n$ are domain variables representing
the *storage locations* of the result and the respective inputs to the operation. These
are typically the registers that can be used for the operation, but also include *virtual
storage locations* which convey that the value is produced as an intermediate result in
a chain of operations (for example, the multiplication term in a multiply-accumulate
instruction is such a result). Then, for every pair of operations that are adjacent in the
program DAG, a set of constraints is added to ensure that there exists a valid data
transfer between the storage locations of D and U_i if these are assigned to different
registers, or that both are identical if one is a virtual storage location. F, C, and T are
all domain variables which collectively represent the *extended resource information
(ERI)* that specifies at which functional unit the operation will be executed (F); at
what cost (C), which is the number of execution cycles; and by which instruction
type (T). A combination of a functional unit and an instruction type is later mapped
to a particular instruction. Multiple RTs can be combined into the same instruction
when the destination of the result is a virtual storage location by setting $C = 0$
and letting the last node in the operation chain account for the required number
of execution cycles. The last entity, *CS*, is the set of constraints for defining the
range of values for the domain variables and the dependencies between D and U_i, as

well as other auxiliary constraints that may be required for the target machine. For example, if the set of RTs matching a node consists of $\{r_c = r_a + r_b, r_a = r_c + r_b\}$, then the corresponding FRT becomes

$$\langle +, D, [U_1, U_2], F, C, T, \{D \in \{r_c, r_a\}, U_1 \in \{r_a, r_c\}, U_2 = r_b, D = r_c \Rightarrow U_1 = r_a\} \rangle.$$

For brevity I have omitted several details such as the constraints concerning the ERI.

This CP model is then solved to optimality using a CP solver. But since optimal covering using FRTs is NP-complete, Bashford and Leupers applied heuristics to curb the complexity by splitting the program DAG into smaller pieces along edges where intermediate results are shared, and then performing instruction selection on each program tree in isolation.

Although the constraints in Bashford and Leupers's CP model appear to be limited to involving only a single FRT at a time—thus hindering support for interdependent instructions—constraint programming in general seems like a promising tool for performing instruction selection. As with integer programming, constraint programming facilitates integrated and potentially optimal code generation. In addition, it allows additional restrictions of the target machine to be included in the CP model, but without the need of expressing these constraints as linear equations. At the time of writing, however, the existing techniques for solving IP models are more mature than those for solving CP models, which potentially makes integer programming a more powerful method than constraint programming for solving instruction selection. Having said that, it is still unclear which technique of combinatorial optimization—which also includes SAT and other methods—is best suited for instruction selection (and code generation in general).

4.9.1 Taking Advantage of Global Constraints

So far we have discussed several techniques that apply constraint programming for solving the problems of pattern matching and pattern selection—namely those by Bashford and Leupers and Martin et al. Recently, Beg [44] introduced another CP model for instruction selection as well as new methods for improving solving. For example, in order to reduce the search space, Beg applied conventional DP-based techniques to compute an upper bound on the cost. However, the CP model mainly deals with the problem of pattern matching rather than pattern selection. Moreover, Beg noticed only a negligible improvement (less than 1%) in code quality compared to LLVM, mainly because the target machines (MIPS and ARM) were simple enough that greedy heuristics generate near-optimal assembly code. In addition, the program DAGs of the benchmark programs were fairly tree-shaped [325], for which optimal code can be generated in linear time. In any case, none of these designs take advantage of a key feature of constraint programming, which is the use of *global constraints*. A global constraint is a restriction that is enforced simultaneously over multiple domain variables and results in more search space pruning than if it had

been expressed using multiple constraints over only a subset of the variables at a
time (see for example [45] for an overview).

Hence, when Floch et al. [131] in 2010 adapted the CP model by Martin et al.
to support processors with reconfigurable cell fabric, they replaced the method of
pattern selection with constraints that are radically different from those incurred by
unate covering. In addition, unlike in the case of Bashford and Leupers, the design by
Floch et al. applies the more direct form of pattern matching instead of first breaking
down the patterns into RTs and then selecting instructions that combine as many RTs
as possible.

As described in their 2010 paper, Floch et al. use the *global cardinality constraint*[6]
to enforce the requirement that every node in the program DAG must be covered by
exactly one pattern. This constraint, which we will refer to as $\text{COUNT}(i, var, val)$, enforces that exactly val number of domain variables from the set var assume the value i,
where val can either be a fixed value or represent another domain variable. Let us
assume that every node in the program DAG has an associated matchset containing all
the patterns that may cover that node, and that each match m appearing in that matchset has been assigned a unique integer value i_m (if m appears in multiple matchsets, it
is still given the same value). We introduce a domain variable $match_n$ for each node n
in the program DAG to represent the match selected to cover n. For each match m,
we also introduce a domain variable $nodecount_m \in \{0, size(m)\}$, where $size(m)$ is
the number of pattern nodes in m. We also define $mset_m = \bigcup_{n \in nodes(m)} match_n$ as the
set of $match_n$ variables in which match m may appear, where $nodes(m)$ is the set of
nodes matched by m. With this we can express the constraint that every node in the
program DAG must be covered exactly once as

$$\text{COUNT}(i_m, mset_m, nodecount_m), \quad \forall m \in M,$$

where M is the total set of matches. This may appear convoluted at first glance, but it
is actually rather simple. $mset_m$ essentially provides the nodes in the program DAG
that may be covered by match m, $nodecount_m$ provides the number of nodes covered
by m, and COUNT ensures that the relation between the two holds. But since the
domain of $nodecount_m$ is initially restricted to only two values—zero and the size
of the pattern—it must be so that either *no* nodes are covered by m, or *all* nodes
are covered by m. To identify which matches have been selected, we simply check
whether $nodecount_m \neq 0$ for every pattern m. Since a domain variable cannot be
assigned more than one value, each node can only be covered by exactly one match
(remember that the $match_n$ variable for node n can appear in multiple $mset_m$ sets).
Hence this constraint is more restrictive than that of unate covering, which results in
more propagation and thus reduces the search space.

This CP model was also further extended by Arslan and Kuchcinski [29, 30]
to accommodate VLIW architectures and disjoint-output instructions. First, every
disjoint-output instructions is split into multiple *subinstructions*, each modeled by
a disjoint pattern. A generic subgraph isomorphism algorithm is used to find all

---

[6] It is also possible to enforce pattern selection through a global set covering developed by
Mouthuy et al. [256], but I have not seen any implementation do so.

matchsets, and pattern selection is then modeled as an instance of the CP model with the additional constraints to schedule the subinstructions such that they can be replaced by the original disjoint-output instruction. Arslan and Kuchcinski's design therefore differs from the previous techniques that we have seen before, where matches of partial patterns are recombined into matches of complex patterns prior to pattern selection (see for example Scharwaechter et al. [303], Ahn et al. [2], Arnold and Corporaal [25, 26, 27]), as it allows these two problems to be solved in tandem. The design is also capable of accepting multiple, disconnected program DAGs as a single input.

However, a limitation inherent to the CP models applied by Martin et al., Floch et al., and Arslan and Kuchcinski is that they do not model the necessary data transfers between different register classes. This in turn means that the cost model is only accurate for target machines equipped with a homogeneous register architecture, which could compromise code quality for more complicated target machines.

4.10 Other DAG-Based Approaches

4.10.1 More Genetic Algorithms

Seemingly independently from the earlier work by Shu et al. [308] (discussed in Chapter 3), Lorenz et al. [241, 242] introduced in 2001 another technique where genetic algorithms are applied to code generation. But unlike the design by Shu et al., the one by Lorenz et al. takes program DAGs instead of trees as input and also incorporates instruction scheduling and register allocation. Lorenz et al. recognized that contemporary compilers struggled with generating efficient assembly code for DSPs equipped with very few registers and typically always spill the results of common subexpressions to memory and reload them when needed. Compared to optimal assembly code, this may incur more memory accesses than needed.

The design by Lorenz et al. is basically an iterative process. First, the operations within a block are scheduled using *list scheduling*, which is a traditional method of scheduling (see for example [290]). For every scheduled operation, a gene is formulated to encode all the possible decisions to take in order to solve the problems of instruction selection and register allocation. These decisions are then taken over multiple steps using standard GA operations, where the values are selected probabilistically. In each step the gene is mutated and crossed over in order to produce new, hopefully better genes, and a fitness function is applied to evaluate each gene in terms of expected execution time. After a certain number of generations, the process stops and the best gene is selected. Certain steps are also followed by a routine based on constraint programming that prunes the search space for the subsequent decisions by removing values which will never appear in any valid gene. Although every gene represents a single node in the program DAG, complex patterns can still be supported through an additional variable for selecting the instruction type for the node. If nodes with the same instruction type have been scheduled to be executed on the same cycle, then they can be implemented using the same instruction during assembly code emission.

Lorenz et al. originally developed this technique in order to reduce power usage of assembly code generated for constrained DSPs, and later extended the design to also incorporate *code compaction* and *address generation*. Experiments indicate that the technique for a selected set of test cases resulted in energy savings of 18 to 36% compared to a traditional tree covering-based compiler, and reduced execution time by up to 51%. According to Lorenz et al., the major contribution to this reduction is due to improved usage of registers for common subexpression values, which in turn leads to less use of power-hungry and long-executing memory operations. But due to the probabilistic nature of GA, optimality cannot be guaranteed, making it unclear how this technique would fare against other DAG covering-based designs which allow a more exhaustive exploration of the search space.

4.10.2 Extending Trellis Diagrams to DAGs

In 1998, Hanono and Devadas [167, 168] proposed a technique that is similar to Wess's use of trellis diagrams, which we discussed in Chapter 3. Implemented in a system called AVIV, Hanono and Devadas's instruction selector takes a program DAG as input and duplicates each operation node according to the number of functional units in the target machine on which that operation can run. Special *split* and *transfer nodes* are inserted before and after each duplicated operation node to allows the data flow to diverge and then reconverge before passing to the next operation node in the program DAG. The use of transfer nodes also allow the cost of transferring data from one functional unit to another to be taken into account. Similarly to the trellis diagram, instruction selection is thus transformed to finding a path from the leaf nodes in the program DAG to its root node. But differently from the optimal, DP-oriented design of Wess, Hanono and Devadas applied a greedy heuristic that starts from the root node and makes it way towards the leaves.

Unfortunately, as in Wess's design, this technique assumes a 1-to-1 mapping between the nodes in the program DAG and the instructions in order to generate efficient assembly code. In fact, the main purpose behind AVIV was to generate efficient assembly code for VLIW architectures, where the focus is on executing as many instructions as possible in parallel.

4.10.3 Hardware Modeling Techniques

In 1984, Marwedel [251] developed a retargetable system called *MIMOLA Software System (MSS)* for *microcode generation,*[7] where a machine description written in *Machine Independent Microprogramming Language (MIMOLA)* [354] is used for modeling the entire data path of the processor, instead of just the instruction set as we have commonly seen. This is commonly used for DSPs where the processor is small but highly irregular. Although MSS consists of several tools, we will concentrate on the MSSQ compiler, as its purpose is most aligned with instruction selection. MSSQ was developed by Leupers and Marwedel [230] as a faster version of MSSC [269], which in turn is an extension of the tree-based MSSV [252].

The MIMOLA specification contains the processor registers as well as all the operations that can be performed on these registers within a single cycle. From this specification, a hardware DAG called the *connection-operation (CO) graph* is automatically derived. An example is given in Fig. 4.7. A pattern matcher then attempts to find subgraphs within the CO graph to cover the program trees. Because the CO graph contains explicit nodes for every register, a match found on this graph— called a *version* — is also an assignment of program variables (and temporaries) to registers. If a match cannot be found (due to a lack of registers), the program tree will be rewritten by splitting assignments and inserting additional temporaries. The

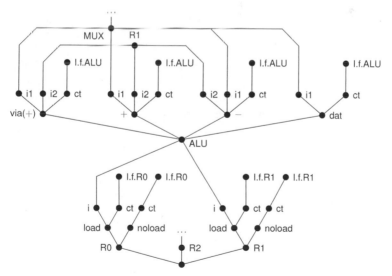

Fig. 4.7: The CO graph of a simple processor containing an arithmetic logic unit, two data registers, a program counter, and a control store [269]

---

[7] *Microcode* is essentially the hardware language that processors use internally for executing instructions. For example, microcode controls how the registers and program counter should be updated for a given instruction.

process then backtracks and repeats in a recursive fashion until the entire program tree is covered. A subsequent process then selects a specific version from each matchset and tries to schedule them so that they can be combined into *bundles* for parallel execution.

Although microcode generation is at a lower hardware level than assembly code generation—which is usually what we refer to with instruction selection—we see several similarities between the problems that must be solved in each, and that is why it is included in this book (further examples include [36, 221, 246]). In Chapter 5 we will see another design that also models the entire processor but applies a more powerful technique.

4.11 Summary

In this chapter we have investigated several methods that rely on the principle of DAG covering, which is a more general form of tree covering. Operating on DAGs instead of trees has several advantages. Most importantly, common subexpressions can be directly modeled, and a larger set of instructions—including multi-output and disjoint-output instructions—can be supported and exploited during instruction selection, leading to improved performance and reduced code size. Consequently, techniques based on DAG covering are today one of the most widely applied methods for instruction selection in modern compilers.

The ultimate cost of transitioning from trees to DAGs, however, is that optimal pattern selection can no longer be achieved in linear time as it is NP-complete. At the same time, DAGs are not expressive enough to allow the proper modeling of all aspects featured in the programs and instructions. For example, statements such as *for* loops incur loops in the graph representing the program, restricting DAG covering to the scope of blocks and excluding the modeling of inter-block instructions. Another disadvantage is that optimization opportunities for storing program variables and temporaries in different forms and at different locations across the function are forfeited.

In the next chapter we will discuss the last and most general principle of instruction selection, which addresses some of the aforementioned deficiencies of DAG covering.

Chapter 5
Graph Covering

Although DAG covering is more general than tree covering—and thus offers a more powerful approach to instruction selection—it is still not enough for handling all aspects featured in the programs and instructions. For example, control flow incurred by loop statements cannot be modeled in a program DAG as it requires the use of cycles, which violates the definition of DAGs. By resorting to *program graphs* we attain *graph covering*, which is the most general form of covering. Unfortunately it also constitutes the shortest chapter among the principles discussed in this book.

5.1 The Principle

In DAG covering-based instruction selection, programs can only be modeled one block at a time as cycles are forbidden to appear in the program DAGs. Lifting this restriction makes it possible to incorporate both data and control-flow information into the program graphs, which in turn enables entire functions to be modeled as a single graph. Selecting instructions for such graphs is known as *global instruction selection* and has several advantages over local instruction selector. First, with an entire function as input, a global instruction selector can account for the effects of local pattern selection across the block boundaries and is thereby better informed when making its decisions. In addition, it can move operations from one block to another if that enables better use of the instruction set (this is known as *global code motion*). Second, to support inter-block instructions—which require modeling of both data and control-flow information—it is imperative that the patterns be expressible using graphs that may contain cycles. This makes graph covering one of the key approaches for making use of fewer but more efficient instructions, which is becoming more and more crucial for modern target machines—especially embedded systems—where both power consumption and heat emission are becoming increasingly important factors.

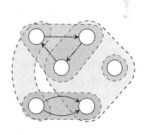

© Springer International Publishing Switzerland 2016
G. Hjort Blindell, *Instruction Selection*,
DOI 10.1007/978-3-319-34019-7_5

	Pattern matching	Optimal pattern selection
Trees	Linear	Linear
DAGs	NP-complete	NP-complete
Graphs	NP-complete	NP-complete

Fig. 5.1: Time complexities for solving the pattern matching and optimal pattern selection problems using various program representations

However, when transitioning from pattern DAGs to *pattern graphs*, we can no longer apply pattern matching techniques designed for trees and DAGs but must resort to methods from the field of subgraph isomorphism in solving this problem (see Fig. 5.1 for a time complexity comparison). The pattern selection problem, on the other hand, can still be solved using many of the techniques which were discussed in Chapter 4. Therefore, in this chapter we will only examine techniques that were originally designated for graph covering.

5.2 Pattern Matching Is a Subgraph Isomorphism Problem

The *subgraph isomorphism problem* is to detect whether an arbitrary graph G_a can be turned, twisted, or mirrored such that it forms a subgraph of another graph G_b. In such cases one says that G_a is an *isomorphic subgraph* of G_b, and deciding this is known to be NP-complete [84]. It should be clear that this is a generalization of the pattern matching problem, and with appropriate constraints a solution to the corresponding subgraph isomorphism problem can be directly translated into a solution for the original pattern matching problem.[1]

As subgraph isomorphism is found in many other fields, a vast amount of research has been devoted to this problem (see for example [86, 119, 120, 143, 166, 178, 217, 311, 324]). In this section we will mainly look at Ullmann's algorithm and another commonly used algorithm by Cordella et al. As a side note, we will also discuss an algorithm that solves the graph isomorphism problem in polynomial time for a certain class of graphs.

It should be noted that although we are now using the most generic graph form for representing the programs and patterns, these methods of pattern matching are still only capable of finding the matchsets where the patterns have matching *structure*, and not matching *semantics*. For example, the expressions $a * (b + c)$ and $a * b + a * c$ are semantically equivalent but will yield differently structured graphs. Hence the patterns selected to cover one program graph may differ from those covering the other—and consequently may yield different code quality—even though both versions of the assembly code will produce the same value in the end. In

---

[1] Most patterns derived from instructions are restrictive in how they can be twisted and turned without changing the semantics. For example, the ingoing edges to a + node can be swapped due to the commutative nature of addition, but the same does not apply to subtraction or division.

an attempt to mitigate this issue Arora et al. [28] introduced a method where the program graphs are first normalized before pattern matching, but the design is limited to arithmetic program DAGs and still does not guarantee that all matches will be found.

5.2.1 Ullmann's Algorithm

One of the first and most well-known methods for deciding subgraph isomorphism is an algorithm developed by Ullmann [324]. In a seminal paper from 1976, Ullmann expresses the problem of determining whether a graph $G_a = (N_a, E_a)$ is subgraph isomorphic to another graph $G_b = (N_b, E_b)$ as a problem of finding a Boolean $|N_a| \times |N_b|$ matrix $\mathbf{M}$ such that the following conditions holds:

$$\mathbf{C} = \mathbf{M} \cdot (\mathbf{M} \cdot \mathbf{B})^T,$$
$$a_{ij} = 1 \Rightarrow c_{ij} = 1, \ \forall 1 \leq i \leq |N_a|, 1 \leq j \leq |N_b|.$$

$\mathbf{A}$ and $\mathbf{B}$ are the respective *adjacency matrices* of G_a and G_b, where a_{ij} is an element of $\mathbf{A}$. Similarly, c_{ij} is an element of $\mathbf{C}$. When these conditions hold, every row in $\mathbf{M}$ will contain exactly one 1, and every column in $\mathbf{M}$ will contain at most one 1.

A simple method for finding $\mathbf{M}$ is to first set every element m_{ij} to 1, and then iteratively reset them to 0 until a solution is found. As expected, this brute-force approach suffers from ensuing combinatorial explosion and will thus not be effective. Ullmann therefore tried to reduce the search space by developing a procedure that eliminates some of the 1s that will never appear in any solution. But according to Cordella et al. [86], even with this improvement the worst-case time complexity of the algorithm is still $O(n!n^2)$.

5.2.2 The VF2 Algorithm

In 2001, Cordella et al. [86] introduced another subgraph isomorphism algorithm called *VF2*—the authors did not say what it stands for—which has been used in several DAG and graph covering-based instruction selectors.

In broad outline, the VF2 algorithm constructs a mapping set consisting of (n, m) pairs, where $n \in G_a$ and $m \in G_b$. This set is grown by recursively adding new pairs, one at a time, until either a solution is found or a dead end is reached. To detect the latter as soon as possible, each new pair is checked against a set of rules before it is added to the mapping set. The rules are composed by a set of syntactic feasibility checks given by F_{syn}, followed by a semantic feasibility check given by F_{sem}. Without going into too much detail, we define F_{syn} as

$$F_{\text{syn}}(s, n, m) = R_{\text{pred}} \lor R_{\text{succ}} \lor R_{\text{in}} \lor R_{\text{out}} \lor R_{\text{new}},$$

where n and m constitute the candidate pair under consideration and s represents the current (partial) mapping set. The first two rules, R_{pred} and R_{succ}, ensure that the new mapping set is consistent with the structures of G_a and G_b, and the remaining three rules are used to prune the search space. R_{in} and R_{out} perform one-step look-aheads in the search process and ensure that there will still exist enough unmapped nodes in G_b to allow the remaining nodes in G_a to be mapped. Similarly, R_{new} performs a two-step look-ahead (but I am not certain about the intuition behind this rule). If necessary, the rules can be modified with minimal effort to check graph isomorphism instead of subgraph isomorphism. In the former the structures of G_a and G_b must be rigid—and thus cannot be twisted and turned in order to match—which is more fitting for our purposes. Additional checks, such as ensuring that the node types are compatible, can be added by customizing the definition of F_{sem}.

Although this algorithm exhibits a worst-case time complexity of $O(n!n)$, its best-case time complexity—which is polynomial—still makes it an efficient method for performing pattern matching over very large graphs. For example, Cordella et al. report in [86] that the VF2 algorithm has been successfully used on graphs containing several thousand nodes.

5.2.3 Graph Isomorphism in Quadratic Time

Jiang and Bunke [188, 189, 190] discovered that if the graphs are ordered, meaning all edges belonging to the same node have a predetermined order among each other, then the graph isomorphism problem can be solved in polynomial time for undirected graphs. This is because ordered graphs contain additional structural information that can be exploited during pattern matching. Although it is unclear whether this discovery can be applied to instruction selection—the reasons will become apparent shortly—I decided to include its discussion out of personal interest.

Jiang and Bunke's algorithm essentially works as follows. Starting from some node, traverse the first graph G_a using breadth-first search in the order dictated by the edge ordering for the current node. When a node n is visited for the first time, assign n a number such that the number of every node is unique for all nodes in G_a. In addition, every time a node n is encountered, no matter if it has already been visited or not, record the number of n onto a sequence. This sequence will always be of length $2m$, where m is the number of edges in G_a, as it can be proven that every edge will be traversed exactly twice (once in each direction). Let us denote the sequence produced for G_a when starting from node n as $S(G_a, n)$. We then do the same for the second graph G_b, and if there exists some node m in G_b such that $S(G_b, m) = S(G_a, n)$, then G_b must be isomorphic to G_a. In the worst case this can be checked in $O(e^2)$, where e is the total number of edges in the two graphs.

This algorithm is clearly a vast improvement over those by Ullmann and Cordella et al., but it also has several significant limitations that make it difficult to use in practice. First, it requires that all program and pattern graphs be ordered, which is not always the case for instruction selection (for example, graphs containing commutative nodes violate this restriction). Second, in its current form it detects graph isomorphism instead of subgraph isomorphism, meaning the algorithm can only be applied on patterns that match the entire program graph. Although the first problem can be mitigated by duplicating patterns with commutative nodes, the second problem is much harder to overcome.

5.3 Graph-Based Intermediate Representations

With tree and DAG covering, it is sufficient to represent the program on block level. Consequently, programs are typically modeled as a forest of program trees or a set of program DAGs. But, as previously stated, this becomes an impediment when applied in graph covering-based techniques, forcing us to instead use a graph-based intermediate representation. We will therefore continue by looking briefly at how programs can be expressed using such representations (an excellent survey of this field was recently made by Stanier and Watson [314]).

5.3.1 Static-Single-Assignment Graphs

Most modern compilers—including GCC and LLVM—use IRs based on *static single assignment (SSA)*, which is a form where each variable or temporary within a function is restricted to being defined only once. This is typically achieved by rewriting the program such that each variable assignment receives its own uniquely named definition, and an example of this is given in Fig. 5.2. One of the main benefits of this is that the *live range* of each variable is contiguous. The live range of a variable can be loosely described as the length within the program where the value of that variable must not be destroyed. This in turn means that each variable corresponds to a single value, which simplifies many program optimization routines.

This *define-only-once* restriction, however, causes problems for variables whose value can come from more than one source. For example, in Fig. 5.2a we see the factorial function (introduced in Chapter 1), which is not in SSA form as n and f are defined multiple times (first at lines 1 and 3, and then at lines 7 and 6, respectively). We could try to rename the variables to avoid redefinition conflicts—n is renamed to n_1 at line 1 and to n_2 at line 7, and f is renamed to f_1 at line 3 and to f_2 at line 6—but which variable do we use for the return at line 10? These situations are addressed through the use of φ-*functions*, which allow variables to be defined using one of several values that originate from a separate block. Hence, by declaring additional variables and inserting φ-functions at the beginning of the loop block, the aforementioned problem of f is resolved as shown in Fig. 5.2b.[2]

---

[2] Although this in turn introduces two new problems—where do we insert these φ-functions, and how do we know which value within the φ-function to choose during execution?—we will ignore these issues as they are out of scope for our purposes. There is also *gated single assignment* [37],

```
1:  int factorial(int n) {
2:      init:
3:          int f = 1;
4:      loop:
5:          if (n <= 1) goto end;
6:              f = f * n;
7:              n = n - 1;
8:          goto loop;
9:      end:
10:         return f;
11: }
```

```
1:  int factorial(int n₁) {
2:      init:
3:          int f₁ = 1;
4:      loop:
5:          int f₂ = φ(f₁, f₃);
6:          int n₂ = φ(n₁, n₃);
7:          if (n₂ <= 1) goto end;
8:              int f₃ = f₂ * n₂;
9:              int n₃ = n₂ - 1;
10:         goto loop;
11:     end:
12:         return f₂;
13: }
```

(a) C function   (b) Same C function in SSA form

Fig. 5.2: Example of converting a regular program into SSA form

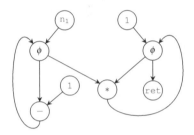

Fig. 5.3: Corresponding SSA graph of the function from Fig. 5.2b. Note that, unlike in program trees and DAGs, the data flows *downwards* along the SSA graph

From the SSA representation we can extract an *SSA graph*, which is basically a program graph where loops are permitted (see for example Fig. 5.2b). Unlike program DAGs, the SSA graph captures the data flow across blocks as well as within them, modeling an entire function which gives a more complete view of the program. But since the SSA graph is devoid of any control-flow information, it is often used as a supplement alongside one or more other IRs. Obviously this also prevents selection of instructions for implementing branches and procedure calls.

5.3.2 Program Dependence Graphs

Another popular intermediate representation is the *program-dependence graph (PDG)*. Introduced by Ferrante et al. [129] in 1987, the PDG only models the *essential* control dependencies of the program—we will soon elaborate on what this means—and several subsequent IR designs, such as the *program dependence web* by Ballance et al. [37] and the *value dependence graph* by Weise et al. [333], are either extensions of the PDG or have been heavily influenced by it.

---

where the φ-functions take a predicate as additional input, which enables executable interpretation of the SSA-based IR code.

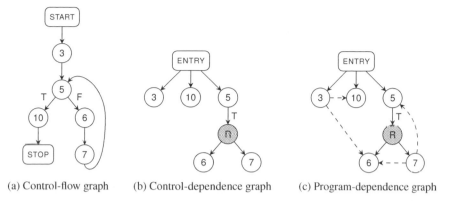

(a) Control-flow graph   (b) Control-dependence graph   (c) Program-dependence graph

Fig. 5.4: Converting the function from Fig. 5.2a into a program-dependence graph.
Node numbers correspond to line numbers in the function. Control flow is shown
using solid lines, and data flow as dashed lines. Shaded nodes represent region nodes

Instead of directly modeling the control flow within a function, the PDG conveys
information about which computational operations are dependent on which predicates.
This information is given as a *control-dependence graph (CDG)*, which is a subgraph
of the PDG. Although it is called a *graph*, the CDG is actually shaped like a tree,
with the operations appearing as leaves and the predicates as intermediate nodes, and
a special node as the root denoting the function entry point. There are also so-called
region nodes, which are used for eliminating common subexpressions that appear as
part of the control flow. Using the CDG, the predicates that an operation depends
on can be found by following the path from the leaf node of that operation to the
root. The PDG is then constructed from the CDG simply by adding the data-flow
dependencies.

An advantage of using a PDG is that program analysis tends to become simpler.
In the factorial function from Fig. 5.2, for example, the end block will always be
executed when the init block is executed. Hence, if there are no data dependencies
between the operations within these blocks, then they could be executed in parallel.
In a control-flow graph (see Fig. 5.4a) this information is not immediately visible, but
in the CDG (see Fig. 5.4b) this fact becomes clear, as these operations only depend
on the function entry. On the other hand, generating correct assembly code directly
from the PDG becomes more complex, as the boundaries of blocks are obscured.

Applications

Despite its widespread use in many program optimization routines, I have not seen any
techniques that use PDGs for selecting instructions, although Paleczny et al. [274]
come close with their implementation of the *Java Hotspot Server Compiler (JHSC)*.
Internally, JHSC uses a graph-based IR format that was originally designed by

Click and Paleczny [80] and is similar to the PDG. The program graphs are covered by a BURS-based instruction selector (see Section 3.6.3) which selects the least-cost patterns for each subtree that is rooted either at a value with multiple uses, or at an operation which may not be duplicated due to side effects. In other words, the program graph is essentially converted into multiple program DAGs that are then covered individually. This, however, may incur overlapping and thus lead to redundant code duplication. After pattern selection the instructions are placed into blocks using a heuristic global code motion method (see [79]).

5.4 Modeling Pattern Selection as a PBQ Problem

In 2003, Eckstein et al. [106] recognized that limiting instruction selection to local scope can decrease code quality of assembly code generated for fixed-point arithmetic digital signal processors. A common idiosyncrasy of such DSPs is that their fixed-point multiplication units will often leave the result shifted one bit to the left. Hence, if a value is computed by accumulating values from fixed-point multiplications—as in the factorial function given in Fig. 5.2—it should remain in shifted mode until all fixed-point multiplications have been performed. Otherwise the accumulated value will needlessly be shifted back and forth. But this is difficult to achieve using local instruction selection.

To overcome this problem, Eckstein et al. developed a design that takes SSA graphs as input—making this technique the first to do so—and transforms the pattern selection problem to a *partitioned Boolean quadratic (PBQ) problem*. The PBQ problem is an extension of the *quadratic assignment (QA) problem*—a fundamental combinatorial optimization problem (see [240] for a recent survey)—and was first introduced Scholz and Eckstein [304] as a means of tackling register allocation. The QA problem and PBQ problem are both NP-complete, and Eckstein et al. therefore developed their own heuristic solver as described in [106]. We will explain the PBQ approach by building the model bottom-up, starting with the definitions.

To begin with, the design assumes that the instructions are given as a linear-form grammar (see Chapter 3, p. 67), where each rule is either a base rule or a chain rule. For each node n in the SSA graph we introduce a Boolean vector $\mathbf{r}_n$, whose length is equal to the number of base rules that match n, and $\mathbf{r}_n[i] = 1$ indicates that the rule i has been selected to cover n. The costs for rule selection are given as another vector $\mathbf{c}_n$ of the same length, where each element is the rule cost times the estimated relative execution frequency of the operation represented by n. This is needed to give higher priority to low-cost instructions for operations that reside in tight loops since those instructions will have a greater impact on performance. With these vectors we can define, for a given SSA graph (N, E), a cost function f as

$$f = \sum_{1 \leq n \leq |N|} \mathbf{r}_n^T \cdot \mathbf{c}_n.$$

We call this the accumulated *base cost* as it gives the total cost of applying base rules to cover the SSA graph. The goal is then to cover each node in the SSA graph exactly once (meaning $\mathbf{r}_n^T \cdot \mathbf{1} = 1$, $\forall n \in N$) such that f is minimized.

Unfortunately this does not necessarily produce a valid covering as there is no connection *between* the base rules. Consequently, the nonterminal to which one selected base rule is reduced may differ from what is expected by another selected base rule. This problem is addressed by introducing a cost matrix $\mathbf{C}_{nm}$ for every pair of nodes n and m in the SSA graph where there exists a directed edge from m to n. An element c_{ij} in $\mathbf{C}_{nm}$ then reflects the aggregated cost of selecting rule i for node n and rule j for node m, which is computed as follows:

1. If rule j reduces m to the nonterminal expected at a certain position on the right-hand side in the production of rule i, then $c_{ij} = 0$.
2. If the previous condition does not hold, but the nonterminal produced by rule j can be reduced to the expected nonterminal using a series of chain rules, then $c_{ij} = \sum c_k$, where c_k denotes the cost of an applied chain rule k.
3. Otherwise $c_{ij} = \infty$, preventing this rule combination from being selected.

The chain costs for the second condition are calculated by first computing the transitive closure for all chain rules (see Chapter 3, p. 49). For this, Eckstein et al. seem to have used the Floyd-Warshall algorithm [132], and Schäfer and Scholz [302] later discovered a method that computes the lowest cost for each c_{ij} by finding the optimal sequence of chain rules. Lastly, the costs are weighted according to the estimated execution frequency for the nodes.

We now extend f by adding the accumulated chain costs, resulting in the following cost function:

$$f = \sum_{1 \le n < m \le |N|} \mathbf{r}_n^T \cdot \mathbf{C}_{nm} \cdot \mathbf{r}_m + \sum_{1 \le n \le |N|} \mathbf{r}_n^T \cdot \mathbf{c}_n.$$

The model is then solved using a heuristic PBQ solver, which was also developed by Eckstein et al. (we will omit details on how it works).

Using a prototype implementation, Eckstein et al. ran experiments on a selected set of fixed-point programs exhibiting the behavior discussed earlier. The results indicate that their scheme improved performance by 40–60% on average—and at most 82% for one program—compared to a traditional tree-based instruction selector. According to Eckstein et al., this considerable gain in performance comes from more efficient use of value modes to which tree covering-based techniques must make premature assignments, and thus could have a detrimental effect on code quality. For example, if chosen poorly, the instruction selector may need to emit additional instructions in order to undo decisions regarding value modes, which obviously reduces performance and needlessly increases the code size. Although the technique by Eckstein et al. clearly mitigates these concerns, their design also has limitations of its own. Most importantly, their PBQ model can only support pattern trees and consequently hinders exploitation of many common target machine features, such as multi-output instructions.

5.4.1 Extending the PBQ Approach to Pattern DAGs

In 2008, Ebner et al. [105] addressed the aforementioned concern by extending the original PBQ model by Eckstein et al. to also support pattern DAGs. When replacing the default instruction selector in LLVM 2.1—which is a greedy DAG rewriter (see Section 4.3.1)—the performance of the assembly code targeting an ARM processor improved by an average of 13% for a selected set of programs. In addition, the impact on compilation time was shown to be negligible.

Ebner et al. first extended the grammar to allow rules to contain multiple productions in a similar fashion to that of Scharwaechter et al. [303] (see Chapter 4, p. 89). We will refer to such rules as *complex rules*, and the productions within a complex rule will be called *proxy rules*. The PBQ model is then augmented to accommodate the selection of complex rules, which essentially entails introducing new vectors and matrices that decide whether a complex rule is selected, together with constraints to enforce that all corresponding proxy rules are also selected.

With more than one cost matrix, it becomes necessary to be able to distinguish one from another. We say that all base and proxy rules belong to category $\mathscr{B}$, and all complex rules belong to category $\mathscr{C}$. A cost matrix written as $\mathbf{C}^{\mathscr{X} \to \mathscr{Y}}$ therefore indicates that it concerns the costs of transitioning from category $\mathscr{X}$ to category $\mathscr{Y}$. As an example, the cost matrix used to compute the accumulated chain cost is henceforth written as $\mathbf{C}_{nm}^{\mathscr{B} \to \mathscr{B}}$ since it only concerns the base rules. We can now proceed with extending the PBQ model.

First, each $\mathbf{r}_n$ vector is extended with the proxy rules that also match at node n in the SSA graph. If a set of identical proxy rules is derived from multiple complex rules, the length of the vector only increases by one element for each such set. Second, we create an instance of a complex rule for every permutation of distinct nodes where the matched proxy rules can be combined into a complex rule. Each such instance i in turn gives rise to a two-element decision vector $\mathbf{d}_i$ which indicates whether i is selected or not (hence a 1 in the first element indicates *not selected*, and a 1 in the second element indicates *selected*).[3] Then, as with the base rules, we accumulate the costs of the selected complex rules by extending f with

$$\sum_{1 \le i \le |I|} \mathbf{d}_i^T \cdot \mathbf{c}_i^{\mathscr{C}},$$

where I is the set of complex rule instances, and $\mathbf{c}_i^{\mathscr{C}}$ is a two-element cost vector whose elements consist of the value 0 and the cost of the complex rule.

Selecting a complex rule means that all of its proxy rules must also be selected. We enforce this through a cost matrix $\mathbf{C}_{ni}^{\mathscr{B} \to \mathscr{C}}$, where n is a particular node in the SSA graph and i is a particular instance of a complex rule. An element c_{mj} in $\mathbf{C}_{ni}^{\mathscr{B} \to \mathscr{C}}$ is then set as follows:

---

[3] A two-element vector is chosen instead of a single Boolean variable as the PBQ model must consist of only matrices and vectors, and for all vectors the sum of its elements must always be exactly 1.

- If j represents that i is not selected, then $c_{mj} = 0$.
- If m is a base rule or proxy rule not associated with the complex rule of i, then $c_{mj} = 0$.
- Otherwise $c_{mj} = \infty$.

We then force the selection of necessary proxy rules by appending the following to f:

$$\sum_{\substack{1 \leq n \leq |N| \\ 1 \leq i \leq |I|}} \mathbf{r}_n^T \cdot \mathbf{C}_{ni}^{\mathcal{B} \to \mathcal{C}} \cdot \mathbf{d}_i.$$

An issue with this model is that if the cost of all proxy rules is 0, then solutions are allowed where all proxy rules of a complex rule are selected but the complex rule itself is not selected. Ebner et al. solved this problem by first setting a high cost M to all proxy rules and then setting the cost of all complex rules to $cost(i) - |l_i|M$, where l_i is the set of proxy rules of a complex rule i. Hence, the overhead of selecting the proxy rules is only offset if the complex rule is also selected.

In some cases, selecting certain complex rules can incur cyclic data dependencies. To prevent this, we introduce a cost matrix $\mathbf{C}_{ij}^{\mathcal{C} \to \mathcal{C}}$ that prevents two instances i and j from being selected simultaneously if such a combination incurs a cyclic data dependency. In their model, Ebner et al. also forbade selection of complex rule instances that overlap. As before, these restrictions are enforced by setting the elements in $\mathbf{C}_{ij}^{\mathcal{C} \to \mathcal{C}}$ corresponding to such situations to ∞, and to 0 for all other elements.

Hence the complete definition of f in the PBQ model by Ebner et al. becomes

$$f = \sum_{1 \leq i < j \leq |I|} \mathbf{d}_i^T \cdot \mathbf{C}_{ij}^{\mathcal{C} \to \mathcal{C}} \cdot \mathbf{d}_j + \sum_{\substack{1 \leq n \leq |N| \\ 1 \leq i \leq |I|}} \mathbf{r}_n^T \cdot \mathbf{C}_{ni}^{\mathcal{B} \to \mathcal{C}} \cdot \mathbf{d}_i + \sum_{1 \leq i \leq |I|} \mathbf{d}_i^T \cdot \mathbf{c}_i^{\mathcal{C}}$$

$$+ \sum_{1 \leq n < m \leq |N|} \mathbf{r}_n^T \cdot \mathbf{C}_{nm}^{\mathcal{B} \to \mathcal{B}} \cdot \mathbf{r}_m + \sum_{1 \leq n \leq |N|} \mathbf{r}_n^T \cdot \mathbf{c}_n^{\mathcal{B}}.$$

5.4.2 Using Rewrite Rules Instead of Production Rules

In 2010, Buchwald and Zwinkau [61] introduced another technique based on PBQ problems. But unlike Eckstein et al. and Ebner et al., Buchwald and Zwinkau approached the task of instruction selection as a formal graph transformation problem, for which much previous work already exist. Hence, in Buchwald and Zwinkau's design the instructions are expressed as rewrite rules instead of production rules. As these rewrite rules are based on a formal foundation, the resulting instruction selector can be automatically verified to handle all possible programs. If this check fails, the verification tool can also provide the necessary rewrite rules that are currently missing from the instruction set.

The technique works as follows. First the SSA graph is converted into a DAG-like form by duplicating each ϕ-node into two nodes, which effectively breaks any cycles appearing in the SSA graph. After finding all applicable rewrite rules for this DAG (this is done using traditional pattern matching), a corresponding instance of the PBQ problem is formulated and solved as before.

Buchwald and Zwinkau also discovered and addressed flaws in the PBQ solver by Eckstein et al., which may fail to find a solution in certain situations due to inadequate propagation of information. However, Buchwald and Zwinkau also cautioned that their own implementation does not scale well when the number of overlapping patterns grows. In addition, since the SSA graph is devoid of control-flow information, none of the PBQ-based techniques can support inter-block instructions.

5.5 Other Graph-Based Approaches

5.5.1 More Hardware Modeling Techniques

In Chapter 4 we saw a technique for performing microcode generation where the entire processor of the target machine is modeled as a graph instead of by just deriving the patterns for the available instructions. Here we will look at a few techniques that rely on the same modeling scheme, but address the more traditional problem of instruction selection.

CHESS

Lanneer et al. [222] developed in 1990 a design that was later adopted by Van Praet et al. [326, 327] in their implementation of CHESS, a well-known compiler targeting DSPs and *application-specific instruction set processors (ASIPs)*.

Comparing CHESS to MSSQ (see Section 4.10.3), we find two striking differences. First, in MSSQ the data paths of the processor are given by a manually written machine description, whereas CHESS derives these automatically from an nML-based specification [123, 124].

Second, the method of *bundling*—which is the task of scheduling operations for parallel execution—is different. The instruction selector in MSSQ uses techniques from DAG covering to find patterns in the hardware graph, which can subsequently be used to cover the program trees. After pattern selection, another routine attempts to schedule the selected instructions for parallel execution. In contrast, CHESS takes a more incremental approach. From the program CHESS first constructs a *chaining graph*, where each node represents an operation in the program that has been annotated with a set of functional units capable of executing that operation. Since the functional units on a DSP are commonly grouped into *functional building blocks (FBBs)*, the chaining graph also contains an edge between every pair of nodes that could potentially be executed on the same FBB. A heuristic algorithm then attempts to collapse the nodes in the chaining graph by selecting an edge, replacing the two nodes with a new node, and then removing the edges between nodes of operations that can no longer be executed on the same FBB as the operations of the new node. This process iterates until no more nodes can be collapsed, and every remaining node in the chaining graph thus constitutes a *bundle*. The same authors later extended this design in [326] to consider selection between *all* possible bundles using branch-and-bound search, and to enable some measure of code duplication by allowing the same operations in the program graph to appear in multiple bundles.

Using this incremental scheme to form the bundles, the design by Van Praet et al. is capable of bundling operations that potentially reside in different blocks. Their somewhat-integrated code generation approach also allows efficient assembly code to be generated for complex architectures, making it suitable for DSPs and ASIPs where the data paths are very irregular. It may be possible to also extend the technique to support inter-block instructions as well, but interdependent instructions are most likely out of reach due to its heuristic nature.

Generating Assembly Code Using Simulated Annealing

Another, albeit unusual, code generation technique was proposed by Visser [328] in 1999. Like MSSQ and CHESS, Visser's approach is an integrated code generation design but solves the problem using *simulated annealing*, which is a meta-heuristic to avoid getting stuck in a local maximum when searching for solutions (see for example [207] for an overview). In brief terms, an initial solution is found by randomly mapping each node in the program graph to a node in the hardware graph—which models the entire processor—and then a schedule is found using traditional list scheduling. A fitness function is then applied to judge the effectiveness of the solution, but the exact details are omitted from the paper. A proof-of-concept prototype was developed and tested on a simple program, but it appears no further research has been conducted on this idea.

5.5.2 *Improving Code Quality with Mutation Scheduling*

The last item we will discuss is a technique called *mutation scheduling*,[4] which was introduced in 1994 by Novack et al. [267, 268]. Mutation scheduling is technically a form of instruction scheduling that primarily targets VLIW architectures, but it also integrates a sufficient amount of instruction selection to warrant being included in this book. On the other hand, the amount of instruction selection that *is* incorporated is in turn not really based on graph covering, but, as with trellis diagrams (see Section 3.7.4 and Section 4.10.2), I decided against discussing it in its own chapter.

Broadly speaking, mutation scheduling essentially tries to reduce the makespan of programs for which assembly code have already been generated (hence instruction se-

---

[4] Despite its name, the idea of mutation scheduling is completely orthogonal to the theory of genetic algorithms.

lection, instruction scheduling, and register allocation has already been performed).[5] This is done by progressively moving the computations, one at a time, such that they can be executed in parallel with other instructions and thus finish sooner. If such a move cannot be made, for example due to violation of some resource constraint or data dependency, then mutation scheduling tries to alter the value—this is called *value mutation*—which means that the current operation is replaced by other, equivalent operations that conform to the restrictions. These operations are selected from a *mutation set*, which is conceptually a recursive data structure, as an expression in the mutation set may use intermediate values that in turn necessitate mutation sets of their own. Novack et al. compute these mutation sets by first taking the original operation and then applying a series of semantic-preserving functions that have been derived from various logical axioms, algebraic theorems, and the characteristics of the target machine. For example, if the value X is computed as $Y + 5$, then Y can later be obtained by computing $X - 5$. Another example is multiplication by powers of 2, which can be replaced with *shift* instructions, provided such instructions are available. If this is beneficial, a value can also be recomputed instead of copied from its current location. This idea is known as *rematerialization*, which is a method for reducing register pressure, as it allows registers to be released at an earlier point in the assembly code.

In mutation scheduling, "shorter" mutations are preferred over longer ones. This is because a value mutation of v can lead to a cascade of new computations, which all will need to be scheduled before v can be is computed. Note that these computations can be scheduled such that they appear in blocks preceding the block in which the computations of v appear. Hence the length of a mutation is loosely defined as the number of instruction bundles that may need to be modified in order to realize the mutation. Moreover, since the new computations of a successful mutation consume resources and incur dependencies of their own, the existing candidates appearing in mutation sets may need to be removed or modified. The "best" combination of mutations is then decided heuristically, but the paper is vague on how this is done exactly.

Novack et al. implemented a prototype by extending an existing scheduler based on *global resource-constrained percolation (GRiP)*, which is another global instruction scheduling technique developed by the same authors (see [265]). Subsequent experiments using a selected set of benchmark programs demonstrated that the mutation scheduling-based design yielded a two- to threefold performance improvement over the GRiP-only-based counterpart, partly due to its ability to apply rematerialization in regions where register pressure is high. Unfortunately the authors neglected to say anything about the time complexity of mutation scheduling, and whether it scales to larger programs.

---

[5] Although it is depicted here primarily as a post-step to code generation, one could just as well design a Davidson-Fraser-style compiler (see Chapter 2) where simple methods are applied to generate correct but naïve assembly code, and then rely on mutation scheduling to improve the code quality.

5.6 Summary

In this chapter we have considered a number of techniques that are founded, in one form or another, on the principle of graph covering. Such techniques are among the most powerful methods of instruction selection since they perform global instruction selection as well as have more extensive instruction support compared to most tree and DAG covering-based designs.

Unfortunately this has not been fully exploited in existing techniques, partly due to limitations in the program representations or to restrictions enforced by the underlying solving techniques. Moreover, performing global instruction selection is computationally much harder compared to local instruction selection, and therefore most likely we will only see these techniques applied in compilers whose users can afford very long compilation times (for example when targeting embedded systems with extremely high demands on performance, code size, power consumption, or a combination thereof).

Chapter 6
Conclusions

In this book we have discussed, examined, and assessed numerous methods of instruction selection. Starting with monolithic instruction selectors, which were typically created ad hoc and by hand, the field advanced into retargetable macro-expanding designs that could be generated from a declarative machine description of the target machine. These were in turn later succeeded by the more powerful principle of tree covering, which led to the introduction of several formal methodologies that made it possible to verify the correctness of the instruction selector. Simultaneous developments were also made to combine macro expansion with peephole optimization, which has proven a very effective methodology. The principle of tree covering later evolved into the more general forms of DAG covering and graph covering, yielding more powerful methods of instruction selection at the expense of increased computational complexity. Since optimal DAG covering and graph covering are both NP-complete, most such designs often applied heuristics to reduce the search space. Lastly, more recent developments have given rise to new approaches where the task of instruction selection is modeled using methods from combinatorial optimization.

An accessible overview of all studied techniques is available in Appendix A, and a publication timeline diagram is shown in Appendix B.

6.1 Open Aspects

Despite the tremendous progress that has been made over the past 40 years, the instruction selection techniques constituting the current state of the art still suffer from several significant shortcomings. Most notably, no technique—at least to my knowledge—is capable of modeling inter-block instructions. Today this impact is mitigated by augmenting the compiler with customized program optimization passes in order to detect and exploit particular instructions, but this is an error-prone and tedious task. A more flexible solution is to use compiler intrinsics, which can be seen as additional node types in the program graph that represent more complicated operations, such as $\sqrt{x}$. Another approach is to implement target-specific library

© Springer International Publishing Switzerland 2016   121
G. Hjort Blindell, *Instruction Selection*,
DOI 10.1007/978-3-319-34019-7_6

functions, written directly as assembly code, and make inlined calls from within the program. But neither is ideal: extending the compiler with additional compiler intrinsics typically requires a significant amount of manual labor, and the library functions must be rewritten every time a new target machine needs to be supported.

Not supporting inter-block instructions often also means that the selection of regular branch instructions must be done separately, typically ad hoc through handwritten routines. In fact, branch instructions in general have been little discussed in the literature, despite the fact that roughly every three to six instructions in most programs is a branch instruction [175]. As discussed by Boender and Sacerdoti Coen [49], code size can be reduced by selecting the appropriate branch instruction, which is imperative when generating assembly code for target machines with extremely small memories.

In addition, the task of supporting disjoint-output instructions such as SIMD instructions is often viewed as a problem that is separate from instruction selection. For example, there exist a number of methods—many of which are based on polyhedral transformations—for making efficient use of such instructions (see for example [10, 39, 180, 206, 213, 214, 323, 342]). Common to most is that they rely on aggressive loop unrolling and are thus restricted to handling *only* these instructions. On the other hand, most instruction selection techniques do not support instructions with this kind of characteristic (the exceptions being of those by Leupers [228] and Arslan and Kuchcinski [30]). Although they are primarily used inside tight loops, disjoint-output instructions could potentially also be used in other situations where an abundance of similar operations exist (see for example [223, 239]).

There has also been little overlap between the techniques for performing instruction selection and the methods for generating assembly code for target machines equipped with reconfigurable hardware, such as ASIP. A compromise between flexibility and performance, ASIPs are processors whose instruction sets can be extended with additional instructions, allowing the processor to be—at least partly—customized for the running program in order to improve code quality. The task of discovering and deciding which instructions to add is commonly referred to as the *instruction set extension (ISE) problem*, and there exists plenty of research on how to solve this problem (see for example [11, 20, 31, 32, 41, 47, 52, 57, 78, 185, 198, 259, 260, 266, 353], and see [144] for a recent survey). However, although the ISE problem can be regarded as a generalization of the instruction selection problem—the main difference is that the pattern set is no longer fixed—the prevalent approach is to treat them separately. As with the selection of SIMD instructions, the instruction set extensions are typically found and selected first—often greedily—and then traditional instruction selection is performed on the remaining parts of the program not covered by the extensions. But this approach often compromises code quality; Murray [259] states in his 2012 doctoral dissertation that it is difficult to accurately estimate the gain of using an instruction set extension when the ISE problem is solved in isolation. In the worst case, it can even lead to a decrease in performance. Hence there is potential in integrating these two problems in order to solve them in unison.

Another relatively unexplored aspect of instruction selection is energy consumption. Some research has been conducted concerning instruction scheduling (see for example [225, 261, 275]) and register allocation (see for example [72, 153]), but there exists very little on power and temperature-aware instruction selection. The only techniques I could find are those by Lorenz et al. [241, 242], Bednarski and Kessler [42], and Schafer et al. [301], and of these only the first is of any real interest (the integrated code generation approach by Bednarski and Kessler is mostly concerned with instruction scheduling and register allocation, and the technique by Schafer et al. only performs functional-unit rebinding of already-selected instructions).

Lastly, as already stated, all three aspects of code generation must be performed simultaneously if truly optimal assembly code is to be attained. Optimal instruction selection in isolation is of limited significance for several reasons. For example, making efficient use of status flags is impossible without taking instruction scheduling into consideration since one must make sure that the flags are not prematurely overwritten by another instruction. The same holds for VLIW architectures, where certain combinations of patterns can increase the number of instructions that can be scheduled together for parallel execution. Another problem is rematerialization, in which a value is recomputed instead of spilled. This can be useful in situations in which there is a shortage of free registers or if the cost of spilling is prohibitively high, but accurate information about whether this will be beneficial can often only be determined by actually performing register allocation. The bond between the instruction selection and register allocation becomes even tighter for target machines equipped with multiple register classes and requires a special set of instructions for transferring data from one register class to another. Having said this, most contemporary techniques only consider instruction selection in isolation, and it is often unclear whether they can be fully and efficiently integrated with instruction scheduling and register allocation.

6.2 Future Challenges

These problems notwithstanding, there do exist several techniques that I believe have shown considerable promise—namely those based on methods for combinatorial optimization (see for example Wilson et al. [340], Bashford and Leupers [40], Bednarski and Kessler [43], Floch et al. [131], and Arslan and Kuchcinski [30]).

First, the underlying modeling mechanisms facilitate the approach of integrated code generation. Second, auxiliary constraints can easily be added to the already existing model, enabling code generation for complicated target machines as well as extending the instruction support to include interdependent instructions. Third, recent advancements in solver technology have made these kinds of techniques viable options for practical use (this is for example showcased by Castañeda Lozano et al. [65, 66]). However, current implementations are still orders-of-magnitude slower than their heuristic counterparts and are thus in need of further research. Moreover, the current program representations inhibit proper modeling of inter-block instructions.

To conclude: although the field has indeed come far since the initial ideas first introduced in the 1960s, instruction selection is still—contrary to common belief—an evasive problem. As the target machines are becoming evermore complex, placing higher demands for more flexible and integrated code generation, the instruction selection problem may be in greater need of study than ever before.

Appendix A
List of Techniques

The list starts on the next page, and its legend appears at the end of the list. The techniques are ordered chronologically.

Note that the capabilities of all techniques have been set to reflect those exhibited by current implementation prototypes and known applications, not the capabilities that could potentially be achieved through extensions of the technique.

© Springer International Publishing Switzerland 2016
G. Hjort Blindell, *Instruction Selection*,
DOI 10.1007/978-3-319-34019-7

REFERENCES	PR	SC	OP	MO	DO	IB	IN	KNOWN APPLICATIONS
Lowry and Medlock [243]	ME	L	○	○	○	○	○	FHC
Orgass and Waite [273]	ME	L	○	○	○	○	○	SIMCMP
Elson and Rake [108]	ME	L	○	○	○	○	○	
Miller [255]	ME	L	○	○	○	○	○	DMACS
Wilcox [338]	ME	L	○	○	○	○	○	
Wasilew [331]	TC	L	○	○	○	○	○	
Donegan [101]	ME	L	○	○	○	○	○	
Tirrell [319]	ME	L	○	○	○	○	○	
Weingart [332]	TC	L	○	○	○	○	○	
Ammann et al. [12, 13]	ME	L	○	○	○	○	○	
Young [350]	ME	L	○	○	○	○	○	
Newcomer [263]	TC	L	○	○	○	○	○	
Simoneaux [309]	ME	L	○	○	○	○	○	
Snyder [310]	ME	L	○	○	○	○	○	
Fraser [140, 141]	ME	L	○	○	○	○	○	
Ripken [294]	TC	L	●	○	○	○	○	
Glanville and Graham [158]	TC	L	○	○	○	○	○	PCC
Johnson [191, 192]	TC	L	○	○	○	○	○	
Harrison [170]	ME$^+$	L	○	○	○	○	○	
Cattell [67, 70, 234]	TC	L	○	○	○	○	○	PQCC
Auslander and Hopkins [33]	ME$^+$	L	○	○	○	○	○	
Ganapathi and Fischer [146, 147, 148, 149]	TC	L	○	○	○	○	○	
Krumme and Ackley [218]	ME	L	○	○	○	○	○	
Deutsch and Schiffman [96]	ME	L	○	○	○	○	○	SMALLTALK-80
Christopher et al. [76]	TC	L	●	○	○	○	○	
Davidson and Fraser [91]	ME$^+$	L	●	●	●	○	○	GCC, ACK, ZEPHYR/VPO
Henry [177]	TC	L	●	○	○	○	○	TWIG
Aho et al. [6, 7, 321]	TC	L	●	○	○	○	○	
Hatcher and Christopher [172]	TC	L	●	○	○	○	○	
Horspool [184]	TC	L	●	○	○	○	○	
Fraser and Wendt [135]	ME$^+$	L	○	○	○	○	○	
Giegerich and Schmal [157]	TC	L	○	○	○	○	○	

REFERENCES	PR	SC	OP	MO	DO	IB	IN	KNOWN APPLICATIONS
Hatcher and Tuller [174]	TC	L	●	○	○	○	○	UNH-CODEGEN
Pelegri-Llopart and Graham [278]	TC	L	●	○	○	○	○	
Yates and Schwartz [348]	TC	L	●	○	○	○	○	
Emmelmann et al. [109]	ME	L	●	●	○	○	○	BEG, COSY
Ganapathi [145]	TC	L	○	●	●	○	○	
Genin et al. [155]	ME$^+$	L	○	●	○	○	○	
Nowak and Marwedel [269]	DC	L	○	●	●	○	○	MSSC
Balachandran et al. [35]	TC	L	○	○	○	○	○	
Despland et al. [63, 94, 95]	TC	L	●	●	○	○	○	FAGODE
Wendt [335]	ME$^+$	L	○	●	○	○	○	
Hatcher [173]	TC	L	●	○	○	○	○	UCG
Fraser et al. [137]	TC	L	●	○	○	○	○	BURG, RECORD, REDACO
Fraser et al. [138, 281, 282, 284, 285]	TC	L	●	○	○	○	○	BURG, HBURG, JBURG, WBURG, OCAMLBURG
Emmelmann [110]	TC	L	●	○	○	○	○	
Wess [336, 337]	TD	L	●	○	○	○	○	
Marwedel [252]	DC	L	●	●	○	○	○	MSSV
Tjiang [320]	TC	L	●	●	○	○	○	OLIVE, SPAM
Engler and Proebsting [114]	TC	L	●	○	○	○	○	DCG
Fauth et al. [125, 258]	DC	L	●	●	●	○	○	C3C
Ferdinand et al. [127]	TC	L	○	○	○	○	○	
Liem et al. [237, 276, 277]	DC	L	●	●	●	○	○	CODESYN
Lanneer et al. [222, 326, 327]	GC	G	●	●	●	○	○	CHESS
Wilson et al. [340]	DC	L	●	●	●	○	○	
Yu and Hu [351, 352]	DC	L	●	●	○	○	○	
Novack et al. [267, 268]	MS	G	●	○	○	○	○	
Hanson and Fraser [169]	TC	L	●	●	○	○	○	LBURG, LCC
Liao et al. [235, 236]	DC	L	●	●	○	○	○	
Adl-Tabatabai et al. [1]	ME	L	○	○	○	○	○	OMNIWARE
Engler [113]	ME	L	○	○	○	○	○	VCODE
Hoover and Zadeck [182]	DC	L	○	●	●	○	○	
Leupers and Marwedel [226, 233]	DC	L	○	●	●	○	○	
Nymeyer et al. [270, 271]	TC	L	○	○	○	○	○	

REFERENCES	PR	SC	OP	MO	DO	IB	IN	KNOWN APPLICATIONS
Shu et al. [308]	TC	L	○	○	○	○	○	
Gough [160, 161, 162]	TC	L	●	○	○	○	○	MBURG, GPBURG
Gebotys [152]	DC	L	●	●	○	○	○	
Hanono and Devadas [167, 168]	TD	L	○	○	○	○	○	AVIV
Leupers and Marwedel [230]	DC	L	●	●	●	○	○	MSSQ
Bashford and Leupers [40]	DC	L	●	●	○	○	○	
Ertl [117]	DC	L	○	○	○	○	○	DBURG
Fraser and Proebsting [139]	ME	L	●	○	○	○	○	GBURG
Fröhlich et al. [142]	TD	L	●	●	●	○	○	
Visser [328]	GC	G	○	●	○	○	○	
Leupers [228]	DC	L	●	●	●	○	○	
Madhavan et al. [245]	TC	L	○	●	○	○	○	
Arnold and Corporaal [25, 26, 27]	DC	L	○	○	○	○	○	
Sarkar et al. [300]	DC	L	○	○	○	○	○	JALAPEÑO
Paleczny et al. [274]	GC	G	●	●	○	○	○	JHSC
Lorenz et al. [241, 242]	DC	L	○	●	●	○	○	
Bravenboer and Visser [56]	TC	L	●	●	○	○	○	
Krishnaswamy and Gupta [216]	ME⁺	L	○	●	○	○	○	
Eckstein et al. [106]	GC	G	○	●	●	○	○	
Tanaka et al. [317]	DC	L	○	○	●	○	○	
Borchardt [50]	TC	L	●	●	○	○	○	
Brisk et al. [58]	DC	L	○	●	○	○	○	
Cong et al. [82]	DC	L	○	○	●	○	○	LLVM
Lattner and Adve [224]	DC	L	●	●	○	○	○	OPTIMIST
Kessler et al. [43, 115, 116]	DC	L	○	●	●	○	○	
Clark et al. [77]	DC	L	●	○	○	○	○	
Dias and Ramsey [98]	ME⁺	L	○	●	●	○	○	
Ertl et al. [118]	TC	L	○	○	○	○	○	
Farfeleder et al. [121]	TC	L	○	●	●	○	○	VISTA
Kulkarni et al. [219]	ME⁺	L	○	●	○	○	○	
Hormati et al. [183]	DC	L	○	●	●	○	○	
Scharwaechter et al. [303]	DC	L	○	○	●	○	○	CBURG

REFERENCES	PR	SC	OP	MO	DO	IB	IN	KNOWN APPLICATIONS
Ebner et al. [105]	GC	G	○	●	●	○	○	
Koes and Goldstein [212]	DC	L	○	●	○	○	○	NOLTIS
Ahn et al. [2]	DC	L	○	●	●	○	○	
Martin et al. [248, 249]	DC	L	●	●	●	○	○	
Buchwald and Zwinkau [61]	GC	G	○	○	○	○	○	
Dias and Ramsey [97, 289]	ME+	L	○	○	○	○	○	
Edler von Koch et al. [107]	TC	L	○	●	●	○	○	
Floch et al. [131]	DC	L	●	○	●	○	○	
Yang [347]	TC	L	●	○	●	○	○	
Youn et al. [349]	DC	L	○	●	●	○	○	CEURG
Arslan and Kuchcinski [29, 30]	DC	L	●	○	●	○	○	
Janoušek and Málek [187]	TC	L	○	○	○	○	○	
Andrade [16]	ME	L	○	○	○	○	○	GNU LIGHTNING

Fundamental principle (PR) on which the technique is based: macro expansion (ME), macro expansion with peephole optimization (ME+), tree covering (TC), trellis diagrams (TD—is actually sorted under TC in this book), DAG covering (DC), graph covering (GC), or mutation scheduling (MS—is actually sorted under GC in this book). Scope of instruction selection (SC): local (L, isolated to a single block), or global (G, considers entire functions). Whether the technique is claimed to be optimal (OP). Supported machine instruction characteristics: single-output (supported by all techniques), multi-output (MO), disjoint-output (DO), inter-block (IB), and interdependent (IN) instructions. The symbols ○, ◐, and ● indicate no, partial, and full support, respectively.

Appendix B
Publication Timeline

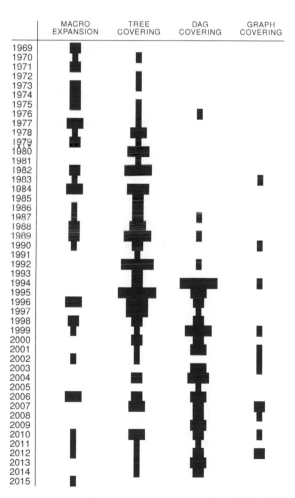

Fig. B.1: Illustrates how research on instruction selection (201 publications in total), with respect to the fundamental principles, has elapsed over time. The widths of the bars indicate the relative numbers of publications for a given year

© Springer International Publishing Switzerland 2016
G. Hjort Blindell, *Instruction Selection*,
DOI 10.1007/978-3-319-34019-7

Appendix C
Graph Definitions

A *graph* is defined as a tuple (N, E) where N is a set of *nodes* (also known as *vertices*) and E is a set of *edges*, each consisting of a pair of nodes $n, m \in N$. A graph is *undirected* if its edges have no direction, and *directed* if they do. In a directed graph we write an edge from a node n to another node m as $n \rightarrow m$, and say that such an edge is *outgoing* with respect to n, and *ingoing* with respect to m. We also introduce the following functions:

$$src : E \rightarrow N \qquad dst : E \rightarrow N$$
$$src(n \rightarrow m) = n \quad dst(n \rightarrow m) = m$$

Edges for which $src(e) = dst(e)$ are known as *loop edges* (or simply *loops*). If there exists more than one edge between the same pair of nodes then the graph is a *multigraph*, otherwise it is a *simple* graph.

A list of edges that describe how to get from one node to another is called a *path*. More formally we define a path between two nodes n and m as an ordered list of edges $p = \langle e_1, \ldots, e_l \rangle$ such that for the directed graph (N, E):

$$e_i \in E \ \forall e_i \in p$$
$$dst(e_i) = src(e_{i+1}) \ \forall 1 \leq i < l - 1$$

Paths for undirected graphs are similarly defined and will thus be skipped. A path for which $src(e_1) = dst(e_l)$ is known as a *cycle*. Two nodes n and m, where $n \neq m$, are said to be *connected* if there exists a path from n to m, and if the path is of length 1 then n and m are also *adjacent*. A directed graph containing no cycles is known as a *directed acyclic graph (DAG)*. An undirected graph is *connected* if and only if there exists a path for every distinct pair of nodes. For completeness, a directed graph is *strongly connected* iff, for every pair of distinct nodes n and m, there exists a path from n to m and a path from m to n. Also, a directed graph is *weakly connected* if replacing all edges with undirected edges yields a connected undirected graph. An example is shown in Fig. C.1.

© Springer International Publishing Switzerland 2016
G. Hjort Blindell, *Instruction Selection*,
DOI 10.1007/978-3-319-34019-7

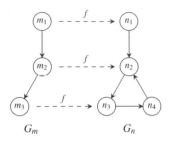

Fig. C.1: An example of two simple directed graphs G_m and G_n. Through the graph homomorphism f we see that G_m is an isomorphic subgraph of G_n. Both graphs are weakly connected, and G_n also has a strongly connected subgraph, consisting of n_2, n_3, and n_4 which form a cycle

A simple, undirected graph that is connected, contains no cycles, and has exactly one path between any two nodes is called a *tree*. A set of trees constitutes a *forest*. Nodes in a tree with exactly one neighbor are known as *leaves*. A *directed tree* is a directed graph that would become a tree when ignoring the direction of its edges. A *rooted directed tree* is a directed tree where one node has been assigned the *root* and all edges either point away or towards the root. In a rooted directed tree a *parent* of a node n is the node adjacent to n that is closest to the root. Likewise, if a node n is the parent of another node m, then m is a *child* of n. In this book we assume all trees to be rooted directed trees, and a tree will always be drawn with its root appearing at the top.

A graph $G = (N, E)$ is a *subgraph* of another graph $G' = (N', E')$, also written as $G \subseteq G'$, iff $N \subseteq N'$ and $E \subseteq E'$. Likewise, a tree T is a *subtree* of another tree T' iff $T \subseteq T'$.

A *graph homomorphism* is a mapping between two graphs such that their structure is preserved. More formally, a graph homomorphism f from a graph $G = (N, E)$ to another graph $G' = (N', E')$ is a mapping $f : N \to N'$ such that $(u, v) \in E$ implies $(f(u), f(v)) \in E'$. If the graph homomorphism f is an injective function, then f is also called a *subgraph isomorphism*. If there exists such a mapping then we say that G is an *isomorphic subgraph* of G', and an example of this is given in Fig. C.1. If f is a bijection, whose inverse function is also a graph homomorphism, then f is also called a *graph isomorphism*.

Lastly we introduce the notion of *topological sort*, where the nodes of a graph (N, E) are arranged in an ordered list $\langle n_1, \ldots, n_n \rangle$ such that $n_i \in N$ $\forall 1 \le i \le n$ and for no pair of nodes n_i and n_j, where $i < j$, does there exist an edge $n_j \to n_i \in E$. In other words, if the edges are added to the list then all edges will go point forward from left to right (hence topological sorts are only defined for DAGs). Several methods exists for achieving a topological sort, see for example Section 22.4 in Cormen et al. [88].

Appendix D
Taxonomy

Technical terms and and their exact definitions often differ from one publication to another, thus making it difficult to discuss and compare techniques without a common foundation. In this book, therefore, a taxonomy with a well-defined vocabulary has been established and is used consistently throughout the book. Although this may seem a bit daunting and superfluous at first, most items in the taxonomy are easy to understand. Most importantly, having explicitly defined these terms will minimize confusions that may otherwise occur.

D.1 Common Terms

Several terms are continuously used when discussing the instruction selection techniques. Most of these are obvious and appear in other literature, while others may require a little explanation.

Program. The code under compilation, and therefore the input to the compiler as well as the instruction selector. In the former this refers to the source code, while in the latter it usually refers to the intermediate representation (IR) code, either in its entirety or parts of it (that is, a function, a basic block, or part of a block), depending on the scope of the instruction selector.

Target machine. The hardware on which the program is compiled to run. Most often this refers to the ISA implemented and understood by its processing unit.

Instruction selector. A component or program responsible for implementing and executing the task of instruction selection. If this program is automatically generated from a machine description, the term refers to the generated *result* and not the *generator* itself.

Frontend. A component or program responsible for parsing, validating, and translating the program into equivalent IR code.

Code generation. The task of generating assembly code for a given program by performing instruction selection, instruction scheduling, and register allocation.

© Springer International Publishing Switzerland 2016
G. Hjort Blindell, *Instruction Selection*,
DOI 10.1007/978-3-319-34019-7

Backend. A component or program responsible for implementing and executing the task of code generation.

Compilation time. The time required to compile a given program.

Pattern matching. The problem of detecting when and where it is possible to use a certain instruction for a given program.

Pattern selection. The problem of deciding which instructions to select from the set of candidates found during pattern matching.

Offline cost analysis. The task of shifting the computation of optimization decisions from the phase of program compilation to the phase of compiler generation, thereby reducing compilation time at the cost of increasing the time it takes to generate the compiler.

D.2 Machine Instruction Characteristics

A machine instruction exhibits one or more machine instruction characteristics. For this study, the following characteristics were identified:

Single-output instructions. An instruction that only produces a single observable output value. In this context observable means a value that can be accessed by the program. This includes instructions that perform typical arithmetic operations such as addition and multiplication as well as bit operations, but it also includes instructions that chain multiple computations (for example, "load into register r_d the value at memory location specified in register r_x plus offset specified in register r_y plus an immediate value"). Note that the instruction must produce only this value and nothing else (compare this with the next characteristic).

Multi-output instructions. An instruction that produces multiple observable output values from the same input values. Examples include `divmod` instructions that produce both the quotient as well as the remainder of two terms, but it also includes instructions that set status flags in addition to computing the arithmetic result. A status flag is a bit that signifies additional information about the result (for example, if there was a carry overflow or the result was equal to 0) and is therefore often a side effect of the instruction. In reality, however, these bits are nothing else but additional output values produced by the instruction.

Disjoint-output instructions. An instruction that produces multiple observable output values from disjoint input value sets. This means that if the expression for computing each observable output value formed a graph, then these graphs would be disjoint. In comparison, single-output and multi-output instructions all form a single graph. Disjoint-output instructions typically include SIMD instructions which execute the same operations simultaneously on many input values.

Inter-block instructions. An instruction whose execution essentially spans multiple blocks. Examples of such instructions are saturated arithmetic instructions and hardware-loop instructions, which repeat a fixed sequence of instructions a certain number of times. As seen in this book, no instruction selection design is yet capable of supporting this kind of instruction.

Interdependent instructions. An instruction that enforces additional constraints when appearing in combination with other instructions in the assembly code. An example is the `add` instruction from the TMS320C55x instruction set which cannot be combined with an `rpt k` instruction if the addressing mode is set to a specific mode. This kind of instruction is very difficult to handle by most instruction selection techniques.

The first three characteristics form sets of instructions that are disjoint from one another, but the last two characteristics can be combined as appropriate with any of the other characteristics. For example, the same instruction can exhibit single-output, inter-block, as well as the characteristics of interdependent instructions.

D.3 Scope

Local instruction selection. Selects instructions for a single block at a time.
Global instruction selection. Selects instructions for several blocks or an entire function at a time.

D.4 Principles

All techniques reviewed in this book have been categorized into one of four principles.

Macro expansion. Each IR node in the program is expanded into one or more instructions using macros. This is a simple strategy but generally produces very inefficient assembly code as an instruction often can implement more than one IR node. Consequently modern instruction selectors that apply this approach also incorporate peephole optimization that combines many instructions into single equivalents.

Tree covering. The program and instructions are represented as trees. Each instruction gives rise to a pattern tree which is then matched over the program tree (this is the pattern matching problem). From the matching set of patterns, a subset is selected such that the entire program tree is covered at the lowest cost.

DAG covering. The same idea as tree covering but operates on DAGs instead of trees. Since DAGs are a more general form of trees, DAG covering supersedes tree covering.

Graph covering. The same idea as DAG covering but operates on general graphs instead of DAGs. Since graphs are a more general form of DAGs, graph covering supersedes DAG covering.

References

[1] A.-R. Adl-Tabatabai, G. Langdale, S. Lucco, and R. Wahbe. "Efficient and Language-Independent Mobile Programs". In: *Proceedings of the SIGPLAN Conference on Programming Language Design and Implementation*. SIGPLAN'96. Philadelphia, Pennsylvania, USA: ACM, 1996, pp. 127–136. ISBN: 0-89791-795-2

[2] M. Ahn, J. M. Youn, Y. Choi, D. Cho, and Y. Paek. "Iterative Algorithm for Compound Instruction Selection with Register Coalescing". In: *Proceedings of the 12th Euromicro Conference on Digital System Design, Architectures, Methods and Tools*. DSD'09. Washington, District of Colombia, USA: IEEE Computer Society, 2009, pp. 513–520. ISBN: 978-0-7695 37825

[3] A. V. Aho and S. C. Johnson. "Optimal Code Generation for Expression Trees". In: *Journal of the ACM* 23.3 (1976), pp. 488–501. ISSN: 0004-5411

[4] A. V. Aho, S. C. Johnson, and J. D. Ullman. "Code Generation for Expressions with Common Subexpressions". In: *Proceedings of the 3rd SIGACT-SIGPLAN Symposium on Principles on Programming Languages*. POPL'76. Atlanta, Georgia, USA: ACM, 1976, pp. 19–31

[5] A. V. Aho and M. J. Corasick. "Efficient String Matching: An Aid to Bibliographic Search". In: *Communications of the ACM* 18.6 (1975), pp. 333–340. ISSN: 0001-0782

[6] A. V. Aho and M. Ganapathi. "Efficient Tree Pattern Matching: An Aid to Code Generation". In: *Proceedings of the 12th SIGACT-SIGPLAN Symposium on Principles of Programming Languages*. POPL'85. New Orleans, Louisiana, USA: ACM, 1985, pp. 334–340. ISBN: 0-89791-147-4

[7] A. V. Aho, M. Ganapathi, and S. W. K. Tjiang. "Code Generation Using Tree Matching and Dynamic Programming". In: *Transactions on Programming Languages and Systems* 11.4 (1989), pp. 491–516. ISSN: 0164-0925

[8] V. A. Aho, R. Sethi, and J. D. Ullman. *Compilers: Principles, Techniques, and Tools*. 2nd ed. Boston, Massachusetts, USA: Addison-Wesley, 2006. ISBN: 978-0321486813

© Springer International Publishing Switzerland 2016
G. Hjort Blindell, *Instruction Selection*,
DOI 10.1007/978-3-319-34019-7

[9]   P. Aigrain, S. L. Graham, R. R. Henry, M. K. McKusick, and E. Pelegrí-Llopart. "Experience with a Graham-Glanville Style Code Generator". In: *Proceedings of the SIGPLAN Symposium on Compiler Construction*. SIGPLAN'84. Montreal, Canada: ACM, 1984, pp. 13–24. ISBN: 0-89791-139-3

[10] R. Allen and K. Kennedy. "Automatic Translation of FORTRAN Programs to Vector Form". In: *Transactions on Programming Language Systems* 9.4 (1987), pp. 491–542. ISSN: 0164-0925

[11] O. Almer, R. Bennett, I. Böhm, A. Murray, X. Qu, M. Zuluaga, B. Franke, and N. Topham. "An End-to-End Design Flow for Automated Instruction Set Extension and Complex Instruction Selection based on GCC". In: *1st International Workshop on GCC Research Opportunities*. GROW'09. Paphos, Cyprus, 2009, pp. 49–60

[12] U. Ammann, K. V. Nori, K. Jensen, and H. Nägeli. *The PASCAL (P) Compiler Implementation Notes*. Tech. rep. Eidgenössische Technishe Hochschule, Zürich, Switzerland: Instituts für Informatik, 1974

[13] U. Ammann. *On Code Generation in a PASCAL Compiler*. Tech. rep. Eidgenössische Technishe Hochschule, Zürich, Switzerland: Instituts für Informatik, 1977

[14] B. Anckaert, B. Sutter, D. Chanet, and K. Bosschere. "Steganography for Executables and Code Transformation Signatures". In: *Proceedings of the 7th International Conference on Information and Communications Security (ICICS'05)*. Ed. by C. Park and S. Chee. Vol. 3506. Lecture Notes in Computer Science. Springer, 2005, pp. 425–439. ISBN: 978-3-540-26226-8

[15] J. P. Anderson. "A Note on Some Compiling Algorithms". In: *Communications of the ACM* 7.3 (1964), pp. 149–150. ISSN: 0001-0782

[16] P. Andrade. *GNU lightning*. 2015. URL: http://www.gnu.org/software/lightning/ (visited on 2015-06-03)

[17] Anonymous reviewer. *Private feedback*. 2015

[18] A. W. Appel and J. Palsberg. *Modern Compiler Implementation in Java*. 2nd ed. Cambridge, England: Cambridge University Press, 2002. ISBN: 0-521-82060-X

[19] A. Appel, J. Davidson, and N. Ramsey. *The Zephyr Compiler Infrastructure*. Tech. rep. Charlottesville, Virginia, USA: University of Virginia, 1998

[20] P. Arató, S. Juhász, Z. A. Mann, A. Orbán, and D. Papp. "Hardware-Software Partitioning in Embedded System Design". In: *International Symposium on Intelligent Signal Processing*. Washington, District of Colombia, USA: IEEE Computer Society, Sept. 2003, pp. 197–202

[21] G. Araujo and S. Malik. "Optimal Code Generation for Embedded Memory Non-Homogeneous Register Architectures". In: *Proceedings of the 8th International Symposium on System Synthesis*. ISSS'95. Cannes, France: ACM, 1995, pp. 36–41. ISBN: 0-89791-771-5

[22] G. Araujo, S. Malik, and M. T.-C. Lee. "Using Register-Transfer Paths in Code Generation for Heterogeneous Memory-Register Architectures". In: *Proceedings of the 33rd Annual Design Automation Conference*. DAC'96. Las Vegas, Nevada, USA: ACM, 1996, pp. 591–596. ISBN: 0-89791-779-0

[23] *ARM11 MPCore Processor.* ARM DDI 0360F. Version r2p0. ARM. Oct. 15, 2018

[24] *ARM Cortex-M7 Devices: Generic User Guide.* ARM DUI 0646A. ARM. Mar. 19, 2015

[25] M. Arnold. *Matching and Covering with Multiple-Output Patterns.* Tech. rep. 1-68340-44. Delft, The Netherlands: Delft University of Technology, 1999

[26] M. Arnold and H. Corporaal. "Automatic Detection of Recurring Operation Patterns". In: *Proceedings of the 7th International Workshop on Hardware/Software Codesign.* CODES'99. Rome, Italy: ACM, 1999, pp. 22–26. ISBN: 1-58113-132-1

[27] M. Arnold and H. Corporaal. "Designing Domain-Specific Processors". In: *Proceedings of the 9th International Symposium on Hardware/Software Codesign.* CODES'01. Copenhagen, Denmark: ACM, 2001, pp. 61–66. ISBN: 1-58113-364-2

[28] N. Arora, K. Chandramohan, N. Pothineni, and A. Kumar. "Instruction Selection in ASIP Synthesis Using Functional Matching". In: *Proceedings of the 23rd International Conference on VLSI Design.* VLSID'10. Washington, District of Colombia, USA: IEEE Computer Society, 2010, pp. 146–151

[29] M. A. Arslan and K. Kuchcinski. "Instruction Selection and Scheduling for DSP Kernels". In: *Microprocessors and Microsystems* 38.8, Part A (2014), pp. 803–813. ISSN: 0141-9331

[30] M. A. Arslan and K. Kuchcinski. "Instruction Selection and Scheduling for DSP Kernels on Custom Architectures". In: *Proceedings of the 16th EUROMICRO Conference on Digital System Design.* DSD'13. Santander, Cantabria, Spain: IEEE Computer Society, Sept. 4–6, 2013

[31] K. Atasu, G. Dündar, and C. özturan. "An Integer Linear Programming Approach for Identifying Instruction-Set Extensions". In: *Proceedings of the 3rd IEEE/ACM/IFIP International Conference on Hardware/Software Codesign and System Synthesis.* CODES+ISSS'05. Jersey City, New Jersey, USA: ACM, 2005, pp. 172–177. ISBN: 1-59593-161-9

[32] K. Atasu, L. Pozzi, and P. Ienne. "Automatic Application-Specific Instruction-Set Extensions Under Microarchitectural Constraints". In: *Proceedings of the 40th Annual Design Automation Conference.* DAC'03. Anaheim, California, USA: ACM, 2003, pp. 256–261. ISBN: 1-58113-688-9

[33] M. Auslander and M. Hopkins. "An Overview of the PL.8 Compiler". In: *Proceedings of the SIGPLAN Symposium on Compiler Construction.* SIGPLAN'82. Boston, Massachusetts, USA: ACM, 1982, pp. 22–31. ISBN: 0-89791-074-5

[34] M. W. Bailey and J. W. Davidson. "Automatic Detection and Diagnosis of Faults in Generated Code for Procedure Calls". In: *Transactions on Software Engineering* 29.11 (2003), pp. 1031–1042. ISSN: 0098-5589

[35] A. Balachandran, D. M. Dhamdhere, and S. Biswas. "Efficient Retargetable Code Generation Using Bottom-Up Tree Pattern Matching". In: *Computer Languages* 15.3 (1990), pp. 127–140. ISSN: 0096-0551

[36]   M. Balakrishnan, P. C. P. Bhatt, and B. B. Madan. "An Efficient Retargetable Microcode Generator". In: *Proceedings of the 19th Annual Workshop on Microprogramming*. MICRO 19. New York, New York, USA: ACM, 1986, pp. 44–53. ISBN: 0-8186-0736-X

[37]   R. A. Ballance, A. B. MacCabe, and K. J. Ottenstein. "The Program Dependence Web: A Representation Supporting Control-, Data-, and Demand-Driven Interpretation of Imperative Languages". In: *Proceedings of the SIGPLAN Conference on Programming Language Design and Implementation*. SIGPLAN'90. White Plains, New York, USA: ACM, 1990, pp. 257–271. ISBN: 0-89791-364-7

[38]   S. Bansal and A. Aiken. "Automatic Generation of Peephole Superoptimizers". In: *Proceedings of the 12th International Conference on Architectural Support for Programming Languages and Operating Systems*. ASPLOS'06. San Jose, California, USA: ACM, 2006, pp. 394–403

[39]   R. Barik, J. Zhao, and V. Sarkar. "Efficient Selection of Vector Instructions Using Dynamic Programming". In: *Proceedings of the 43rd Annual IEEE/ACM International Symposium on Microarchitecture*. MICRO. Washington, District of Colombia, USA: IEEE Computer Society, 2010, pp. 201–212

[40]   S. Bashford and R. Leupers. "Constraint Driven Code Selection for Fixed-Point DSPs". In: *Proceedings of the 36th Annual ACM/IEEE Design Automation Conference*. DAC'99. New Orleans, Louisiana, USA: ACM, 1999, pp. 817–822. ISBN: 1-58113-109-7

[41]   L. Bauer, M. Shafique, and J. Henkel. "Run-Time Instruction Set Selection in a Transmutable Embedded Processor". In: *Design Automation Conference, 2008. DAC 2008. 45th ACM/IEEE*. Washington, District of Colombia, USA: IEEE Computer Society, June 2008, pp. 56–61

[42]   A. Bednarski and C. Kessler. "Energy-Optimal Integrated VLIW Code Generation". In: *Proceedings of the 11th Workshop on Compilers for Parallel Computers*. CPC'04. Chiemsee, Bavaria, Germany, 2004, pp. 227–238

[43]   A. Bednarski and C. W. Kessler. "Optimal Integrated VLIW Code Generation with Integer Linear Programming". In: *Proceedings of the 12th International Euro-Par Conference*. Vol. 4128. Lecture Notes in Computer Science. Dresden, Germany: Springer, 2006, pp. 461–472

[44]   M. O. Beg. "Combinatorial Problems in Compiler Optimization". Doctoral thesis. Ontario, Canada: University of Waterloo, 2013

[45]   N. Beldiceanu, M. Carlsson, and J. Rampon. *Global Constraint Catalog*. Feb. 24, 2014. URL: http://www.emn.fr/z-info/sdemasse/gccat/ (visited on 2014-04-15)

[46]   E. Bendersky. *A Deeper Look into the LLVM Code Generator: Part 1*. Feb. 25, 2013. URL: http://eli.thegreenplace.net/2013/02/25/a-deeper-look-into-the-llvm-code-generator-part-1/ (visited on 2013-05-10)

[47] R. V. Bennett, A. C. Murray, B. Franke, and N. Topham. "Combining Source-to-Source Transformations and Processor Instruction Set Extensions for the Automated Design-Space Exploration of Embedded Systems". In: *Proceedings of the SIGPLAN/SIGBED Conference on Languages, Compilers, and Tools for Embedded Systems*. LCTES'07. San Diego, California, USA: ACM, 2007, pp. 83–92. ISBN: 978-1-59593-632-5

[48] I. Boehm. *HBURG*. 2007. URL: http://www.bytelabs.org/hburg.html (visited on 2014-02-11)

[49] J. Boender and C. Sacerdoti Coen. "On the Correctness of a Branch Displacement Algorithm". In: *Proceedings of the 20th International Conference on Tools and Algorithms for the Construction and Analysis of Systems (TACAS'14)*. Ed. by E. Ábrahám and K. Havelund. Vol. 8413. Lecture Notes in Computer Science. Springer, 2014, pp. 605–619. ISBN: 978-3-642-54861-1

[50] B. Borchardt. "Code Selection by Tree Series Transducers". In: *Proceedings of the 9th International Conference on Implementation and Application of Automata*. CIAA'04. Sophia Antipolis, France: Springer, 2004, pp. 57–67. ISBN: 978-3-540-24318-2

[51] A. Bougacha. *[LLVMdev] [RFC] Integer Saturation Intrinsics*. 2015-01-14. URL: https://groups.google.com/forum/#!topic/llvm-dev/fHThmnh8zkI (visited on 2015-06-09)

[52] D. Boulytchev. "BURS-Based Instruction Set Selection". In: *Proceedings of the 6th International Andrei Ershov Memorial Conference on Perspectives of Systems Informatics*. PSI'06. Novosibirsk, Russia: Springer, 2007, pp. 431–437. ISBN: 978-3-540-70880-3

[53] D. Boulytchev and D. Lomov. "An Empirical Study of Retargetable Compilers". In: *Proceedings of the 4th International Andrei Ershov Memorial Conference on Perspectives of System Informatics (PSI'01)*. Ed. by D. Bjørner, M. Broy, and A. V. Zamulin. Vol. 2244. Lecture Notes in Computer Science. Springer, 2001, pp. 328–335. ISBN: 978-3-540-43075-9

[54] F. Brandner. "Completeness of Automatically Generated Instruction Selectors". In: *Proceedings of the 21st International Conference on Application-Specific Systems, Architectures and Processors*. ASAP'10. Washington, District of Colombia, USA: IEEE Computer Society, 2010, pp. 175–182

[55] F. Brandner, D. Ebner, and A. Krall. "Compiler Generation from Structural Architecture Descriptions". In: *Proceedings of the International Conference on Compilers, Architecture, and Synthesis for Embedded Systems*. CASES'07. Salzburg, Austria: ACM, 2007, pp. 13–22. ISBN: 978-1-59593-826-8

[56] M. Bravenboer and E. Visser. "Rewriting Strategies for Instruction Selection". In: *Proceedings of the 13th International Conference on Rewriting Techniques and Applications (RTA'02)*. Ed. by S. Tison. Vol. 2378. Lecture Notes in Computer Science. Springer, 2002, pp. 237–251. ISBN: 978-3-540-43916-5

[57]   P. Brisk, A. Kaplan, R. Kastner, and M. Sarrafzadeh. "Instruction Generation and Regularity Extraction for Reconfigurable Processors". In: *Proceedings of the International Conference on Compilers, Architecture, and Synthesis for Embedded Systems*. CASES'02. Grenoble, France: ACM, 2002, pp. 262–269. ISBN: 1-58113-575-0

[58]   P. Brisk, A. Nahapetian, and M. Sarrafzadeh. "Instruction Selection for Compilers That Target Architectures with Echo Instructions". In: *Proceedings of the 8th International Workshop on Software and Compilers for Embedded Systems (SCOPES'04)*. Ed. by H. Schepers. Vol. 3199. Lecture Notes in Computer Science. Springer, 2004, pp. 229–243. ISBN: 978-3-540-23035-9

[59]   P. Brown. "A Survey of Macro Processors". In: *Annual Review in Automatic Programming* 6.2 (1969), pp. 37–88. ISSN: 0066-4138

[60]   J. Bruno and R. Sethi. "Code Generation for a One-Register Machine". In: *Journal of the ACM* 23.3 (1976), pp. 502–510. ISSN: 0004-5411

[61]   S. Buchwald and A. Zwinkau. "Instruction Selection by Graph Transformation". In: *Proceedings of the International Conference on Compilers, Architectures and Synthesis for Embedded Systems*. CASES'10. Scottsdale, Arizona, USA: ACM, 2010, pp. 31–40. ISBN: 978-1-60558-903-9

[62]   J. Cai, R. Paige, and R. Tarjan. "More Efficient Bottom-Up Multi-pattern Matching in Trees". In: *Theoretical Computer Science* 106.1 (1992), pp. 21–60. ISSN: 0304-3975

[63]   P. Canalda, L. Cognard, A. Despland, M. Jourdan, M. Mazaud, D. Parigot, F. Thomasset, and D. de Voluceau. *PAGODE: A Realistic Back-End Generator*. Tech. rep. Rocquencourt, France: INRIA, 1995

[64]   Z. Cao, Y. Dong, and S. Wang. "Compiler Backend Generation for Application Specific Instruction Set Processors". In: *Proceedings of the 9th Asian Symposium on Programming Languages and Systems (APLAS'11)*. Ed. by H. Yang. Vol. 7078. Lecture Notes in Computer Science. Springer, 2011, pp. 121–136. ISBN: 978-3-642-25317-1

[65]   R. Castañeda Lozano, M. Carlsson, F. Drejhammar, and C. Schulte. "Constraint-Based Register Allocation and Instruction Scheduling". In: *Proceedings of the 18th International Conference on the Principles and Practice of Constraint Programming (CP'12)*. Ed. by M. Milano. Vol. 7514. Lecture Notes in Computer Science. Springer, 2012, pp. 750–766. ISBN: 978-3-642-33557-0

[66]   R. Castañeda Lozano, M. Carlsson, G. Hjort Blindell, and C. Schulte. "Combinatorial Spill Code Optimization and Ultimate Coalescing". In: *Proceedings of the 14th SIGPLAN/SIGBED Conference on Languages, Compilers and Tools for Embedded Systems*. LCTES'14. Edinburgh, United Kingdom, 2014, pp. 23–32

[67]   R. G. Cattell. "Automatic Derivation of Code Generators from Machine Descriptions". In: *Transactions on Programming Languages and Systems* 2.2 (1980), pp. 173–190. ISSN: 0164-0925

[68]   R. G. G. Cattell. *A Survey and Critique of Some Models of Code Generation*. Tech. rep. Pittsburgh, Pennsylvania, USA: School of Computer Science, Carnegie Mellon University, 1979

[69] R. G. G. Cattell. "Formalization and Automatic Derivation of Code Generators". AAI7815197. Doctoral thesis. Pittsburgh, Pennsylvania, USA: Carnegie Mellon University, 1978

[70] R. G. Cattell, J. M. Newcomer, and B. W. Leverett. "Code Generation in a Machine-Independent Compiler". In: *Proceedings of the SIGPLAN Symposium on Compiler Construction*. SIGPLAN'79. Denver, Colorado, USA: ACM, 1979, pp. 65–75. ISBN: 0-89791-002-8

[71] P. E. Ceruzzi. *A History of Modern Computing*. 2nd ed, Cambridge, Massachusetts, USA: MIT Press, 2003. ISBN: 978-0262532037

[72] J.-M. Chang and M. Pedram. "Register Allocation and Binding for Low Power". In: *Proceedings of the 32nd Annual ACM/IEEE Design Automation Conference*. DAC'95. San Francisco, California, USA: ACM, 1995, pp. 29–35. ISBN: 0-89791-725-1

[73] D. R. Chase. "An Improvement to Bottom-Up Tree Pattern Matching". In: *Proceedings of the 14th SIGACT-SIGPLAN Symposium on Principles of Programming Languages*. POPL'87. Munich, West Germany: ACM, 1987, pp. 168–177. ISBN: 0-89791-215-2

[74] T. Chen, F. Lai, and R. Shang. "A Simple Tree Pattern Matching Algorithm for Code Generator". In: *Proceedings of the 19th Annual International Conference on Computer Software and Applications*. COMPSAC'95. Dallas, Texas, USA: IEEE Computer Society, 1995, pp. 162–167

[75] D. Cho, A. Ravi, G.-R. Uh, and Y. Paek. "Instruction Re-selection for Iterative Modulo Scheduling on High Performance Multi issue DSPs". In: *Emerging Directions in Embedded and Ubiquitous Computing*. Ed. by X. Zhou, O. Sokolsky, L. Yan, E.-S. Jung, Z. Shao, Y. Mu, D. Lee, D. Kim, Y.-S. Jeong, and C.-Z. Xu. Vol. 4097. Lecture Notes in Computer Science. Springer, 2006, pp. 741–754. ISBN: 978-3-540-36850-2

[76] T. W. Christopher, P. J. Hatcher, and R. C. Kukuk. "Using Dynamic Programming to Generate Optimized Code in a Graham-Glanville Style Code Generator". In: *Proceedings of the SIGPLAN Symposium on Compiler Construction*. SIGPLAN'84. Montreal, Canada: ACM, 1984, pp. 25–36. ISBN: 0-89791-139-3

[77] N. Clark, A. Hormati, S. Mahlke, and S. Yehia. "Scalable Subgraph Mapping for Acyclic Computation Accelerators". In: *Proceedings of the International Conference on Compilers, Architecture and Synthesis for Embedded Systems*. CASES'06. Seoul, Korea: ACM, 2006, pp. 147–157. ISBN: 1-59593-543-6

[78] N. Clark, H. Zhong, and S. Mahlke. "Processor Acceleration Through Automated Instruction Set Customization". In: *Proceedings of the 36th Annual IEEE/ACM International Symposium on Microarchitecture*. MICRO 36. Washington, District of Colombia, USA: IEEE Computer Society, 2003, pp. 129–140. ISBN: 0-7695-2043-X

[79] C. Click and K. D. Cooper. "Combining Analyses, Combining Optimizations". In: *Transactions on Programming Languages and Systems* 17.2 (Mar. 1995), pp. 181–196. ISSN: 0164-0925

[80]   C. Click and M. Paleczny. "A Simple Graph-based Intermediate Representation". In: *Papers from the SIGPLAN Workshop on Intermediate Representations*. IR'95. San Francisco, California, USA: ACM, 1995, pp. 35–49. ISBN: 0-89791-754-5

[81]   R. Cole and R. Hariharan. "Tree Pattern Matching and Subset Matching in Randomized $O(n \log^3 m)$ Time". In: *Proceedings of the 29th Annual Symposium on Theory of Computing*. STOC'97. El Paso, Texas, USA: ACM, 1997, pp. 66–75. ISBN: 0-89791-888-6

[82]   J. Cong, Y. Fan, G. Han, and Z. Zhang. "Application-Specific Instruction Generation for Configurable Processor Architectures". In: *Proceedings of the ACM/SIGDA 12th International Symposium on Field Programmable Gate Arrays*. FPGA'04. Monterey, California, USA: ACM, 2004, pp. 183–189. ISBN: 1-58113-829-6

[83]   M. E. Conway. "Proposal for an UNCOL". In: *Communications of the ACM* 1.10 (1958), pp. 5–8. ISSN: 0001-0782

[84]   S. A. Cook. "The Complexity of Theorem-Proving Procedures". In: *Proceedings of the 3rd Annual Symposium on Theory of Computing*. STOC'71. Shaker Heights, Ohio, USA: ACM, 1971, pp. 151–158

[85]   K. D. Cooper and L. Torczon. *Engineering a Compiler*. 2nd ed. Burlington, Massachusetts, USA: Morgan Kaufmann, 2011. ISBN: 978-0120884780

[86]   L. P. Cordella, P. Foggia, C. Sansone, and M. Vento. "An Improved Algorithm for Matching Large Graphs". In: *Proceedings of the 3rd IAPR-TC15 Workshop on Graph-based Representations in Pattern Recognition*. Springer, 2001, pp. 149–159

[87]   R. Cordone, F. Ferrandi, D. Sciuto, and R. Wolfler Calvo. "An Efficient Heuristic Approach to Solve the Unate Covering Problem". In: *Proceedings of the Conference and exhibition on Design, Automation and Test in Europe*. DATE'00. Washington, District of Colombia, USA: IEEE Computer Society, 2000, pp. 364–371

[88]   T. H. Cormen, C. E. Leiserson, R. L. Rivest, and C. Stein. *Introduction to Algorithms*. 3rd ed. Cambridge, Massachusetts, USA: MIT Press, 2009. ISBN: 978-0262033848

[89]   *CoSy Compilers: Overview of Construction and Operation*. CoSy-8004-construct. ACE Associated Compiler Experts. 2003

[90]   T. Crick, M. Brain, M. Vos, and J. Fitch. "Generating Optimal Code Using Answer Set Programming". In: *Proceedings of the 10th International Conference on Logic Programming and Nonmonotonic Reasoning*. LPNMR'09. Potsdam, Germany: Springer, 2009, pp. 554–559. ISBN: 978-3-642-04237-9

[91]   J. W. Davidson and C. W. Fraser. "Code Selection Through Object Code Optimization". In: *Transactions on Programming Languages and Systems* 6.4 (1984), pp. 505–526. ISSN: 0164-0925

[92]   J. W. Davidson and C. W. Fraser. "Eliminating Redundant Object Code". In: *Proceedings of the 9th SIGPLAN-SIGACT Symposium on Principles of Programming Languages*. POPL'82. Albuquerque, New Mexico, USA: ACM, 1982, pp. 128–132. ISBN: 0-89791-065-6

[93] J. W. Davidson and C. W. Fraser. "The Design and Application of a Retargetable Peephole Optimizer". In: *Transactions on Programming Languages and Systems* 2.2 (1980), pp. 191–202. ISSN: 0164-0925

[94] A. Despland, M. Mazaud, and R. Rakotozafy. "Code Generator Generation Based on Template-Driven Target Term Rewriting". In: *Rewriting Techniques and Applications*. Bordeaux, France: Springer, 1987, pp. 105–120. ISBN: 0-387-17220-3

[95] A. Despland, M. Mazaud, and R. Rakotozafy. "Using Rewriting Techniques to Produce Code Generators and Proving Them Correct". In: *Science of Computer Programming* 15.1 (1990), pp. 15–54. ISSN: 0167-6423

[96] L. P. Deutsch and A. M. Schiffman. "Efficient Implementation of the Smalltalk-80 System". In: *Proceedings of the 11th SIGACT-SIGPLAN Symposium on Principles of Programming Languages*. POPL'84. Salt Lake City, Utah, USA: ACM, 1984, pp. 297–302. ISBN: 0-89791-125-3

[97] J. Dias and N. Ramsey. "Automatically Generating Instruction Selectors Using Declarative Machine Descriptions". In: *Proceedings of the 37th Annual SIGPLAN-SIGACT Symposium on Principles of Programming Languages*. POPL'10. Madrid, Spain: ACM, 2010, pp. 403–416. ISBN: 978-1-60558-479-9

[98] J. Dias and N. Ramsey "Converting Intermediate Code to Assembly Code Using Declarative Machine Descriptions". In: *Proceedings of the 15th International Conference on Compiler Construction*. CC'06. Vienna, Austria: Springer, 2006, pp. 217–231. ISBN: 3-540-33050-X, 978-3-540-33050-9

[99] A. Dold, T. Gaul, V. Vialard, and W. Zimmermann. "ASM-Based Mechanized Verification of Compiler Back-Ends". In: *Proceedings of the 5th International Workshop on Abstract State Machines*. Ed. by U. Glässer and P. H. Schmitt. Magdeburg, Germany, 1998, pp. 50–67

[100] M. K. Donegan, R. E. Noonan, and S. Feyock. "A Code Generator Generator Language". In: *Proceedings of the 1979 SIGPLAN Symposium on Compiler Construction*. SIGPLAN'79. Denver, Colorado, USA: ACM, 1979, pp. 58–64

[101] M. K. Donegan. "An Approach to the Automatic Generation of Code Generators". AAI7321548. Doctoral thesis. Houston, Texas, USA: Rice University, 1973

[102] M. Dorigo and T. Stützle. "Ant Colony Optimization: Overview and Recent Advances". In: *Handbook of Metaheuristics*. Ed. by M. Gendreau and J.-Y. Potvin. 2nd ed. Vol. 146. International Series in Operations Research & Management Science. Springer, 2010. Chap. 8, pp. 227–263. ISBN: 978-1-4419-116-1

[103] M. Dubiner, Z. Galil, and E. Magen. "Faster Tree Pattern Matching". In: *Journal of the ACM* 41.2 (1994), pp. 205–213. ISSN: 0004-5411

[104] J. Earley. "An Efficient Context-Free Parsing Algorithm". In: *Communications of the ACM* 13.2 (1970), pp. 94–102. ISSN: 0001-0782

[105]   D. Ebner, F. Brandner, B. Scholz, A. Krall, P. Wiedermann, and A. Kadlec. "Generalized Instruction Selection Using SSA-Graphs". In: *Proceedings of the SIGPLAN-SIGBED Conference on Languages, Compilers, and Tools for Embedded Systems*. LCTES'08. Tucson, Arizona, USA: ACM, 2008, pp. 31–40. ISBN: 978-1-60558-104-0

[106]   E. Eckstein, O. König, and B. Scholz. "Code Instruction Selection Based on SSA-Graphs". In: *Proceedings of the 7th International Workshop on Software and Compilers for Embedded Systems (SCOPES'03)*. Ed. by A. Krall. Vol. 2826. Lecture Notes in Computer Science. Springer, 2003, pp. 49–65. ISBN: 978-3-540-20145-8

[107]   T. J. Edler von Koch, I. Böhm, and B. Franke. "Integrated Instruction Selection and Register Allocation for Compact Code Generation Exploiting Freeform Mixing of 16- and 32-bit Instructions". In: *Proceedings of the 8th Annual IEEE/ACM International Symposium on Code Generation and Optimization*. CGO'10. Toronto, Ontario, Canada: ACM, 2010, pp. 180–189. ISBN: 978-1-60558-635-9

[108]   M. Elson and S. T. Rake. "Code-Generation Technique for Large-Language Compilers". In: *IBM Systems Journal* 9.3 (1970), pp. 166–188. ISSN: 0018-8670

[109]   H. Emmelmann, F.-W. Schröer, and R. Landwehr. "BEG: A Generator for Efficient Back Ends". In: *Proceedings of the SIGPLAN Conference on Programming Language Design and Implementation*. SIGPLAN'89. Portland, Oregon, USA: ACM, 1989, pp. 227–237. ISBN: 0-89791-306-X

[110]   H. Emmelmann. "Code Selection by Regularly Controlled Term Rewriting". In: *Code Generation—Concepts, Tools, Techniques*. Ed. by R. Giegerich and S. L. Graham. Springer, 1992, pp. 3–29. ISBN: 978-3-540-19757-7

[111]   H. Emmelmann. "Testing Completeness of Code Selector Specifications". In: *Proceedings of the 4th International Conference on Compiler Construction*. CC'92. Springer, 1992, pp. 163–175. ISBN: 3-540-55984-1

[112]   J. Engelfriet, Z. Fülöp, and H. Vogler. "Bottom-Up and Top-Down Tree Series Transformations". In: *Journal of Automata, Languages and Combinatorics* 7.1 (July 2001), pp. 11–70. ISSN: 1430-189X

[113]   D. R. Engler. "VCODE: A Retargetable, Extensible, Very Fast Dynamic Code Generation System". In: *Proceedings of the SIGPLAN Conference on Programming Language Design and Implementation*. SIGPLAN'96. Philadelphia, Pennsylvania, USA: ACM, 1996, pp. 160–170. ISBN: 0-89791-795-2

[114]   D. R. Engler and T. A. Proebsting. "DCG: An Efficient, Retargetable Dynamic Code Generation System". In: *Proceedings of the 6th International Conference on Architectural Support for Programming Languages and Operating Systems*. ASPLOS VI. San Jose, California, USA: ACM, 1994, pp. 263–272. ISBN: 0-89791-660-3

[115]   M. V. Eriksson, O. Skoog, and C. W. Kessler. "Optimal vs. Heuristic Integrated Code Generation for Clustered VLIW Architectures". In: *Proceedings of the 11th International Workshop on Software & Compilers for Embedded Systems*. SCOPES'08. Munich, Germany: ACM, 2008, pp. 11–20

[116]   M. Eriksson and C. Kessler. "Integrated Code Generation for Loops". In: *Transactions on Embedded Computing Systems* 11S.1 (June 2012), 19:1–19:24. ISSN: 1539-9087

[117]   M. A. Ertl. "Optimal Code Selection in DAGs". In: *Proceedings of the 26th SIGPLAN-SIGACT Symposium on Principles of Programming Languages*. POPL'99. San Antonio, Texas, USA: ACM, 1999, pp. 242–249. ISBN: 1-58113-095-3

[118]   M. A. Ertl, K. Casey, and D. Gregg. "Fast and Flexible Instruction Selection with On-Demand Tree-Parsing Automata". In: *Proceedings of the SIGPLAN Conference on Programming Language Design and Implementation*. PLDI'06. Ottawa, Ontario, Canada: ACM, 2006, pp. 52–60. ISBN: 1-59593-320-4

[119]   W. Fan, J. Li, J. Luo, Z. Tan, X. Wang, and Y. Wu. "Incremental Graph Pattern Matching". In: *Proceedings of the SIGMOD International Conference on Management of Data*. SIGMOD'11. Athens, Greece: ACM, 2011, pp. 925–936. ISBN: 978-1-4503-0661-4

[120]   W. Fan, J. Li, S. Ma, N. Tang, Y. Wu, and Y. Wu. "Graph Pattern Matching: From Intractable to Polynomial Time". In: *Proceedings of the VLDB Endowment* 3,1-2 (2010), pp. 264–275. ISSN: 2150-8097

[121]   S. Farfeleder, A. Krall, E. Steiner, and F. Brandner. "Effective Compiler Generation by Architecture Description". In: *Proceedings of the SIGPLAN/SIGBED Conference on Language, Compilers, and Tool support for Embedded Systems*. LCTES'06. Ottawa, Ontario, Canada: ACM, 2006, pp. 145–152. ISBN: 1-59593-362-X

[122]   R. Farrow. "Experience with an Attribute Grammar-based Compiler". In: *Proceedings of the 9th SIGPLAN-SIGACT Symposium on Principles of Programming Languages*. POPL'82. Albuquerque, New Mexico, USA: ACM, 1982, pp. 95–107. ISBN: 0-89791-065-6

[123]   A. Fauth, M. Freericks, and A. Knoll. "Generation of Hardware Machine Models from Instruction Set Descriptions". In: *Proceedings of the Workshop on VLSI Signal Processing*. VI'93. Washington, District of Colombia, USA: IEEE Computer Society, 1993, pp. 242–250

[124]   A. Fauth, J. Van Praet, and M. Freericks. "Describing Instruction Set Processors Using nML". In: *Proceedings of the European Conference on Design and Test*. EDTC'95. Washington, District of Colombia, USA: IEEE Computer Society, 1995, pp. 503–507. ISBN: 0-8186-7039-8

[125]   A. Fauth, G. Hommel, A. Knoll, and C. Müller. "Global Code Selection of Directed Acyclic Graphs". In: *Proceedings of the 5th International Conference on Compiler Construction*. CC'94. Springer, 1994, pp. 128–142. ISBN: 3-540-57877-3

[126]   J. Feldman and D. Gries. "Translator Writing Systems". In: *Communications of the ACM* 11.2 (1968), pp. 77–113. ISSN: 0001-0782

[127]   C. Ferdinand, H. Seidl, and R. Wilhelm. "Tree Automata for Code Selection". In: *Acta Informatica* 31.9 (1994), pp. 741–760. ISSN: 0001-5903

[128] M. Fernández and N. Ramsey. "Automatic Checking of Instruction Specifi-
       cations". In: *Proceedings of the 19th International Conference on Software
       Engineering*. ICSE'97. Boston, Massachusetts, USA: ACM, 1997, pp. 326–
       336. ISBN: 0-89791-914-9

[129] J. Ferrante, K. J. Ottenstein, and J. D. Warren. "The Program Dependence
       Graph and Its Use in Optimization". In: *Transactions on Programming
       Languages and Systems* 9.3 (July 1987), pp. 319–349. ISSN: 0164-0925

[130] C. N. Fischer, R. K. Cytron, and R. J. J. LeBlanc. *Crafting a Compiler*.
       London, England: Pearson, 2009. ISBN: 978-0138017859

[131] A. Floch, C. Wolinski, and K. Kuchcinski. "Combined Scheduling and
       Instruction Selection for Processors with Reconfigurable Cell Fabric". In:
       *Proceedings of the 21st International Conference on Application-Specific
       Systems, Architectures and Processors*. ASAP'10. Washington, District of
       Colombia, USA: IEEE Computer Society, 2010, pp. 167–174

[132] R. W. Floyd. "Algorithm 97: Shortest Path". In: *Communications of the ACM*
       5.6 (1962), p. 345. ISSN: 0001-0782

[133] R. W. Floyd. "An Algorithm for Coding Efficient Arithmetic Operations".
       In: *Communications of the ACM* 4.1 (1961), pp. 42–51. ISSN: 0001-0782

[134] C. W. Fraser. "A Language for Writing Code Generators". In: *Proceedings
       of the SIGPLAN Conference on Programming Language Design and Im-
       plementation*. PLDI'89. Portland, Oregon, USA: ACM, 1989, pp. 238–245.
       ISBN: 0-89791-306-X

[135] C. W. Fraser and A. L. Wendt. "Automatic Generation of Fast Optimizing
       Code Generators". In: *Proceedings of the SIGPLAN Conference on Program-
       ming Language Design and Implementation*. PLDI'88. Atlanta, Georgia,
       USA: ACM, 1988, pp. 79–84. ISBN: 0-89791-269-1

[136] C. W. Fraser. "A Compact, Machine-Independent Peephole Optimizer".
       In: *Proceedings of the 6th SIGACT-SIGPLAN Symposium on Principles of
       Programming Languages*. POPL'79. San Antonio, Texas, USA: ACM, 1979,
       pp. 1–6

[137] C. W. Fraser, D. R. Hanson, and T. A. Proebsting. "Engineering a Simple,
       Efficient Code-Generator Generator". In: *Letters on Programming Languages
       and Systems* 1.3 (1992), pp. 213–226. ISSN: 1057-4514

[138] C. W. Fraser, R. R. Henry, and T. A. Proebsting. "BURG—Fast Optimal
       Instruction Selection and Tree Parsing". In: *SIGPLAN Notices* 27.4 (1992),
       pp. 68–76. ISSN: 0362-1340

[139] C. W. Fraser and T. A. Proebsting. "Finite-State Code Generation". In: *Pro-
       ceedings of the SIGPLAN Conference on Programming Language Design
       and Implementation*. PLDI'99. Atlanta, Georgia, USA: ACM, 1999, pp. 270–
       280. ISBN: 1-58113-094-5

[140] C. W. Fraser. "A Knowledge-Based Code Generator Generator". In: *Proceed-
       ings of the Symposium on Artificial Intelligence and Programming Languages*.
       New York, New York, USA: ACM, 1977, pp. 126–129

[141] C. W. Fraser. "Automatic Generation of Code Generators". Doctoral thesis.
       New Haven, Connecticut, USA: Yale University, 1977

[142] S. Fröhlich, M. Gotschlich, U. Krebelder, and B. Wess. "Dynamic Trellis Diagrams for Optimized DSP Code Generation". In: *Proceedings of the International Symposium on Circuits and Systems*. ISCAS'99. Washington, District of Colombia, USA: IEEE Computer Society, 1999, pp. 492–495

[143] B. Gallagher. *The State of the Art in Graph-Based Pattern Matching*. Tech. rep. UCRL-TR-220300. Livermore, California, USA: Lawrence Livermore National Laboratory, Mar. 31, 2006

[144] C. Galuzzi and K. Bertels. "The Instruction-Set Extension Problem: A Survey". In: *Transactions on Reconfigurable Technology and Systems* 4.2 (May 2011), 18:1–18:28. ISSN: 1936-7406

[145] M. Ganapathi. "Prolog Based Retargetable Code Generation". In: *Computer Languages* 14.3 (1989), pp. 193–204. ISSN: 0096-0551

[146] M. Ganapathi. "Retargetable Code Generation and Optimization Using Attribute Grammars". AAI8107834. Doctoral thesis. Madison, Wisconsin, USA: The University of Wisconsin–Madison, 1980

[147] M. Ganapathi and C. N. Fischer. "Affix Grammar Driven Code Generation". In: *Transactions on Programming Languages and Systems* 7.4 (1985), pp. 560–599. ISSN: 0164-0925

[148] M. Ganapathi and C. N. Fischer. "Description-Driven Code Generation Using Attribute Grammars". In: *Proceedings of the 9th SIGPLAN-SIGACT Symposium on Principles of Programming Languages*. POPL'82. Albuquerque, New Mexico, USA: ACM, 1982, pp. 108–119. ISBN: 0-89791-065-6

[149] M. Ganapathi and C. N. Fischer. *Instruction Selection by Attributed Parsing*. Tech. rep. No. 84-256. Stanford, California, USA: Stanford University, 1984

[150] M. Ganapathi, C. N. Fischer, and J. L. Hennessy. "Retargetable Compiler Code Generation". In: *Computing Surveys* 14.4 (1982), pp. 573–592. ISSN: 0360-0300

[151] M. R. Garey and D. S. Johnson. *Computers and Intractability*. New York, New York, USA: W. H. Freeman and Company, 1979

[152] C. H. Gebotys. "An Efficient Model for DSP Code Generation: Performance, Code Size, Estimated Energy". In: *Proceedings of the 10th International Symposium on System Synthesis*. ISSS'97. Antwerp, Belgium: IEEE Computer Society, 1997, pp. 41–47. ISBN: 0-8186-7949-2

[153] C. H. Gebotys. "Low Energy Memory and Register Allocation Using Network Flow". In: *Proceedings of the 34th Annual Design Automation Conference*. DAC'97. Anaheim, California, USA: ACM, 1997, pp. 435–440. ISBN: 0-89791-920-3

[154] F. Gecseg and M. Steinby. *Tree Automata*. Budapest, Hungary: Akadémiai Kiadó, 1984. ISBN: 978-96305317-02

[155] D. Genin, J. De Moortel, D. Desmet, and E. Van de Velde. "System Design, Optimization and Intelligent Code Generation for Standard Digital Signal Processors". In: *Proceedings of the International Symposium on Circuits and Systems*. ISCAS'90. Washington, District of Colombia, USA: IEEE Computer Society, 1989, pp. 565–569

[156]   R. Giegerich. "A Formal Framework for the Derivation of Machine-Specific Optimizers". In: *Transactions on Programming Languages and Systems* 5.3 (1983), pp. 478–498. ISSN: 0164-0925

[157]   R. Giegerich and K. Schmal. "Code Selection Techniques: Pattern Matching, Tree Parsing, and Inversion of Derivors". In: *Proceedings of the 2nd European Symposium on Programming*. Ed. by H. Ganzinger. Vol. 300. ESOP'88. Nancy, France: Springer, 1998, pp. 247–268. ISBN: 978-3-540-19027-1

[158]   R. S. Glanville and S. L. Graham. "A New Method for Compiler Code Generation". In: *Proceedings of the 5th SIGACT-SIGPLAN Symposium on Principles of Programming Languages*. POPL'78. Tucson, Arizona, USA: Springer, 1978, pp. 231–254

[159]   E. I. Goldberg, L. P. Carloni, T. Villa, R. K. Brayton, and A. L. Sangiovanni-Vincentelli. "Negative Thinking in Branch-and-Bound: The Case of Unate Covering". In: *Transactions of Computer-Aided Design of Integrated Ciruits and Systems* 19.3 (2006), pp. 281–294. ISSN: 0278-0070

[160]   K. J. Gough. *Bottom-Up Tree Rewriting Tool MBURG*. Tech. rep. Brisbane, Australia: Faculty of Information Technology, Queensland University of Technology, July 18, 1995

[161]   K. J. Gough and J. Ledermann. "Optimal Code-Selection using MBURG". In: *Proceedings of the 20th Australasian Computer Science Conference*. ACSC'97. Sydney, Australia, 1997

[162]   K. Gough. "Reconceptualizing Bottom-Up Tree Rewriting". In: *Patterns, Programming and Everything*. Ed. by K. K. Breitman and R. N. Horspool. Springer, 2012, pp. 31–44. ISBN: 978-1-4471-2349-1

[163]   S. L. Graham. "Table-Driven Code Generation". In: *Computer* 13.8 (1980), pp. 25–34. ISSN: 0018-9162

[164]   S. L. Graham, R. R. Henry, and R. A. Schulman. "An Experiment in Table Driven Code Generation". In: *Proceedings of the SIGPLAN Symposium on Compiler Construction*. SIGPLAN'82. Boston, Massachusetts, USA: ACM, 1982, pp. 32–43. ISBN: 0-89791-074-5

[165]   T. Granlund and R. Kenner. "Eliminating Branches Using a Superoptimizer and the GNU C Compiler". In: *Proceedings of the SIGPLAN Conference on Programming Language Design and Implementation*. PLDI'92. San Francisco, California, USA: ACM, 1992, pp. 341–352. ISBN: 0-89791-4759

[166]   Y. Guo, G. J. Smit, H. Broersma, and P. M. Heysters. "A Graph Covering Algorithm for a Coarse Grain Reconfigurable System". In: *Proceedings of the SIGPLAN Conference on Language, Compiler, and Tools for Embedded Systems*. LCTES'03. San Diego, California, USA: ACM, 2003, pp. 199–208. ISBN: 1-58113-647-1

[167]   S. Z. Hanono. "AVIV: A Retargetable Code Generator for Embedded Processors". AAI7815197. Doctoral thesis. Cambridge, Massachusetts, USA: Massachusetts Institute of Technology, 1999

[168] S. Hanono and S. Devadas. "Instruction Selection, Resource Allocation, and
       Scheduling in the AVIV Retargetable Code Generator". In: *Proceedings of
       the 35th Annual Design Automation Conference*. DAC'98. San Francisco,
       California, USA: ACM, 1998, pp. 510–515. ISBN: 0-89791-964-5

[169] D. R. Hanson and C. W. Fraser. *A Retargetable C Compiler: Design
       and Implementation*. Boston, Massachusetts, USA: Addison-Wesley, 1995.
       ISBN: 978-0805316704

[170] W. H. Harrison. "A New Strategy for Code Generation the General-Purpose
       Optimizing Compiler". In: *Transactions Software Engineering* 5.4 (1979),
       pp. 367–373. ISSN: 0098-5589

[171] T. Harwood, K. Kumar, and N. Bereton. *JBURG*. 2013. URL: http://
       jburg.sourceforge.net/ (visited on 2014-02-11)

[172] P. J. Hatcher and T. W. Christopher. "High-Quality Code Generation via
       Bottom-Up Tree Pattern Matching". In: *Proceedings of the 13th SIGACT-
       SIGPLAN Symposium on Principles of Programming Languages*. POPL'86.
       St. Petersburg Beach, Florida, USA: ACM, 1986, pp. 119–130

[173] P. Hatcher. "The Equational Specification of Efficient Compiler Code Gener-
       ation". In: *Computer Languages* 16.1 (1991), pp. 81–95. ISSN: 0096-0551

[174] P. Hatcher and J. W. Tuller. "Efficient Retargetable Compiler Code Gen-
       eration". In: *Proceedings for the International Conference on Computer
       Languages*. Miami Beach, Florida, USA: IEEE Computer Society, 1988,
       pp. 25–30. ISBN: 0-8186-0874-9

[175] J. L. Hennessy and D. A. Patterson. *Computer Architecture: A Quantitative
       Approach*. 5th ed. Burlington, Massachusetts, USA: Morgan Kaufmann, 2011

[176] R. R. Henry. *Encoding Optimal Pattern Selection in Table-Driven Bottom-
       Up Tree-Pattern Matcher*. Tech. rep. 89-02-04. Seattle, Washington, USA:
       University of Washington, 1989

[177] R. R. Henry. "Graham-Glanville Code Generators". UCB/CSD-84-184. Doc-
       toral thesis. Berkeley, California, USA: EECS Department, University of
       California, May 1984

[178] T. Hino, Y. Suzuki, T. Uchida, and Y. Itokawa. "Polynomial Time Pattern
       Matching Algorithm for Ordered Graph Patterns". In: *Proceedings of the
       22nd International Conference on Inductive Logic Programming*. ILP'12.
       Dubrovnik, Croatia: Springer, 2012, pp. 86–101

[179] C. M. Hoffmann and M. J. O'Donnell. "Pattern Matching in Trees". In:
       Journal of the ACM 29.1 (1982), pp. 68–95. ISSN: 0004-5411

[180] M. Hohenauer, C. Schumacher, R. Leupers, G. Ascheid, H. Meyr, and H.
       van Someren. "Retargetable Code Optimization with SIMD Instructions".
       In: *Proceedings of the 4th International Conference on Hardware/Software
       Codesign and System Synthesis*. CODES+ISSS'06. Seoul, Korea: ACM,
       2006, pp. 148–153. ISBN: 1-59593-370-0

[181] J. N. Hooker. "Resolution vs. Cutting Plane Solution of Inference Problems:
       Some Computational Experience". In: *Operations Research Letters* 7.1 (Feb.
       1988), pp. 1–7. ISSN: 0167-6377

[182]   R. Hoover and K. Zadeck. "Generating Machine Specific Optimizing Compilers". In: *Proceedings of the 23rd SIGPLAN-SIGACT Symposium on Principles of Programming Languages*. POPL'96. St. Petersburg Beach, Florida, USA: ACM, 1996, pp. 219–229. ISBN: 0-89791-769-3

[183]   A. Hormati, N. Clark, and S. Mahlke. "Exploiting Narrow Accelerators with Data-Centric Subgraph Mapping". In: *Proceedings of the International Symposium on Code Generation and Optimization*. CGI'07. Washington, District of Colombia, USA: IEEE Computer Society, 2007, pp. 341–353

[184]   R. N. Horspool. "An Alternative to the Graham-Glanville Code-Generation Method". In: *Software* 4.3 (May 1987), pp. 33–39. ISSN: 0740-7459

[185]   I. Huang and A. M. Despain. "Synthesis of Application Specific Instruction Sets". In: *Transactions on Computer Aided Design of Integrated Circuits and Systems* 14.6 (June 1995), pp. 663–675

[186]   *Intel 64 and IA-32 Architectures: Software Developer's Manual*. Intel. Apr. 2015

[187]   J. Janoušek and J. Málek. "Target Code Selection by Tilling AST with the Use of Tree Pattern Pushdown Automaton". In: *Proceedings of the 3rd Symposium on Languages, Applications and Technologies*. Ed. by M. J. V. Pereira, J. P. Leal, and A. Simões. Vol. 38. SLATE'14. Dagstuhl, Germany: Schloss Dagstuhl–Leibniz-Zentrum fuer Informatik, 2014, pp. 159–165. ISBN: 978-3-939897-68-2

[188]   X. Jiang and H. Bunke. "On the Coding of Ordered Graphs". In: *Computing* 61.1 (1998), pp. 23–38. ISSN: 0010-485X

[189]   X. Jiang and H. Bunke. "Marked Subgraph Isomorphism of Ordered Graphs". In: *Advances in Pattern Recognition*. Ed. by A. Amin, D. Dori, P. Pudil, and H. Freeman. Vol. 1451. Lecture Notes in Computer Science. Springer, 1998, pp. 122–131. ISBN: 978-3-540-64858-1

[190]   X. Jiang and H. Bunke. "Including Geometry in Graph Representations: A Quadratic-Time Graph Isomorphism Algorithm and Its Applications". In: *Advances in Structural and Syntactical Pattern Recognition*. Ed. by P. Perner, P. Wang, and A. Rosenfeld. Vol. 1121. Lecture Notes in Computer Science. Springer, 1996, pp. 110–119. ISBN: 978-3-540-61577-4

[191]   S. C. Johnson. "A Portable Compiler: Theory and Practice". In: *Proceedings of the 5th SIGACT-SIGPLAN Symposium on Principles of Programming Languages*. POPL'78. Tucson, Arizona, USA: ACM, 1978, pp. 97–104

[192]   S. C. Johnson. "A Tour Through the Portable C Compiler". In: *Unix Programmer's Manual*. 7th ed. Vol. 2B. Murray Hill, New Jersey, USA: AT&T Bell Laboratories, 1981. Chap. 33

[193]   R. Joshi, G. Nelson, and K. Randall. "Denali: A Goal-Directed Superoptimizer". In: *Proceedings of the SIGPLAN Conference on Programming Language Design and Implementation*. PLDI'02. Berlin, Germany: ACM, 2002, pp. 304–314. ISBN: 1-58113-463-0

[194]   R. Joshi, G. Nelson, and Y. Zhou. "Denali: A Practical Algorithm for Generating Optimal Code". In: *Transactions on Programming Languages and Systems* 28.6 (2006), pp. 967–989. ISSN: 0164-0925

[195] K. Kang. "A Study on Generating an Efficient Bottom-Up Tree Rewrite Machine for JBURG". In: *Proceedings of the International Conference on Computational Science and Its Applications (ICCSA'04)*. Ed. by A. Laganá, M. Gavrilova, V. Kumar, Y. Mun, C. Tan, and O. Gervasi. Vol. 3043. Lecture Notes in Computer Science. Assisi, Italy: Springer, 2004, pp. 65–72. ISBN: 978-3-540-22054-1

[196] K. Kang and K. Choe. *On the Automatic Generation of Instruction Selector Using Bottom-Up Tree Pattern Matching*. Tech. rep. CS/TR-95-93. Daejeon, South Korea: Korea Advanced Institute of Science and Technology, 1995

[197] R. M. Karp, R. E. Miller, and A. L. Rosenberg. "Rapid Identification of Repeated Patterns in Strings, Trees and Arrays". In: *Proceedings of the 4th Annual Symposium on Theory of Computing*. STOC'72. Denver, Colorado, USA: ACM, 1972, pp. 125–136

[198] R. Kastner, A. Kaplan, S. O. Memik, and E. Bozorgzadeh. "Instruction Generation for Hybrid Reconfigurable Systems". In: *Transactions on Design Automation of Electronic Systems* 7.4 (2002), pp. 605–627. ISSN: 1084-4309

[199] C. W. Kessler and A. Bednarski. "A Dynamic Programming Approach to Optimal Integrated Code Generation". In: *Proceedings of the Conference on Languages, Compilers, and Tools for Embedded Systems*. LCTES'01. New York, New York, USA: ACM, 2001, pp. 165–174

[200] C. W. Kessler and A. Bednarski. "Optimal Integrated Code Generation for Clustered VLIW Architectures". In: *Proceedings of the SIGPLAN Joint Conference on Languages, Compilers, and Tools for Embedded Systems and Software and Compilers for Embedded Systems*. LCTES/SCOPES'02. New York, New York, USA: ACM, 2002, pp. 102–111

[201] P. B. Kessler. "Discovering Machine-Specific Code Improvements". In: *Proceedings of the SIGPLAN Symposium on Compiler Construction*. SIGPLAN'86. Palo Alto, California, USA: ACM, 1986, pp. 249–254. ISBN: 0-89791-197-0

[202] R. R. Kessler. "PEEP: An Architectural Description Driven Peephole Optimizer". In: *Proceedings of the SIGPLAN Symposium on Compiler Construction*. SIGPLAN'84. Montreal, Canada: ACM, 1984, pp. 106–110. ISBN: 0-89791-139-3

[203] K. Keutzer. "DAGON: Technology Binding and Local Optimization by DAG Matching". In: *Proceedings of the 24th ACM/IEEE Design Automation Conference*. DAC'87. New York, New York, USA: ACM, 1987, pp. 341–347

[204] R. El-Khalil and A. D. Keromytis. "Hydan: Hiding Information in Program Binaries". In: *Proceedings of the 6th International Conference on Information and Communications Security (ICICS'04)*. Ed. by J. Lopez, S. Qing, and E. Okamoto. Vol. 3269. Lecture Notes in Computer Science. Springer, 2004, pp. 187–199. ISBN: 978-3-540-23563-7

[205] U. Khedker. "Workshop on Essential Abstractions in GCC". Lecture. GCC Resource Center, Department of Computer Science and Engineering, IIT Bombay. Bombay, India, June 30–July 3, 2012

[206]   S. Kim and H. Han. "Efficient SIMD Code Generation for Irregular Kernels". In: *Proceedings of the 17th SIGPLAN Symposium on Principles and Practice of Parallel Programming*. PPoPP'12. New Orleans, Louisiana, USA: ACM, 2012, pp. 55–64. ISBN: 978-1-4503-1160-1

[207]   S. Kirkpatrick, C. D. Gelatt, and M. P. Vecchi. "Optimization by Simulated Annealing". In: *Science* 220.4598 (1983), pp. 671–680

[208]   D. E. Knuth. "On the Translation of Languages From Left to Right". In: *Information and Control* 8 (6 Dec. 1965), pp. 607–639

[209]   D. E. Knuth. "Semantics of Context-Free Languages". In: *Mathematical Systems Theory* 2.2 (1968), pp. 127–145

[210]   D. E. Knuth, J. H. J. Morris, and V. R. Pratt. "Fast Pattern Matching in Strings". In: *SIAM Journal of Computing* 6.2 (1977), pp. 323–350. ISSN: 0097-5397

[211]   D. Koes. "Towards a More Principled Compiler: Register Allocation and Instruction Selection Revisited". Doctoral thesis. Pittsburgh, Pennsylvania, USA: Carnegie Mellon University, 2009

[212]   D. R. Koes and S. C. Goldstein. "Near-Optimal Instruction Selection on DAGs". In: *Proceedings of the 6th Annual IEEE/ACM International Symposium on Code Generation and Optimization*. CGO'08. Boston, Massachusetts, USA: ACM, 2008, pp. 45–54. ISBN: 978-1-59593-978-4

[213]   M. Kong, R. Veras, K. Stock, F. Franchetti, L.-N. Pouchet, and P. Sadayappan. "When Polyhedral Transformations Meet SIMD Code Generation". In: *Proceedings of the 34th SIGPLAN Conference on Programming Language Design and Implementation*. PLDI'13. Seattle, Washington, USA: ACM, 2013, pp. 127–138. ISBN: 978-1-4503-2014-6

[214]   A. Krall and S. Lelait. "Compilation Techniques for Multimedia Processors". In: *International Journal of Parallel Programming* 28.4 (2000), pp. 347–361. ISSN: 0885-7458

[215]   W. Kreuzer, W. Gotschlich, and B. Wess. "REDACO: A Retargetable Data Flow Graph Compiler for Digital Signal Processors". In: *Proceedings of the International Conference on Signal Processing Applications and Technology*. ICSPAT'96. Alameda, California, USA: Miller Freeman, 1996, pp. 742–746

[216]   A. Krishnaswamy and R. Gupta. "Profile Guided Selection of ARM and Thumb Instructions". In: *Proceedings of the Joint Conference on Languages, Compilers and Tools for Embedded Systems: Software and Compilers for Embedded Systems*. LCTES/SCOPES'02. Berlin, Germany: ACM, 2002, pp. 56–64. ISBN: 1-58113-527-0

[217]   E. B. Krissinel and K. Henrick. "Common Subgraph Isomorphism Detection by Backtracking Search". In: *Software–Practice & Experience* 34.6 (2004), pp. 591–607. ISSN: 0038-0644

[218]   D. W. Krumme and D. H. Ackley. "A Practical Method for Code Generation Based on Exhaustive Search". In: *Proceedings of the SIGPLAN Symposium on Compiler Construction*. SIGPLAN'82. Boston, Massachusetts, USA: ACM, 1982, pp. 185–196. ISBN: 0-89791-074-5

[219]   P. Kulkarni, W. Zhao, S. Hines, D. Whalley, X. Yuan, R. v. Engelen, K. Gallivan, J. Hiser, J. Davidson, B. Cai, M. Bailey, H. Moon, K. Cho, and Y. Paek. "VISTA: VPO Interactive System for Tuning Applications". In: *Transactions on Embedded Computer Systems* 5.4 (Nov. 2006), pp. 819–863. ISSN: 1539-9087

[220]   R. Landwehr, H.-S. Jansohn, and G. Goos. "Experience with an Automatic Code Generator Generator". In: *Proceedings of the 1982 SIGPLAN Symposium on Compiler Construction*. SIGPLAN'82. Boston, Massachusetts, USA: ACM, 1982, pp. 56–66. ISBN: 0-89791-074-5

[221]   M. Langevin and E. Cerny. "An Automata-Theoretic Approach to Local Microcode Generation". In: *Proceedings of the 4th European Conference on Design Automation with the European Event in ASIC Design*. EDAC'93. Washington, District of Colombia, USA: IEEE Computer Society, 1993, pp. 94–98

[222]   D. Lanneer, F. Catthoor, G. Goossens, M. Pauwels, J. Van Meerbergen, and H. De Man. "Open-Ended System for High-Level Synthesis of Flexible Signal Processors". In: *Proceedings of the Conference on European Design Automation*. EURO-DAC'90. Glasgow, Scotland: IEEE Computer Society, 1990, pp. 272–276. ISBN: 0-8186-2024-2

[223]   S. Larsen and S. Amarasinghe. "Exploiting Superword Level Parallelism with Multimedia Instruction Sets". In: *Proceedings of the ACM SIGPLAN Conference on Programming Language Design and Implementation*. PLDI'00. Vancouver, British Columbia, Canada: ACM, 2000, pp. 145–156. ISBN: 1-58113-199-2

[224]   C. Lattner and V. Adve. "LLVM: A Compilation Framework for Lifelong Program Analysis & Transformation". In: *Proceedings of the International Symposium on Code Generation and Optimization: Feedback-Directed and Runtime Optimization*. CGO'04. Palo Alto, California, USA: IEEE Computer Society, 2004, pp. 75–86. ISBN: 0-7695-2102-9

[225]   C. Lee, J. K. Lee, T. Hwang, and S. Tsai. "Compiler Optimization on VLIW Instruction Scheduling for Low Power". In: *Transactions on Design Automation of Electronic Systems* 8.2 (Apr. 2003), pp. 252–268. ISSN: 1084-4309

[226]   R. Leupers and P. Marwedel. "Instruction Selection for Embedded DSPs with Complex Instructions". In: *Proceedings of the Conference on European Design Automation*. EURO-DAC/EURO-VHDL'96. Geneva, Switzerland: IEEE Computer Society, 1996, pp. 200–205. ISBN: 0-8186-7573-X

[227]   R. Leupers. "Code Generation for Embedded Processors". In: *Proceedings of the 13th International Symposium on System Synthesis*. ISSS'00. Madrid, Spain: IEEE Computer Society, 2000, pp. 173–178. ISBN: 1-58113-267-0

[228]   R. Leupers. "Code Selection for Media Processors with SIMD Instructions". In: *Proceedings of the Conference on Design, Automation and Test in Europe*. DATE'00. Paris, France: ACM, 2000, pp. 4–8. ISBN: 1-58113-244-1

[229]   R. Leupers and S. Bashford. "Graph-Based Code Selection Techniques for Embedded Processors". In: *Transactions on Design Automation of Electronic Systems* 5 (4 2000), pp. 794–814. ISSN: 1084-4309

[230] R. Leupers and P. Marwedel. "Retargetable Code Generation Based on Structural Processor Description". In: *Design Automation for Embedded Systems* 3.1 (1998), pp. 75–108. ISSN: 0929-5585

[231] R. Leupers and P. Marwedel. *Retargetable Compiler Technology for Embedded Systems*. Dordrecht, Netherlands: Kluwer Academic Publishers, 2001. ISBN: 0-7923-7578-5

[232] R. Leupers and P. Marwedel. "Retargetable Generation of Code Selectors from HDL Processor Models". In: *Proceedings of the European Design and Test Conference*. EDTC'97. Paris, France: IEEE Computer Society, 1997, pp. 140–144

[233] R. Leupers and P. Marwedel. "Time-Constrained Code Compaction for DSPs". In: *Proceedings of the 8th International Symposium on System Synthesis*. ISSS'95. Cannes, France: ACM, 1995, pp. 54–59. ISBN: 0-89791-771-5

[234] B. W. Leverett, R. G. G. Cattell, S. O. Hobbs, J. M. Newcomer, A. H. Reiner, B. R. Schatz, and W. A. Wulf. "An Overview of the Production-Quality Compiler-Compiler Project". In: *Computer* 13.8 (1980), pp. 38–49. ISSN: 0018-9162

[235] S. Liao, K. Keutzer, S. Tjiang, and S. Devadas. "A New Viewpoint on Code Generation for Directed Acyclic Graphs". In: *Transactions on Design Automation of Electronic Systems* 3.1 (1998), pp. 51–75. ISSN: 1084-4309

[236] S. Liao, S. Devadas, K. Keutzer, and S. Tjiang. "Instruction Selection Using Binate Covering for Code Size Optimization". In: *Proceedings of the IEEE/ACM International Conference on Computer-Aided Design*. ICCAD'95. San Jose, California, USA: IEEE Computer Society, 1995, pp. 393–399. ISBN: 0-8186-7213-7

[237] C. Liem, T. May, and P. Paulin. "Instruction-Set Matching and Selection for DSP and ASIP Code Generation". In: *Proceedings of European Design and Test Conference (EDAC/ETC/EUROASIC'94)*. Washington, District of Colombia, USA: IEEE Computer Society, 1994, pp. 31–37

[238] C. Lindig and N. Ramsey. *OCamlBURG*. 2006. URL: http://www.cminusminus.org/ (visited on 2014-02-11)

[239] J. Liu, Y. Zhang, O. Jang, W. Ding, and M. Kandemir. "A Compiler Framework for Extracting Superword Level Parallelism". In: *Proceedings of the 33rd ACM SIGPLAN Conference on Programming Language Design and Implementation*. PLDI'12. Beijing, China: ACM, 2012, pp. 347–358. ISBN: 978-1-4503-1205-9

[240] E. M. Loiola, N. M. Maia de Abreu, P. O. Boaventura-Netto, P. Hahn, and T. Querido. "A Survey for the Quadratic Assignment Problem". In: *European Journal of Operational Research* 176.2 (2007), pp. 657–690. ISSN: 0377-2217

[241] M. Lorenz, R. Leupers, P. Marwedel, T. Drager, and G. Fettweis. "Low-Energy DSP Code Generation Using a Genetic Algorithm". In: *Proceedings of the International Conference on Cmoputer Design*. ICCD'01. Washington, District of Colombia, USA: IEEE Computer Society, 2001, pp. 431–437

[242] M. Lorenz and P. Marwedel. "Phase Coupled Code Generation for DSPs Using a Genetic Algorithm". In: *Proceedings of the 9th Conference and Exhibition on Design, Automation and Test in Europe.* Vol. 2. DATE'04. Washington, District of Colombia, USA: IEEE Computer Society, Feb. 2004, pp. 1270–1275

[243] E. S. Lowry and C. W. Medlock. "Object Code Optimization". In: *Communications of the ACM* 12.1 (1969), pp. 13–22. ISSN: 0001-0782

[244] H. Lunell. "Code Generator Writing Systems". No. 94. Doctoral thesis. Linköping, Sweden: Linkoping University, 1983

[245] M. Madhavan, P. Shankar, S. Rai, and U. Ramakrishna. "Extending Graham-Glanville Techniques for Optimal Code Generation". In: *Transactions on Programming Languages and Systems* 22.6 (2000), pp. 973–1001. ISSN: 0164-0925

[246] M. Mahmood, F. Mavaddat, and M. Elmastry. "Experiments with an Efficient Heuristic Algorithm for Local Microcode Generation". In: *Proceedings of the International Conference on Computer Design: VLSI in Computers and Processors.* ICCD'90. Washington, District of Colombia, USA: IEEE Computer Society, 1990, pp. 319–323

[247] I. J. Maltz. "Implementation of a Code Generator Preprocessor". MA thesis. Berkeley, California, USA: University of California, 1978

[248] K. Martin, C. Wolinski, K. Kuchcinski, A. Floch, and F. Charot. "Constraint Programming Approach to Reconfigurable Processor Extension Generation and Application Compilation". In: *Transactions on Reconfigurable Technology and Systems* 5.2 (2012), 10:1–10:38. ISSN: 1936-7406

[249] K. Martin, C. Wolinski, K. Kuchcinski, A. Floch, and F. Charot. "Constraint-Driven Instructions Selection and Application Scheduling in the DURASE System". In: *Proceedings of the 20th International Conference on Application-Specific Systems, Architectures and Processors.* ASAP'09. Washington, District of Colombia, USA: IEEE Computer Society, 2009, pp. 145–152. ISBN: 978-0-7695-3732-0

[250] P. Marwedel. "Code Generation for Core Processors". In: *Proceedings of the Design Automation Conference.* DAC'97. Anaheim, California, USA: IEEE Computer Society, 1997, pp. 232–237. ISBN: 0-7803-4093-0

[251] P. Marwedel. "The MIMOLA Design System: Tools for the Design of Digital Processors". In: *Proceedings of the 21st Design Automation Conference.* DAC'84. Albuquerque, New Mexico, USA: IEEE Computer Society, 1984, pp. 587–593. ISBN: 0-8186-0542-1

[252] P. Marwedel. "Tree-Based Mapping of Algorithms to Predefined Structures". In: *Proceedings of the IEEE/ACM International Conference on Computer-Aided Design.* ICCAD'93. Santa Clara, California, USA: IEEE Computer Society, 1993, pp. 586–593. ISBN: 0-8186-4490-7

[253]   H. Massalin. "Superoptimizer: A Look at the Smallest Program". In: *Proceedings of the 2nd International Conference on Architectual Support for Programming Languages and Operating Systems*. ASPLOS II. Palo Alto, California, USA: IEEE Computer Society, 1987, pp. 122–126. ISBN: 0-8186-0805-6

[254]   W. M. McKeeman. "Peephole Optimization". In: *Communications of the ACM* 8.7 (July 1965), pp. 443–444. ISSN: 0001-0782

[255]   P. L. Miller. "Automatic Creation of a Code Generator from a Machine Description". MA thesis. Cambridge, Massachusetts, USA: Massachusetts Institute of Technology, 1971

[256]   S. Mouthuy, Y. Deville, and G. Dooms. "Global Constraint for the Set Covering Problem". In: *Proceedings of the 3rd French-Speaking Conference on Constraint Programming*. JFPC'07. INRIA, Domaine de Voluceau, Rocquencourt, Yvelines, France, June 2007, pp. 183–192

[257]   S. Muchnick. *Advanced Compiler Design & Implementation*. Burlington, Massachusetts, USA: Morgan Kaufmann, 1997. ISBN: 978-1558603202

[258]   C. Müller. *Code Selection from Directed Acyclic Graphs in the Context of Domain Specific Digital Signal Processors*. Tech. rep. Berlin, Germany: Humboldt-Universität, 1994

[259]   A. C. Murray. "Customising Compilers for Customisable Processors". Doctoral thesis. Edinburgh, Scotland: University of Edinburgh, 2012

[260]   A. Murray and B. Franke. "Compiling for Automatically Generated Instruction Set Extensions". In: *Proceedings of the 10th International Symposium on Code Generation and Optimization*. CGO'12. San Jose, California, USA: ACM, 2012, pp. 13–22. ISBN: 978-1-4503-1206-6

[261]   M. Mutyam, F. Li, V. Narayanan, M. Kandemir, and M. J. Irwin. "Compiler-Directed Thermal Management for VLIW Functional Units". In: *Proceedings of the SIGPLAN/SIGBED Conference on Language, Compilers, and Tool Support for Embedded Systems*. LCTES'06. Ottawa, Ontario, Canada: ACM, 2006, pp. 163–172. ISBN: 1-59593-362-X

[262]   I. Nakata. "On Compiling Algorithms for Arithmetic Expressions". In: *Communications of the ACM* 10.8 (1967), pp. 492–494. ISSN: 0001-0782

[263]   J. M. Newcomer. "Machine-Independent Generation of Optimal Local Code". Order number: AAI7521781. Doctoral thesis. Pittsburgh, Pennsylvania, USA: Carnegie Mellon University, 1975

[264]   A. Newell and H. A. Simon. *The Simulation of Human Thought*. Tech. rep. Santa Monica, California, USA: Mathematics Devision, RAND Corporation, June 1959

[265]   A. Nicolau and S. Novack. "An Efficient Global Resource Constrained Technique for Exploiting Instruction Level Parallelism". In: *Proceedings of the International Conference on Parallel Processing*. Ed. by K. G. Shin. Vol. 2. ICPP'92. University of Michigan, Ann Arbor, Michigan, USA, 1992, pp. 297–301

[266] R. Niemann and P. Marwedel. "An Algorithm for Hardware/Software Parti-
       tioning Using Mixed Integer Linear Programming". In: *Design Automation
       for Embedded Systems* 2.2 (1997), pp. 165–193. ISSN: 0929-5585

[267] S. Novack, A. Nicolau, and N. Dutt. "A Unified Code Generation Approach
       Using Mutation Scheduling". In: *Code Generation for Embedded Processors*.
       Ed. by P. Marwedel and G. Goossens. Vol. 317. Springer, 2002. Chap. 12,
       pp. 203–218. ISBN: 978-1-4613-5983-8

[268] S. Novack and A. Nicolau. "Mutation Scheduling: A Unified Approach to
       Compiling for Fine-Grain Parallelism". In: *Proceedings of the 7th Inter-
       national Workshop on Languages and Compilers for Parallel Computing*.
       LCPC'94. Springer, 1995, pp. 16–30. ISBN: 3-540-58868-X

[269] L. Nowak and P. Marwedel. "Verification of Hardware Descriptions by
       Retargetable Code Generation". In: *Proceedings of the 26th ACM/IEEE
       Design Automation Conference*. DAC'89. Las Vegas, Nevada, USA: ACM,
       1989, pp. 441–447. ISBN: 0-89791-310-8

[270] A. Nymeyer and J.-P. Katoen. "Code Generation Based on Formal Bottom-
       Up Rewrite Systems Theory and Heuristic Search". In: *Acta Informatica*
       34.4 (1997), pp. 597–635

[271] A. Nymeyer, J.-P. Katoen, Y. Westra, and H. Alblas. "Code Generation = A^{*}
       | BURS". In: *Proceedings of the 6th International Conference on Compiler
       Construction (CC'96)*. Ed. by T. Gyimóthy. Vol. 1060. Lecture Notes in
       Computer Science. Springer, 1996, pp. 160–176. ISBN: 978-3-540-61053-3

[272] M. J. O'Donnell. *Equational Logic as a Programming Language*. Cambridge,
       Massachusetts, USA: MIT Press, 1985. ISBN: 978-0262150286

[273] R. J. Orgass and W. M. Waite. "A Base for a Mobile Programming System".
       In: *Communications of the ACM* 12.9 (1969), pp. 507–510. ISSN: 0001-0782

[274] M. Paleczny, C. Vick, and C. Click. "The Java Hotspot^{TM} Server Com-
       piler". In: *Proceedings of the Symposium on Java Virtual Machine Research
       and Technology Symposium*. JVM'01. Monterey, California, USA: USENIX
       Association, 2001

[275] A. Parikh, S. Kim, M. Kandemir, N. Vijaykrishnan, and M. Irwin. "Instruc-
       tion Scheduling for Low Power". In: *Journal of VLSI Signal Processing
       Systems for Signal, Image and Video Technology* 37.1 (2004), pp. 129–149.
       ISSN: 0922-5773

[276] P. G. Paulin, C. Liem, T. C. May, and S. Sutarwala. "DSP Design Tool
       Requirements for Embedded Systems: A Telecommunications Industrial
       Perspective". In: *Journal of VLSI Signal Processing Systems for Signal,
       Image and Video Technology* 9.1–2 (1995), pp. 23–47. ISSN: 0922-5773

[277] P. P. Paulin, C. Liem, T. May, and S. Sutarwala. "CodeSyn: A Retargetable
       Code Synthesis System". In: *Proceedings of the 7th International Symposium
       on High Level Synthesis*. San Diego, California, USA: IEEE Computer
       Society, 1994, pp. 94–95

[278]   E. Pelegrí-Llopart and S. L. Graham. "Optimal Code Generation for Ex-
        pression Trees: An Application of BURS Theory". In: *Proceedings of the
        15th SIGPLAN-SIGACT Symposium on Principles of Programming Lan-
        guages*. POPL'88. San Diego, California, USA: ACM, 1988, pp. 294–308.
        ISBN: 0-89791-252-7

[279]   T. J. Pennello. "Very Fast LR Parsing". In: *Proceedings of the SIGPLAN
        Symposium on Compiler Construction*. SIGPLAN'86. Palo Alto, California,
        USA: ACM, 1986, pp. 145–151. ISBN: 0-89791-197-0

[280]   D. R. Perkins and R. L. Sites. "Machine-Independent PASCAL Code Opti-
        mization". In: *Proceedings of the SIGPLAN Symposium on Compiler Con-
        struction*. SIGPLAN'79. Denver, Colorado, USA: ACM, 1979, pp. 201–207.
        ISBN: 0-89791-002-8

[281]   T. A. Proebsting. "BURS Automata Generation". In: *Transactions on Pro-
        gramming Language Systems* 17.3 (1995), pp. 461–486. ISSN: 0164-0925

[282]   T. A. Proebsting. "Code Generation Techniques". #1119. Doctoral thesis.
        Madison, Wisconsin, USA: The University of Wisconsin–Madison, Nov.
        1992

[283]   T. A. Proebsting. *Least-Cost Instruction Selection in DAGs is NP-Complete.*
        1995. URL: http://web.archive.org/web/20081012050644/http:
        //research.microsoft.com/~toddpro/papers/proof.htm (visited on
        2013-04-23)

[284]   T. A. Proebsting. "Simple and Efficient BURS Table Generation". In: *Pro-
        ceedings of the SIGPLAN Conference on Programming Language Design
        and Implementation*. PLDI'92. San Francisco, California, USA: ACM, 1992,
        pp. 331–340. ISBN: 0-89791-475-9

[285]   T. A. Proebsting and B. R. Whaley. "One-Pass, Optimal Tree Parsing—With
        or Without Trees". In: *Proceedings of the 6th International Conference on
        Compiler Construction (CC'06)*. Ed. by T. Gyimóthy. Vol. 1060. Lecture
        Notes in Computer Science. Springer, 1996, pp. 294–306. ISBN: 978-3-540-
        61053-3

[286]   P. W. Purdom Jr. and C. A. Brown. "Fast Many-to-One Matching Algorithms".
        In: *Proceedings of the 1st International Conference on Rewriting Techniques
        and Applications*. Dijon, France: Springer, 1985, pp. 407–416. ISBN: 0-387-
        15976-2

[287]   R. Ramesh and I. V. Ramakrishnan. "Nonlinear Pattern Matching in Trees".
        In: *Journal of the ACM* 39.2 (1992), pp. 295–316. ISSN: 0004-5411

[288]   N. Ramsey and J. W. Davidson. "Machine Descriptions to Build Tools for
        Embedded Systems". In: *Proceedings of the SIGPLAN Workshop on Lan-
        guages, Compilers, and Tools for Embedded Systems*. LCTES'98. Springer,
        1998, pp. 176–192. ISBN: 3-540-65075-X

[289]   N. Ramsey and J. Dias. "Resourceable, Retargetable, Modular Instruction
        Selection Using a Machine-Independent, Type-Based Tiling of Low-Level
        Intermediate Code". In: *Proceedings of the 38th Annual SIGPLAN-SIGACT
        Symposium on Principles of Programming Languages*. POPL'11. Austin,
        Texas, USA: ACM, 2011, pp. 575–586. ISBN: 978-1-4503-0490-0

[290]   B. R. Rau and J. A. Fisher. "Instruction-Level Parallel Processing: History, Overview, and Perspective". In: *Journal of Supercomputing* 7.1–2 (May 1993), pp. 9–50. ISSN: 0920-8542

[291]   R. R. Redziejowski. "On Arithmetic Expressions and Trees". In: *Communications of the ACM* 12.2 (1969), pp. 81–84. ISSN: 0001-0782

[292]   C. R. Reeves. "Genetic Algorithms". In: *Handbook of Metaheuristics*. Ed. by M. Gendreau and J.-Y. Potvin. 2nd ed. Vol. 146. International Series in Operations Research & Management Science. Springer, 2010. Chap. 5, pp. 109–139. ISBN: 978-1-4419-116-1

[293]   J. F. Reiser. "Compiling Three-Address Code for C Programs". In: *The Bell System Technical Journal* 60.2 (1981), pp. 159–166

[294]   K. Ripken. *Formale Beschreibung von Maschinen, Implementierungen und Optimierender Maschinencodeerzeugung aus Attributierten Programmgraphen*. Tech. rep. TUM-INFO-7731. Munich, Germany: Institut für Informatik, Technical University of Munich, July 1977

[295]   F. Rossi, P. Van Beek, and T. Walsh, eds. *Handbook of Constraint Programming*. Amsterdam, Netherlands: Elsevier, 2006. ISBN: 978-0-444-52726-4

[296]   R. L. Rudell. "Logic Synthesis for VLSI Design". AAI9006491. Doctoral thesis. Berkeley, California, USA: University of California, 1989

[297]   S. J. Russell and P. Norvig. *Artificial Intelligence: A Modern Approach*. 3rd ed. London, England: Pearson Education, 2010. ISBN: 0-13-604259-7

[298]   E. D. Sacerdoti. "Planning in a Hierarchy of Abstraction Spaces". In: *Proceedings of the 3rd International Joint Conference on Artificial Intelligence*. Ed. by N. J. Nilsson. IJCAI'73. Stanford, California, USA: Morgan Kaufmann, 1973, pp. 412–422

[299]   S. Sakai, M. Togasaki, and K. Yamazaki. "A Note on Greedy Algorithms for the Maximum Weghted Independent Set Problem". In: *Discrete Applied Mathematics* 126.2-3 (2003), pp. 313–322. ISSN: 0166-218X

[300]   V. Sarkar, M. J. Serrano, and B. B. Simons. "Register-Sensitive Selection, Duplication, and Sequencing of Instructions". In: *Proceedings of the 15th International Conference on Supercomputing*. ICS'01. Sorrento, Italy: ACM, 2001, pp. 277–288. ISBN: 1-58113-410-X

[301]   B. Schafer, Y. Lee, and T. Kim. "Temperature-Aware Compilation for VLIW Processors". In: *Proceedings for the 13th International Conference on Embedded and Real-Time Computing Systems and Applications*. RTCSA'07. Daegu, Korea: IEEE Computer Society, Aug. 2007, pp. 426–431

[302]   S. Schäfer and B. Scholz. "Optimal Chain Rule Placement for Instruction Selection Based on SSA Graphs". In: *Proceedings of the 10th International Workshop on Software and Compilers for Embedded Systems*. SCOPES'07. Nice, France: ACM, 2007, pp. 91–100

[303]   H. Scharwaechter, J. M. Youn, R. Leupers, Y. Pack, G. Ascheid, and H. Meyr. "A Code-Generator Generator for Multi-Output Instructions". In: *Proceedings of the 5th IEEE/ACM International Conference on Hardware/Software Codesign and System Synthesis*. CODES+ISSS'07. Salzburg, Austria: ACM, 2007, pp. 131–136. ISBN: 978-1-59593-824-4

[304] B. Scholz and E. Eckstein. "Register Allocation for Irregular Architectures". In: *Proceedings of the joint Conference on Languages, Compilers and Tools for Embedded Systems and Software and Compilers for Embedded Systems*. LCTES/SCOPES'02. Berlin, Germany: ACM, 2002, pp. 139–148. ISBN: 1-58113-527-0

[305] R. Sethi and J. D. Ullman. "The Generation of Optimal Code for Arithmetic Expressions". In: *Journal of the ACM* 17.4 (1970), pp. 715–28. ISSN: 0004-5411

[306] R. Shamir and D. Tsur. "Faster Subtree Isomorphism". In: *Journal of Algorithms* 33.2 (1999), pp. 267–280. ISSN: 0196-6774

[307] P. Shankar, A. Gantait, A. R. Yuvaraj, and M. Madhavan. "A New Algorithm for Linear Regular Tree Pattern Matching". In: *Theoretical Computer Science* 242.1-2 (2000), pp. 125–142. ISSN: 0304-3975

[308] J. Shu, T. C. Wilson, and D. K. Banerji. "Instruction-Set Matching and GA-based Selection for Embedded-Processor Code Generation". In: *Proceedings of the 9th International Conference on VLSI Design: VLSI in Mobile Communication*. VLSID'96. Washington, District of Colombia, USA: IEEE Computer Society, 1996, pp. 73–76. ISBN: 0-8186-7228-5

[309] D. C. Simoneaux. "High-Level Language Compiling for User-Defineable Architectures". Doctoral thesis. Monterey, California, USA: Naval Postgraduate School, 1975

[310] A. Snyder. "A Portable Compiler for the Language C". MA thesis. Cambridge, Massachusetts, USA, 1975

[311] S. Sorlin and C. Solnon. "A Global Constraint for Graph Isomorphism Problems". In: *Proceedings of the 1st International Conference on Integration of AI and OR Techniques in Constraint Programming for Combinatorial Optimization Problems (CPAIOR'04)*. Ed. by J.-C. Régin and M. Rueher. Vol. 3011. Lecture Notes in Computer Science. Springer, 2004, pp. 287–301. ISBN: 978-3-540-21836-4

[312] V. Srinivasan and T. Reps. "Synthesis of Machine Code from Semantics". In: *Proceedings of the 36th SIGPLAN Conference on Programming Language Design and Implementation*. PLDI'15. Portland, OR, USA: ACM, 2015, pp. 596–607. ISBN: 978-1-4503-3468-6

[313] R. Stallman. *Internals of GNU CC*. Version 1.21. Free Software Foundation, Inc. Apr. 24, 1988. URL: http://trinity.engr.uconn.edu/~vamsik/ internals.pdf (visited on 2013-05-29)

[314] J. Stanier and D. Watson. "Intermediate Representations in Imperative Compilers: A Survey". In: *Computing Surveys* 45.3 (July 2013), 26:1–26:27. ISSN: 0360-0300

[315] J. Strong, J. Wegstein, A. Tritter, J. Olsztyn, O. Mock, and T. Steel. "The Problem of Programming Communication with Changing Machines: A Proposed Solution". In: *Communications of the ACM* 1.8 (1958), pp. 12–18. ISSN: 0001-0782

[316] A. Sudarsanam, S. Malik, and M. Fujita. "A Retargetable Compilation Methodology for Embedded Digital Signal Processors Using a Machine-Dependent Code Optimization Library". In: *Design Automation for Embedded Systems* 4.2–3 (1999), pp. 187–206. ISSN: 0929-5585

[317] H. Tanaka, S. Kobayashi, Y. Takeuchi, K. Sakanushi, and M. Imai. "A Code Selection Method for SIMD Processors with PACK Instructions". In: *Proceedings of the 7th International Workshop on Software and Compilers for Embedded Systems (SCOPES'03)*. Ed. by A. Krall, Vol. 2826. Lecture Notes in Computer Science. Springer, 2003, pp. 66–80. ISBN: 978-3-540-20145-8

[318] A. S. Tanenbaum, H. van Staveren, E. G. Keizer, and J. W. Stevenson. "A Practical Tool Kit for Making Portable Compilers". In: *Communications of the ACM* 26.9 (1983), pp. 654–660. ISSN: 0001-0782

[319] A. K. Tirrell. "A Study of the Application of Compiler Techniques to the Generation of Micro-Code". In: *Proceedings of the SIGPLAN/SIGMICRO Interface Meeting*. Harriman, New York, USA: ACM, 1973, pp. 67–85

[320] S. W. K. Tjiang. *An Olive Twig*. Tech. rep. Synopsys Inc., 1993

[321] S. W. K. Tjiang. *Twig Reference Manual*. Tech. rep. Murray Hill, New Jersey, USA: AT&T Bell Laboratories, 1986

[322] *TMS320C55x DSP Mnemonic Instruction Set Reference Guide*. SPRU374G. Texas Instruments. Oct. 2002

[323] K. Trifunovic, D. Nuzman, A. Cohen, A. Zaks, and I. Rosen. "Polyhedral-Model Guided Loop-Nest Auto-Vectorization". In: *Proceedings of the 2009 18th International Conference on Parallel Architectures and Compilation Techniques*. PACT'09. Washington, District of Colombia, USA: IEEE Computer Society, 2009, pp. 327–337. ISBN: 978-0-7695-3771-9

[324] J. R. Ullmann. "An Algorithm for Subgraph Isomorphism". In: *Journal of the ACM* 23.1 (1976), pp. 31–42. ISSN: 0004-5411

[325] P. Van Beek. Private correspondence. Nov. 2014

[326] J. Van Praet, D. Lanneer, W. Geurts, and G. Goossens. "Processor Modeling and Code Selection for Retargetable Compilation". In: *Transactions on Design Automation of Electronic Systems* 6.3 (2001), pp. 277–307. ISSN: 1084-4309

[327] J. Van Praet, G. Goossens, D. Lanneer, and H. De Man. "Instruction Set Definition and Instruction Selection for ASIPs". In: *Proceedings of the 7th International Symposium on Systems Synthesis*. ISSS'94. Niagara-on-the-Lake, Ontario, Canada: IEEE Computer Society, 1994, pp. 11–16. ISBN: 0-8186-5785-5

[328] B.-S. Visser. "A Framework for Retargetable Code Generation Using Simulated Annealing". In: *Proceedings of the 25th EUROMICRO'99 Conference on Informatics: Theory and Practice for the New Millennium*. Washington, District of Colombia, USA: IEEE Computer Society, 1999, pp. 1458–1462. ISBN: 0-7695-0321-7

[329] E. Visser. "A Survey of Strategies in Rule-Based Program Transformation Systems". In: *Journal of Symbolic Computation* 40.1 (2005), pp. 831–873

[330] E. Visser. "Stratego: A Language for Program Transformation Based on Rewriting Strategies - System Description of Stratego 0.5". In: *Rewriting Techniques and Applications*. Vol. 2051. RTA'01. Springer, 2001, pp. 357–361

[331] S. G. Wasilew. "A Compiler Writing System with Optimization Capabilities for Complex Object Order Structures". AAI7232604. Doctoral thesis. Evanston, Illinois, USA: Northwestern University, 1972

[332] S. W. Weingart. "An Efficient and Systematic Method of Compiler Code Generation". AAI7329501. Doctoral thesis. New Haven, Connecticut, USA: Yale University, 1973

[333] D. Weise, R. F. Crew, M. Ernst, and B. Steensgaard. "Value Dependence Graphs: Representation Without Taxation". In: *Proceedings of the 21st SIGPLAN-SIGACT Symposium on Principles of Programming Languages*. POPL'94. Portland, Oregon, USA: ACM, 1994, pp. 297–310. ISBN: 0-89791-636-0

[334] B. Weisgerber and R. Wilhelm. "Two Tree Pattern Matchers for Code Selection". In: *Proceedings of the 2nd CCHSC Workshop on Compiler Compilers and High Speed Compilation*. Springer, 1989, pp. 215–229. ISBN: 3-540-51364-7

[335] A. L. Wendt. "Fast Code Generation Using Automatically-Generated Decision Trees". In: *Proceedings of the SIGPLAN Conference on Programming Language Design and Implementation*. PLDI'90. White Plains, New York, USA: ACM, 1990, pp. 9–15. ISBN: 0-89791-364-7

[336] B. Wess. "Automatic Instruction Code Generation Based on Trellis Diagrams". In: *Proceedings of the International Symposium on Circuits and Systems*. Vol. 2. ISCAS'92. Washington, District of Colombia, USA: IEEE Computer Society, 1992, pp. 645–648

[337] B. Wess. "Code Generation Based on Trellis Diagrams". In: *Code Generation for Embedded Processors*. Ed. by P. Marwedel and G. Goossens. Springer, 1995. Chap. 11, pp. 188–202. ISBN: 978-0-7923-9577-5

[338] T. R. Wilcox. "Generating Machine Code for High-Level Programming Languages". AAI7209959. Doctoral thesis. Ithaca, New York, USA: Cornell University, 1971

[339] R. Wilhelm and D. Maurer. *Compiler Design*. Boston, Massachusetts, USA: Addison-Wesley, 1995. ISBN: 978-0201422-900

[340] T. Wilson, G. Grewal, B. Halley, and D. Banerji. "An Integrated Approach to Retargetable Code Generation". In: *Proceedings of the 7th International Symposium on High-Level Synthesis*. ISSS'94. Niagara-on-the-Lake, Ontario, Canada: IEEE Computer Society, 1994, pp. 70–75. ISBN: 0-8186-5785-5

[341] L. A. Wolsey. *Integer Programming*. Hoboken, New Jersey, USA: Wiley, 1998

[342] P. Wu, A. E. Eichenberger, and A. Wang. "Efficient SIMD Code Generation for Runtime Alignment and Length Conversion". In: *Proceedings of the International Symposium on Code Generation and Optimization*. CGO'05. Washington, District of Colombia, USA: IEEE Computer Society, 2005, pp. 153–164. ISBN: 0-7695-2298-X

[343] S. Wu and S. Li. "Instruction Selection for ARM/Thumb Processors Based on a Multi-objective Ant Algorithm". In: *Computer Science—Theory and Applications*. Ed. by D. Grigoriev, J. Harrison, and E. A. Hirsch. Vol. 3967. Lecture Notes in Computer Science. Springer, 2006, pp. 641–651. ISBN: 978-3-540-34166-6

[344] W. A. Wulf, R. K. Johnsson, C. B. Weinstock, S. O. Hobbs, and C. M. Geschke. *The Design of an Optimizing Compiler*. Amsterdam, Netherlands: Elsevier, 1975. ISBN: 0444001581

[345] H.-T. L. Wuu and W. Yang. "A Simple Tree Pattern-Matching Algorithm". In: *Proceedings of the Workshop on Algorithms and Theory of Computation*. Chiyayi, Taiwan, 2000, pp. 1–8

[346] M. Xie, C. Pan, J. Hu, C. Xue, and Q. Zhuge. "Non-Volatile Registers Aware Instruction Selection for Embedded Systems". In: *Proceedings of the 20th International Conference on Embedded and Real-Time Computing Systems and Applications (RTCSA)*. RTCSA'14. Washington, District of Colombia, USA: IEEE Computer Society, Aug. 2014, pp. 1–9

[347] W. Yang. "A Fast General Parser for Automatic Code Generation". In: *Proceedings of the 2nd Russia-Taiwan Conference on Methods and Tools of Parallel Programming Multicomputers*. MTPP'10. Vladivostok, Russia: Springer, 2010, pp. 30–39. ISBN: 978-3-642-14821-7

[348] J. S. Yates and R. A. Schwartz. "Dynamic Programming and Industrial-Strength Instruction Selection: Code Generation by Tiring, but not Exhaustive, Search". In: *SIGPLAN Notices* 23.10 (1988), pp. 131–140. ISSN: 0362-1340

[349] J. M. Youn, J. Lee, Y. Paek, J. Lee, H. Scharwaechter, and R. Leupers. "Fast Graph-Based Instruction Selection for Multi-Output Instructions". In: *Software—Practice & Experience* 41.6 (2011), pp. 717–736. ISSN: 0038-0644

[350] R. Young. "The Coder: A Program Module for Code Generation in High Level Language Compilers". MA thesis. Urbana-Champaign, Illinois, USA: Computer Science Department, University of Illinois, 1974

[351] K. H. Yu and Y. H. Hu. "Artificial Intelligence in Scheduling and Instruction Selection for Digital Signal Processors". In: *Applied Artificial Intelligence* 8.3 (1994), pp. 377–392

[352] K. H. Yu and Y. H. Hu. "Efficient Scheduling and Instruction Selection for Programmable Digital Signal Processors". In: *Transactions on Signal Processing* 42.12 (1994), pp. 3549–3552. ISSN: 1053-587X

[353] P. Yu and T. Mitra. "Scalable Custom Instructions Identification for Instruction-Set Extensible Processors". In: *Proceedings of the International Conference on Compilers, Architecture, and Synthesis for Embedded Systems*. CASES'04. Washington, District of Colombia, USA: ACM, 2004, pp. 69–78

[354] G. Zimmermann. "The MIMOLA Design System: A Computer Aided Digital Processor Design Method". In: *Proceedings of the 16th Design Automation Conference*. DAC'79. San Diego, California, USA: IEEE Computer Society, 1979, pp. 53–58

[355] W. Zimmermann and T. Gaul. "On the Construction of Correct Compiler Back-Ends: An ASM-Approach". In: *Journal of Universal Computer Science* 3.5 (May 28, 1997), pp. 504–567

[356] J. Ziv and A. Lempel. "A Universal Algorithm for Sequential Data Compression". In: *Transactions on Information Theory* 23.3 (1977), pp. 337–343

[357] V. Živojnović, J. Martínez Velarde, C. Schläger, and H. Meyr. "DSPstone: A DSP-Oriented Benchmarking Methodology". In: *Proceedings of the International Conference on Signal Processing Applications and Technology*. ICSPAT'94. Dallas, Texas, USA, Oct. 1994, pp. 715–720

Index

© Springer International Publishing Switzerland 2016
G. Hjort Blindell, *Instruction Selection*,
DOI 10.1007/978-3-319-34019-7

Printed in the United States
By Bookmasters